Modernism and ...

Series Editor: **Roger Griffin**, Professor in Modern History, Oxford Brookes University, UK.

The series *Modernism and...* invites experts in a wide range of cultural, social, scientific and political phenomena to explore the relationship between a particular topic in modern history and 'modernism'. Apart from their intrinsic value as short but groundbreaking specialist monographs, the books aim through their cumulative impact to expand the application of this highly contested term beyond its conventional remit of art and aesthetics. Our definition of modernism embraces the vast profusion of creative acts, reforming initiatives and utopian projects that, since the late nineteenth century, have sought either to articulate, and so symbolically transcend, the spiritual malaise or decadence of modernity, or to find a radical solution to it through a movement of spiritual, social, political – even racial – regeneration and renewal. The ultimate aim is to foster a spirit of transdisciplinary collaboration in shifting the structural forces that define modern history beyond their conventional conceptual frameworks.

Titles include:

Ben Hutchinson
MODERNISM AND STYLE

Marius Turda
MODERNISM AND EUGENICS

Shane Weller
MODERNISM AND NIHILISM

Forthcoming titles:

Tamir Bar-On
MODERNISM AND THE EUROPEAN NEW RIGHT

Maria Bucur
MODERNISM AND GENDER

Frances Connelly
MODERNISM AND THE GROTESQUE

Elizabeth Darling
MODERNISM AND DOMESTICITY

Matthew Feldman
MODERNISM AND PROPAGANDA

Claudio Fogu
MODERNISM AND MEDITERRANEANISM

Roger Griffin
MODERNISM AND TERRORISM

Carmen Kuhling
MODERNISM AND NEW RELIGIONS

Patricia Leighten
MODERNISM AND ANARCHISM

Thomas Linehan
MODERNISM AND BRITISH SOCIALISM

Gregory Maertz
MODERNISM AND NAZI PAINTING

Paul March-Russell
MODERNISM AND SCIENCE FICTION

Anna Katharina Schaffner
MODERNISM AND PERVERSION

Richard Shorten
MODERNISM AND TOTALITARIANISM

Mihai Spariosu
MODERNISM, EXILE AND UTOPIA

Roy Starrs
MODERNISM AND JAPANESE CULTURE

Erik Tonning
MODERNISM AND CHRISTIANITY

Veronica West-Harling
MODERNISM AND THE QUEST

Modernism and ...
Series Standing Order ISBN 978–0–230–20332–7 (Hardback)
978–0–230–20333–4 (Paperback)
(*outside North America only*)

You can receive future titles in this series as they are published by placing a standing order. Please contact your bookseller or, in case of difficulty, write to us at the address below with your name and address, the title of the series and the ISBN quoted above.

Customer Services Department, Macmillan Distribution Ltd, Houndmills, Basingstoke, Hampshire RG21 6XS, England

---

Modernism and Style

Ben Hutchinson

Reader in Modern German and Comparative Literature,
University of Kent

First published 2011 by
PALGRAVE MACMILLAN

Palgrave Macmillan in the UK is an imprint of Macmillan Publishers Limited,
registered in England, company number 785998, of Houndmills, Basingstoke,
Hampshire RG21 6XS.

Palgrave Macmillan in the US is a division of St Martin's Press LLC,
175 Fifth Avenue, New York, NY 10010.

Palgrave Macmillan is the global academic imprint of the above companies
and has companies and representatives throughout the world.

Palgrave® and Macmillan® are registered trademarks in the United States,
the United Kingdom, Europe and other countries.

ISBN 978-0-230-23096-5 hardback
ISBN 978-0-230-23097-2 paperback

This book is printed on paper suitable for recycling and made from fully
managed and sustained forest sources. Logging, pulping and manufacturing
processes are expected to conform to the environmental regulations of the
country of origin.

A catalogue record for this book is available from the British Library.

Library of Congress Cataloging-in-Publication Data
Hutchinson, Ben, 1976–
    Modernism and style / Ben Hutchinson.
        p.   cm.
    Includes index.
    ISBN 978-0-230-23097-2 (pbk.)
    1. European literature—19th century—History and criticism.
    2. European literature—20th century—History and criticism.
    3. Modernism (Literature)—Europe.   4. Creation (Literary, artistic, etc.)
    I. Title.
    PN760.5H88 2011
    809′.9112—dc23   2011024171

10   9   8   7   6   5   4   3   2   1
20   19   18   17   16   15   14   13   12   11

Printed and bound in Great Britain by
CPI Antony Rowe, Chippenham and Eastbourne

This book is dedicated to Max, for slowing me down and speeding me up.

Contents

Series Editor Preface

As the title 'Modernism and...' implies, this series has been conceived in an open-ended, closure-defying spirit, more akin to the soul of jazz than to the rigour of a classical score. Each volume provides an experimental space allowing both seasoned professionals and aspiring academics to investigate familiar areas of modern social, scientific or political history from the defamiliarizing vantage point afforded by a term not routinely associated with it: 'modernism'. Yet this is no contrived make-over of a clichéd concept for the purposes of scholastic bravado. Nor is it a gratuitous theoretical exercise in expanding the remit of an 'ism' already notorious for its polyvalence – not to say its sheer nebulousness – in a transgressional fling of postmodern *jouissance*.

Instead this series is based on the *empirically* orientated hope that a deliberate enlargement of the semantic field of 'modernism', to embrace a whole range of phenomena apparently unrelated to the radical innovation in the arts it normally connotes, will do more than contribute to scholarly understanding of those topics. Cumulatively the volumes that appear are meant to contribute to a perceptible paradigm shift slowly becoming evident in the way modern history is approached. It is one which, while indebted to 'the cultural turn', is if anything 'post-post-modern', for it attempts to use transdisciplinary perspectives and the conscious clustering of concepts often viewed as unconnected – or even antagonistic to each other – to consolidate and deepen the reality principle on which historiography is based, to move closer to the experience of history of its actors. Only those with a stunted, myopic (and actually *unhistorical*) view of what constitutes historical 'fact' and 'causation' will be predisposed to dismiss the 'Modernism and...' project as mere 'culturalism', a term which due to unexamined prejudices and sometimes sheer ignorance has, particularly in the vocabulary of more than one eminent 'archival' historian, acquired a reductionist, pejorative meaning.

Compared with several volumes in this series, in the case of the present text there is little to disconcert the reader in the juxtaposition of the term modernism with the key theme. After all, style and modernism both belong to the realm of aesthetics. Yet readers should be aware that the broader context for this book is a radical extension of the term modernism to embrace a wide range of phenomena many of which have little to do with aesthetics or culture in the artistic sense. The conceptual ground for works such as *Modernism and Eugenics* or *Modernism and the New Right* or *Modernism and Propaganda* has been prepared by such seminal texts as Marshall Berman's *All That is Solid Melts into Air: The Experience of Modernity* (1982), Modris Eksteins' *Rites of Spring* (1989), Peter Osborne's *The Politics of Time: Modernity and Avant-Garde* (1995), Emilio Gentile's *The Struggle for Modernity* (2003) and more recently Mark Antliff's *Avant-Garde Fascism: The Mobilization of Myth, Art, and Culture in France, 1909–1939* (2007). In each case modernism is revealed as the long-lost sibling (twin or maybe even father) of historical phenomena rarely mentioned in the same breath.

Yet the real pioneers of such a 'maximalist' interpretation of modernism were none other than some of the major modernists. For them the art and thought that subsequently earned them this title was a creative force – passion even – of revelatory power which, in a crisis-ridden West where *anomie* was reaching pandemic proportions, was capable of regenerating not just 'cultural production', but 'socio-political production', and for some even society *tout court*. Figures such as Friedrich Nietzsche, Richard Wagner, Wassily Kandinsky, Walter Gropius, Pablo Picasso and Virginia Woolf never accepted that the art and thought of 'high culture' were to be treated as self-contained spheres of activity peripheral to – and cut off from – the main streams of contemporary social and political events. Instead they assumed them to be laboratories of visionary thought vital to the spiritual salvation of a world being systematically drained of higher meaning and ultimate purpose by the dominant, 'nomocidal' forces of modernity. If we accept Max Weber's thesis of the gradual *Entzauberung*, or 'disenchantment' of the world through rationalism, such creative individuals can be seen as setting themselves the task – each in his or her own idiosyncratic way – of *re-enchanting* and re-sacralizing the world. Such modernists consciously sought to restore a sense of higher purpose, transcendence and *Zauber* to a spiritually starved modern humanity condemned by 'progress' to live in a permanent state of existential exile, of *liminoid transition*, now that the forces of the divine seemed to have

withdrawn in what Martin Heidegger's muse, the poet
Friedrich Hölderlin, called 'the flight of the gods'. If the
hero of modern popular nationalism is the Unknown
Warrior, perhaps the patron saint of modernism itself
is *Deus Absconditus*.

Approached from this oblique angle, modernism is
thus a revolutionary force, but in a manner only dis-
tantly related to the one made familiar by standard
accounts of the (political or social) revolutions on
which modern historians cut their teeth. It is primarily a 'hidden' revolution of the sort referred to by the
'arch-'aesthetic modernist Vincent van Gogh, musing
to his brother Theo in his letter of 24 September 1888
about the sorry plight of the world. In one passage he
waxes ecstatic about the impression made on him by
the work of another spiritual seeker disturbed by the
impact of 'modern progress', Leo Tolstoy:

> It seems that in the book, *My Religion*, Tolstoy
> implies that whatever happens in a violent rev-
> olution, there will also be an inner and hidden
> revolution in the people, out of which a new reli-
> gion will be born, or rather, something completely
> new which will be nameless, but which will have the
> same effect of consoling, of making life possible, as
> the Christian religion used to.
>
> The book must be a very interesting one, it seems
> to me. In the end, we shall have had enough of
> cynicism, scepticism and humbug, and will want to
> live – more musically. How will this come about,
> and what will we discover? It would be nice to be
> able to prophesy, but it is even better to be fore-
> warned, instead of seeing absolutely nothing in the

future other than the disasters that are bound to strike the modern world and civilization like so many thunderbolts, through revolution, or war, or the bankruptcy of worm-eaten states.

In the series 'Modernism and...' the key term has been experimentally expanded and 'heuristically modified' to embrace any movement for change which set out to give a name and a public identity to the 'nameless' and 'hidden' revolutionary principle that van Gogh saw as necessary to counteract the rise of nihilism. He was attracted to Tolstoy's vision because it seemed to offer a remedy to the impotence of Christianity and the insidious spread of a literally soul-destroying cynicism, which if unchecked would ultimately lead to the collapse of civilization. Modernism thus applies in this series to all concerted attempts in any sphere of activity to enable life to be lived more 'musically', to resurrect the sense of transcendent communal and individual purpose being palpably eroded by the chaotic unfolding of events in the modern world even if the end result would be 'just' to make society physically and mentally healthy.

What would have probably appalled van Gogh is that some visionaries no less concerned than he by the growing crisis of the West sought a manna of spiritual nourishment emanating not from heaven, nor even from an earthly beauty still retaining an aura of celestial otherworldliness, but from strictly secular visions of an alternative modernity so radical in conception that attempts to enact them inevitably led to disasters of their own, following the law of unintended consequences. Such solutions were to be realized not by a withdrawal from history into the realm of art (the sphere of 'epiphanic' modernism), but by applying a utopian artistic, mythopoeic, religious or technocratic consciousness to the task of harnessing the dynamic forces of modernity itself in such spheres as the natural sciences and social engineering in order to establish a new social, political and biological order. It is initiatives conceived in this 'programmatic' mode of modernism that the series sets out to explore. Its results are intended to benefit not just a small coterie of like-minded academics, but mainstream teaching and research in modern history and literature, thereby becoming part of the 'common sense' of the discipline even of self-proclaimed 'empiricists'.

Some of the deep-seated psychological, cultural and 'anthropological' mechanisms underlying the futural revolts against modernity here termed 'modernism' are explored at length in my *Modernism and Fascism: The Sense of a Beginning under Mussolini and Hitler* (2007). The premise of this book could be taken to be Phillip E. Johnson's assertion that 'Modernism is typically defined as the condition that begins when people realize God is truly dead, and we are therefore on our own.' It presents the wellsprings of modernism in the primordial human need for transcendental meaning in a godless universe, in the impulse to erect a 'sacred canopy' of culture which not only aesthetically veils the infinity of time and space surrounding human existence to make this existence feasible, but provides a totalizing world-view within which to locate individual life narratives, thus investing it with the illusion of cosmic significance. By eroding or destroying that canopy, modernity creates a protracted spiritual crisis which provokes the proliferation of countervailing impulses to restore a 'higher meaning' to historical time, collectively termed by the book (ideal-typically) as 'modernism'.

Johnson's statement seems to make a perceptive point by associating modernism not just with art, but with a general 'human condition' consequent on what Nietzsche, the first great modernist philosopher, called 'the death of God'. Yet in the context of this series his statement requires significant qualification. Modernism is *not* a general historical condition (any more than 'post-modernism' is), but a generalized revolt against even the *intuition* made possible by a secularizing modernization that we are spiritual orphans in a godless and ultimately meaningless universe. Its hallmark is the bid to find a new home, a new community and a new source of transcendence.

Nor is modernism itself necessarily secular. On the contrary: both the wave of occultism and the Catholic revival of the 1890s and the emergence of radicalized, Manichaean forms of Christianity, Hinduism, Islam and even Buddhism in the 1990s demonstrate that modernist impulses need not take the form of secular utopianism, but may readily assume religious (some would say 'post-secular') forms. In any case, within the cultural force field of modernism even the most secular entities are sacralized to acquire an aura of numinous significance. Ironically, Johnson himself offers a fascinating case study in this fundamental aspect of the modernist rebellion against the empty skies of a disenchanted, anomic world. A retired Berkeley law professor, books like *The Wedge of Truth* made him one of the major protagonists of 'Intelligent Design', a

Christian(ized) version of creationism that offers a pro-
phylactic against the allegedly nihilistic implications
of Darwinist science.

Naturally no attempt has been made to impose the
'reflexive metanarrative' developed in *Modernism and
Fascism* on the various authors of this series. Each
has been encouraged to tailor the term modernism
to fit their own epistemological cloth, as long as
they broadly agree in seeing it as the expression of a
reaction against modernity not restricted to art and
aesthetics, and driven by the aspiration to create a spiritually or physically 'healthier' modernity through a
new cultural, political and ultimately biological order.
Naturally, the blueprint for the ideal society varies sig-
nificantly according to each diagnosis of what makes
actually existing modernity untenable, 'decadent' or
doomed to self-destruction.

The ultimate aim of the series is to help bring about
a paradigm shift in the way 'modernism' is used, and
hence to stimulate fertile new areas of research and
teaching with an approach which enables methodological empathy and causal analysis to be applied
even to events and processes ignored by or resistant
to the explanatory powers of conventional historiography. Though 'style' does not strike a discordant note in
the context of modernism, Ben Hutchinson has shown
that there are deeper societal and historical factors at
work shaping developments in modern literary style
than aesthetic considerations, and that, far from being
a decorative appendage or accessory to 'real' innovations, modernism itself can be seen as largely or
even essentially stylistic. It is a claim that casts a new
light on the ritual style of politics that emerged with

Bolshevism, Fascism and Nazism, and the increasing domination of the mental space of the inhabitants of the 'modern world' by images and spectacles. But that is a subject for another volume.

Roger Griffin
Oxford

Acknowledgements

This book was written in Canterbury, Albi and Paris. In Canterbury, I am indebted to colleagues in the Department of German and in the Centre for Modern European Literature. Above all, I owe a great debt of gratitude to Shane Weller, countless discussions with whom made this book possible, from initial conception to final redrafting. A more severe, more harassing friend is hard to imagine. In Albi, I would like to thank Michèle and Pierre Paycha for their hospitality during a period of gestation, as well as Claire and Alwin Hutchinson for their quiet forbearance in a time of noise. In Paris, staff at the Bibliothèque nationale were unfailingly helpful.

In all of these places, Marie and Max make everything possible.

All translations in the present work are my own, unless otherwise acknowledged. Part of Chapter 3 has appeared in *Modern Language Review* 106.3 (July 2011).

List of Abbreviations

Crucefix   Rainer Maria Rilke, *Duino Elegies*, trans.
             Martyn Crucefix (London: Enitharmon,
             2006)

EP   Ezra Pound, 'A Few Don'ts by an
             Imagiste', in *Manifesto: A Century of Isms*,
             ed. Mary Ann Caws (London: University
             of Nebraska Press, 2001)

FT   Jean Paulhan, *The Flowers of Tarbes*, trans.
             Michael Syrotinski (Urbana and Chicago:
             University of Illinois Press, 2006)

KSA   Friedrich Nietzsche, *Kritische
             Studienausgabe in 15 Bänden*, ed.
             Giorgio Colli and Mazzino Montinari
             (Berlin/New York: de Gruyter, 1967ff.)

LLB   *The Lost Lunar Baedeker: Poems of Mina
             Loy*, ed. Roger L. Conover (New York:
             Farrar, Straus, Giroux, 1996)

MD   Kurt Pinthus (ed.), *Menschheits-
             dämmerung*, trans. Joanna M. Ratych,
             Ralph Ley and Robert C. Conard
             (Rochester, NY: Camden House, 1994)

MS   André Breton, *Manifestos of Surrealism*
             (Ann Arbor: University of Michigan
             Press, 1972)

Notebooks Paul Valéry, *Cahiers/Notebooks*, ed. Brian
             Stimpson, trans. Norma Rinsler, Brian
             Stimpson, Rima Joseph and Paul Ryan
             (Frankfurt: Peter Lang, 2010), vol. IV

Œuvres	Paul Valéry, *Œuvres*, ed. Jean Hytier (Paris: Gallimard, 1957–60)
TS	Louis Aragon, *Traité du style* (Paris: Gallimard, 1928)
Young	Rainer Maria Rilke, *Sonnets to Orpheus*, trans. David Young (Middletown, CT: Wesleyan University Press, 1987)

Introduction

From 'pure style' to purely style

In the introduction to their widely read essay collection *Modernism* (1976), Malcolm Bradbury and James McFarlane describe modernism as 'less a style than a search for a style'.[1] Does this search constitute its defining topos?

This study contends that the self-conception of modernism is fundamentally determined by its relationship to its own notions of style. That this is a plural concept, that there are a wide range of theories of style from the earliest roots of modernism in the nineteenth century to its zenith in the 1920s, is one of the main reasons for writing such a book. As Fredric Jameson has observed, 'the great modernisms were [...] predicated on the invention of a personal, private style'.[2] Whilst attempting to survey a representative range of these private styles, this study will argue that modernist views of style are united by an underlying double movement: on the one hand, style is increasingly foregrounded as its own subject matter, rather than as a transparent window onto a supposedly 'real' world; on the other hand, there is a concomitant suspicion of *mere* style, a fear that secular modernity may have been voided of any meaningful content.

In order to navigate between these two positions, this study traces the development of modernism from 'pure' style to what one could call 'purely' style. It argues that this dialectical transition is inherent to the aesthetics of modernism: in foregrounding its own stylistic surfaces, modernism flirts with a self-destructive narcissism. Where the cultivation of pure style becomes purely style, the standard critical concept of modernism as a primarily aesthetic response to modernity turns against itself, since its very aestheticism threatens to occlude any broader engagement with the 'conditions of modernity'.[3] Roger Griffin's understanding of modernism as a reaction *against* modernity[4] can be pursued into the enduring obsession with style: from Gustave Flaubert's conception of an 'absolute style' in the 1850s, through the 'decadent style' of the 1880s, to the hypertrophied late modernism of the 1940s, time and again the reification of style threatens to reduce modernity to a mere pretext for hermetic, 'pure' aestheticism.

What are the roots of this dialectic? The origins of the modernist notion of purity go back at least as far as Kant. The notion of 'disinterest', as Kant develops it in the *Critique of Judgement* (1790), is the forerunner of Walter Pater's fin-de-siècle doctrine of *l'art pour l'art*: at the end of both the eighteenth and the nineteenth centuries, art is to be judged purely on its own terms, to the exclusion of all external criteria or vested interests. The key term 'pure' looks back to the first of the three critiques, the *Critique of Pure Reason* (1781), where 'pure' reason is distinguished from empirical (i.e. Humean) reason; in the later critique, this notion of purity is transposed from the epistemo-logical and moral concerns of the earlier work onto the aesthetic sphere. As Kant writes: 'A judgement of taste which is uninfluenced by charm or emotion [...] and whose determining ground, therefore, is simply finality of form, is a pure judgement of taste.'[5] Strik-ing here is Kant's insistence on a 'finality of form' as the defining criterion of 'pure judgement'. The brack-eting off of external, contingent criteria such as 'charm or emotion' places the burden of aesthetic proof on the formal aspects of art; the preponderance of a rhetoric of 'purity' in modernist literature, art and thought can thus be read as a foregrounding of form. Schopenhauer, whose influence on modernist concep-tions of style will be considered in Chapter 1, develops a similar argument in his post-Kantian philosophy of the 'will', repeatedly falling back on the adjective 'pure' as a marker of forms of perception unsullied by vulgar, 'phenomenal' content. Walter Pater's state-ment, in his seminal essay 'On Style' (1889), that style exposes 'that inward sense of things, the purity of this medium',[6] descends directly from this lineage.

Moreover, it is easy to show that modernist poetry is preoccupied with the issue of purity. Stéphane Mallarmé's famous desire of 1877 to 'give a purer sense to the language of the tribe' (*donner un sens plus pur aux mots de la tribu*)[7] is echoed at the other end of modernism by T.S. Eliot, who wrote 65 years later, in the final section of *Four Quartets*, of how 'speech impelled us | To purify the dialect of the tribe'.[8] Paul Valéry says something very similar when he writes in 1939 of *'everyday language*, from which we must draw a pure, ideal Voice',[9] whilst for R.M. Rilke the adjective 'pure' is one of the key aesthetic terms, starting with his rebaptism in 1897 as 'Rainer' (echoing the German word *rein*, pure) and finishing in 1926 with the famous reference on his tombstone to 'pure contradiction' (*reiner Widerspruch*).

If the urge to 'purity' that unites these disparate poets, as well as many others of the period, can thus be seen as one of the fundamental impulses of the modernist age, the foregrounding of form that it implies inevitably leads to its dialectical counterpart, to the *crisis* of form whose patron saint in the modernist era is Hugo von Hofmannsthal's Lord Chandos. Increased attention to the formal surfaces of art brings these very surfaces into question. Indeed, the crisis of representation characteristic of the turn of the century is often given expression through precisely this rhetoric of surface and depth, a rhetoric that can be seen to run through the various movements of the modernist period across Europe. One version of the traditional narrative, for instance, has the 'Sprachkrise' developing out of the *Wiener Moderne* of the turn of the century, from Hofmannsthal, Schnitzler and Musil in literature, through Freud in psychoanalysis, to the logical positivists and the 'linguistic turn' in philosophy which their thought did so much to prepare. Yet even a cursory examination reveals the cross-currents at work in late nineteenth-century Europe. The young Hofmannsthal, for instance, started out as a symbolist, yet his sense of dissatisfaction with the distance between world and word – between lived life and its aesthetic expression – implicit in the prevailing idea of the 'symbol', can be felt time and again in the early verse of 'Loris' (as the young Hofmannsthal styled himself). Poems such as 'World Secret' ('Weltgeheimnis'), 'Your Face' ('Dein Antlitz') and 'Ballad of External Life' ('Ballade des äusseren Lebens') all attest to an essential *décalage* between the external and the internal, surface and depth, the contingent and the essential. Similarly, Robert Musil takes as his epigraph to *The Confusions of Young Törless* (1906) a quotation from the Belgian symbolist Maurice Maeterlinck:

> As soon as we put something into words, we devalue it in a strange way. We think we have plunged into the depths of the abyss, and when we return to the surface the drop of water on our pale fingertips no longer resembles the sea from which it comes.[10]

This questioning of aesthetic 'surfaces' as somehow detached from their ostensible referent can be seen as the logical consequence of the Kantian foregrounding of 'form': where pure form is perceived as having become purely form, dissatisfaction is sure to follow. This study starts from the premiss that modernism is defined by this primacy of the signifier over the signified: in an increasingly secular, post-realist era, it is *manners of meaning* that assume centre stage, rather than simply meaning itself. Where previously the world being described (signified) was the focus of interest, modernism in all its manifestations shifts the emphasis back a stage to the ways of describing it (signifier). As William Carlos Williams wrote in his *Autobiography*, it is 'the words themselves beyond the mere thought expressed that distinguish [...] the modern'.[11]

This preoccupation with 'the words themselves' brings with it an increasing interest in questions of style, since style is precisely that which enacts these manners of meaning. In an age in which art can be broadly characterized as being as interested in its own aesthetic and epistemological processes as in any given subject matter, it is inevitable that questions of style become foregrounded. Indeed, one logical conclusion of what Roland Barthes and others[12] have identified as the linguistic turn that started around the middle of the nineteenth century is a reduction of art purely to style, where 'purely' is to be understood in both its senses, both as absolute style (in the manner of 'absolute poetry' à la Mallarmé) and as *only* style. In a letter that forms one of the founding documents of modernism, Flaubert famously wrote to Louise Colet in 1852:

> What I should like to write is a book about nothing, a book dependent on nothing external, which would be held together by the strength of its style, just as the earth, suspended in the void, depends on nothing external for its support; a book which would have almost no subject, or at least in which the subject would be almost invisible, if such a thing is possible.[13]

The ambition to produce a work reduced to a kind of non-representational, intransitive style – a style that is 'about nothing' but itself – is one of the enduring impulses of modernist art, which from Flaubert onwards increasingly seeks to bracket off the external referent in favour of making itself its own subject matter.

Yet if Flaubert thus elides signifier and signified, one can also see this as *suppressing* the signified, as dismissing it as unimportant. This criticism comports, moreover, a moral and socio-political aspect: the hermetic self-regard of the so-called 'decadent style' – in many ways a microcosm of modernist style more broadly, as we shall see – was criticized by a range of contemporary thinkers, from Nietzsche to Nordau, as symptomatic of the ways in which modernity was perceived to be abrogating responsibility for anything beyond purely aesthetic surfaces. Theodor W. Adorno captures something of this in his claim that 'every step toward the perfection of artworks is a step toward their self-alienation':[14] when style is polished to opacity, one can no longer look through it. Much of the work of Thomas Mann – from early texts such as *Tonio Kröger* (1903) to late work such as *Doctor Faustus* (1947) – can be understood in these terms, as an attempt to negotiate between the aesthetic temptations of a pure formalism on the one hand, and the moral imperative not to succumb to a *purely* formalistic world-view on the other. As Gustav von Aschenbach muses in *Death in Venice* (1912):

> And is form not two-faced? Is it not at one and the same time moral and immoral – moral as the product and expression of discipline, but immoral and even anti-moral inasmuch as it harbours within itself an innate moral indifference, and indeed

essentially strives for nothing less than to bend morality under its proud and absolute sceptre?[15]

This study argues that style is as 'two-faced' as form. The relationship between the two terms thus needs immediate clarification.

Style and form

In her study *On Form*, Angela Leighton suggests that 'style' is one of the 'more than twenty definitions' of the word 'form' (alongside, amongst others, 'shape, design, outline, frame, ideal, figure, image, [...] genre, order, etiquette, body, beauty, mould, lair, print-type, format').[16] For better or for worse, the two terms are often used interchangeably: when Leighton writes that form answers 'to at least three different opposites: form and matter, form and content, form and formlessness',[17] one could plausibly substitute the word 'style' for form. The basic opposition between form and content is certainly at the heart of any discussion of the concept of style: 'What haunts all contemporary use of the notion of style', wrote Susan Sontag in 1965 in her influential essay 'On Style', 'is the putative opposition between form and content.'[18]

If there is common ground to the many different definitions of style and form, it can be said in the first instance to lie in the foregrounding of *modes* of meaning, rather than meaning itself. 'The knowledge we gain through art is an experience of the form or style of knowing something, rather than a knowledge of something (like a fact or a moral judgment) in itself,' writes Sontag.[19] If one provisionally allows the 'putative opposition' between form and content, one can say that the style of a given work of art is essentially its *how*, as opposed to its *what*. Indeed, it is tempting to posit style as that which reconciles form and content. In the opening words of Peter Gay's study *Style in History* (1974): 'Style is a centaur [...]. It is form and content, woven into the texture of every art.'[20] In any successful work of art, manner and matter will necessarily be inseparable, as Sontag acknowledges when she defines style as 'an epistemological decision, an interpretation of how and what we perceive'.[21] The artist chooses a certain style since it is appropriate to both the subject s/he wishes to depict and the form in which s/he wishes to depict it. 'An artist's style is [...] nothing other than the particular idiom in which he deploys the forms of his art,' writes Sontag; 'it is for this reason that the problems raised by the concept of "style" overlap with those raised by the concept of "form".'[22] Yet this artist-centred perspective arguably marginalizes the question of historical and artistic context: in his *Reflections of a Nonpolitical Man*, for instance, Thomas Mann defines style as 'a mysterious adjustment of the personal to the objective',[23] whilst more recently the poet Geoffrey Hill has restated this position in similar terms, commenting that 'style marks the success an author may have in forging a personal utterance between the hammer of self-being and the anvil of those impersonal forces that a given time possesses'.[24]

For the purposes of this book, style can be provisionally understood, in the words of Paul Valéry, as 'the manner in which one expresses oneself, *whatever one is expressing*'.[25] Of course, this it not to suggest that one should distinguish apodictically between manner and meaning; in the successful work of art, the manner conveys the meaning. Indeed, modernist style since Flaubert can be understood in the first instance as essentially performative,[26] in the sense that it enacts its own concerns with the possibilities – but also with the limits – of aesthetic expression. As Roland Barthes observes, 'around 1850 [...] classical writing disintegrated, and the whole of literature, from Flaubert to the present day, became the problematics of language'.[27] Modernist style is in this sense both self-theorizing and self-actualizing: if the whole of literature becomes 'the problematics of language', then the whole of literature becomes a question of style. Analogous movements can be discerned in the visual arts: the drive to abstraction in painting, and the increasing obsession with 'surface' and 'planes' in sculpture, suggest a preoccupation with stylistic surface comparable to the 'linguistic' turn in literature.

In his posthumously published *Aesthetic Theory*, Adorno reflects at some length on questions of style and form. Although it did not appear until 1970, the book's frame of reference is mainly that of high modernism, reflecting the engagement of the Frankfurt School with aesthetic modernism as a critique of modern society. Adorno does not explicitly distinguish between style and form, but his discussion of the two concepts makes it clear that he sees them as ideologically distinct.[28] 'Form' receives its most sustained exposition in chapter eight, 'Coherence and Meaning'. After defining aesthetic success as 'measured by whether the formed object is able to awaken the content sedimented in the form', he contends that 'the concept of form marks out art's sharp antithesis to an empirical world in which art's right to exist is uncertain'.[29] Adorno sees form, in the Marxist manner, as a force of resistance to affirmative, bourgeois culture; his dismissal of Lukács' claim that 'in modern art the importance of form has been greatly overestimated' as the 'philistine call to arms' of a 'cultural conservative'[30] underlines this. For Adorno, 'form converges with critique. It is that through which artworks prove to be self-critical.'[31]

In chapter eleven, 'Universal and Particular', Adorno introduces the concept of style. What confuses the issue is that he immediately conflates the theoretical notion of *style* with the 'conventions' of pre-established *styles*:

> When conventions are in an ever unstable equilibrium with the subject they are called styles. The concept of style refers as much to the inclusive element through which art becomes language – for style is the quintessence of all language in art – as to a constraining element that was somehow compatible with particularization.[32]

This conflation of style and styles means that where he saw 'form' as radical and revolutionary, Adorno sees 'style' in the first instance as bourgeois and conservative: 'in the copy of style – one of the primal aesthetic phenomena of the nineteenth century – that specifically bourgeois trait of promising freedom while prohibiting it can be sought'.[33] Adorno associates this normative sense of styles as 'conventions' with nineteenth-century bourgeois realism; with the modernist period, things become more complicated. In keeping with his broader view of the artwork as a constellation of 'irreconcilable' tensions,[34] Adorno sees modernist art as defined by its contradictory relationship to style:

> Authentic artists like Schoenberg protested fiercely against the concept of style; it is a criterion of radical modernism that modernism reject the concept. The concept of style never fully did justice to the quality of works; those works that seem most exactly to represent their style have always fought through the conflict with it; style itself was the unity of style and its suspension. Every work is a force field, even in its relation to style, and this continues to be the case in modernism, where, unbeknownst to modernism and precisely there where it renounced all will to style, something resembling style formed under the pressure of the immanent elaboration of works.[35]

In his typically dense dialectical idiom, Adorno here sketches out the paradoxical centrality of style to high modernism. In rejecting the 'unity of style', in asserting the radical sovereignty, the 'immanent lawfulness of the individual artwork',[36] modernism smuggles style in through the back door, since this very resistance to 'styles' becomes in turn its own style: 'The complete negation of style seems to reverse dialectically into style.'[37] The stylistic self-consciousness that characterizes modernism is born of this transition from plural to singular, from styles to style: it is precisely because it fights to reject conventional, 'bourgeois' notions of style that modernism comes to be defined by this 'conflict'.[38] 'If technique is the quintessence of art's language', writes Adorno, 'it at the same time inescapably liquidates its language.'[39] 'Pure' style, in other words, is both utopian and totalitarian; it is both a promise and a threat.

If conventional 'styles' and modernist 'style' are understood in this dialectical fashion, then the Flaubertian attempt to reduce art to pure style, to 'nothing' but style, must indeed be taken to inaugurate what Adorno calls 'the double character of art'[40] in the modernist era. The way in which Flaubert explicitly understands the foregrounding of style as contingent on having 'almost no subject' makes Adorno's statement that 'the concept of subject-matter [...] has, since Kandinsky, Proust, and Joyce, incontrovertibly declined',[41] seem belated: one needs to look for the roots of modernist style much earlier. Before doing this, however, it will be helpful to give an overview of the contemporary critical discourse.

Modernist criticism and style

From the earliest stirrings of modernism in the mid-nineteenth century, the roles of artist and critic became increasingly intertwined; almost all of the leading modernist writers of Europe were also active as critics. As Jean-Yves Tadié suggests in his history of modern literary criticism, this can be linked to an increased self-consciousness about the epistemological status of language:

> In the twentieth century in particular, when art and language come to view themselves as their

own objects and to operate as much through their conscious as through their subconscious, there is perhaps not a single author who did not also write criticism, from Proust to Butor, Malraux to D.H. Lawrence or Faulkner.[42]

As Tadié goes on to point out, however, there is of course a basic methodological problem with taking the criticism of one artist about another at face value: 'the criticism of artists is a work of art, the reconstitution of one style by another, the metamorphosis of one language into another'.[43] In the first instance, then, it seems expedient to seek an objective correlative in some of the leading European critics of the high modernist period who, whilst not necessarily artists themselves, exercised a decisive influence on the reception of theories of style in modernism.

Histories of literary criticism in the twentieth century tend to start with the Russian formalists. As early as page two of his influential *Literary Theory: An Introduction* (1983), Terry Eagleton quotes Roman Jakobson's famous definition of literature as 'organized violence committed on ordinary speech', and much of his subsequent introduction is dedicated to an exposition of the tenets of the best-known formalists. 'Formalists', Eagleton writes, 'passed over the analysis of literary "content" [...] for the study of literary form. Far from seeing form as the expression of content, they stood the relationship on its head: content was merely the motivation of form.'[44] The key formalist concept of 'estrangement', of 'defamiliarizing' ordinary language, seeks to foreground in Saussurian terms the signifier rather than the signified, and thus leads to an obvious emphasis on questions of linguistic style. Jean-Yves Tadié, who also opens his account of literary criticism in the twentieth century with a consideration of the formalists, quotes Viktor Shklovsky as saying that the central principle of formalism was 'pure form, the relationship of elements',[45] and cites Yury Tynyanov claiming that their goal was the establishment of a link 'between elements of style envisaged up until now separately'.[46] Although the reference to structural correspondence anticipates the later developments of structuralism, both Shklovsky's and Tynyanov's statements bring out the inevitable interest that the formalists had in questions of style, with Shklovsky's notion of 'pure form' echoing once again the modernist rhetoric of purity.

Perhaps one of the less celebrated aspects of Roman Jakobson's work is the extent to which it emphasizes the cross-fertilization of the arts in the early twentieth century. Jakobson, who worked with both Shklovsky and Tynyanov, stressed in his 'Retrospect' that their interest in surfaces and structures stemmed not only from the linguistics of Saussure, but more broadly from the whole range of the 'turbulent artistic movement' of the early twentieth century:

> The great men of art born in the 1880s – Picasso, Joyce, Braque, Stravinsky, Xlebnikov, Le Corbusier – [...] keenly anticipated the upheavals that were to come and met them while still young enough to test their own creative power in this crucible. The extraordinary capacity of these discoverers to overcome again and again the faded habits of their own yesterdays, together with an unprecedented

gift for seizing and shaping anew every older tradition or foreign model without sacrificing the stamp
of their own permanent individuality in the amazing polyphony of ever new creations, is intimately
allied to their unique feeling for the dialectic tension between the parts and the uniting whole, and
between the conjugated parts, primarily between
the two aspects of any artistic sign, its *signans* and
its *signatum*.[47]

Jakobson explicitly interprets the modernist urge to
'make it new' in terms of the Saussurian distinction
between signifier and signified, and links this to what
was happening in painting, music and architecture at
the time. Key to all these forms was the prioritization
of motion: 'The overcoming of *statics*, the discarding
of the absolute, is the main thrust of modern times,
the order of the day,' writes Jakobson in a 1919 essay
on futurism.[48] From Baudelaire's famous definition of
the modern as 'the transient, the fleeting, the contingent' onwards,[49] this emphasis on 'pure motion', as
Rilke would say,[50] is one of the consistent motifs of
the various forms of modernism. It brought with it the
need for a new means of expression, a 'new style', as
Jakobson quotes from the physicist N.A. Umov:

The newly discovered offers a sufficient quantity of
images for the construction of the world, but they
break its former architecture, so familiar to us, and
can be fit only within the boundaries of a new style,
one which far out-distances in its free lines the borders not only of the old external world, but also of
the basic forms of our thinking.[51]

The formalist urge to problematize, defamiliarize and disassemble the signifier can thus be seen as the critical counterpart to what was happening in the creative arts. 'Making it new' meant taking things apart in order to see them differently – and seeing things differently required a stylistic self-consciousness as to how things are seen anew.

In England, these fractious, dynamic impulses of modernism gave rise to the school of close reading – or what, in the United States, later became known as 'New Criticism' – as the dominant methodology of the 1920s and 1930s. In 1924, I.A. Richards published *The Principles of Literary Criticism*, followed in 1929 by *Practical Criticism*; in 1930, his pupil William Empson published *Seven Types of Ambiguity*, and in 1932, F.R. Leavis published *New Bearings in English Poetry*. These three figures established a particular way of reading literary texts through bracketing off their biographical and contextual circumstances and concentrating on the images, tensions and structures of the texts themselves. This close attention to language and syntax brought with it a revivification of what may have been thought to be the fairly old-fashioned notion of style: yet rather than adhering to the classical, Aristotelian concepts of 'high' and 'low' style, of the tragic and comic, etc.,[52] style was no longer imagined to be predetermined by conventions of genre or form, but rather emerged on a case-by-case basis through careful analysis of linguistic ambiguities. As we have seen Adorno imply, this transition from classical *styles* à la Winckelmann[53] to modernist *style* had been one of the key tenets of the whole late nineteenth-century period of early modernism: Flaubert, for instance, had written as early as

1853 that 'rather than persist in copying old modes we should exert ourselves to invent new ones', attacking what he saw as more old-fashioned writers precisely in these terms: 'I think Leconte de Lisle [...] has no instinct for modern life; he lacks heart. [...] Thorough-bred horses and thoroughbred styles have plenty of blood in their veins, and it can be seen pulsing every-where beneath the skin and the words.'[54] Nearly 50 years later, in 1902, the Spanish novelist and drama-tist Ramón del Valle-Inclán echoed Flaubert's words, in the wake of Rubén Dario's importation of the term *el modernismo* into Spanish literary discourse: 'I have pre-ferred to struggle to create for myself a personal style, instead of looking for a ready-made one by imitating the writers of the seventeenth century. [...] This is how I became a professional modernist.'[55]

What is thus important to remember about the rise of 'new criticism' in the English-speaking world in the 1920s and 1930s is that it came towards the end of the modernist era – that is to say, it grew out of the innovative energy of modernist art. In reaction to the Victorians and Georgians, the early imagists had put forward a particular notion of poetic style as the enactment of a kind of tactile, visual intensity, as con-veying the 'intellectual and emotional complex in an instant of time' of Pound's famous phrase. T.E. Hulme wrote in 1907 in his so-called 'Notes on Language and Style' that

> with perfect style, the solid leather for reading, each sentence should be a lump, a piece of clay, a vision seen; rather, a wall touched with soft fingers. Never

should one feel light vaporous bridges between one solid sense and another. [...] Style short, being forced by the coming together of many different thoughts, and generated by their contact.[56]

Empson for his part took some of the key examples in *Seven Types of Ambiguity* from Eliot's *The Waste Land*; indeed, in the preface to the 1930 edition, Empson implied that his whole technique was essentially modernist when he claimed that 'I derive the method I am using from Mr Robert Graves' analysis of a Shakespeare sonnet, "The expense of spirit in a waste of shame", in *A Survey of Modernist Poetry.*'[57] Leavis, as is well known, was heavily influenced by Eliot's own theoretical pronouncements. Not only did he do much to quicken the reception of the leading modernists Eliot and Pound through his discussion of their work, he also shared their insistence on the 'new' and their dislike for what they saw as the rigidly codified style of much nineteenth-century poetry. Leavis' influential attack on the cultivation of the self-consciously 'poetical' in Victorian verse in the first two chapters of *New Bearings in English Poetry* owes much to Eliot's tastes, as he later acknowledged ('It was Mr. Eliot who made us fully conscious of the weakness of that tradition'),[58] and can be read as a continuation of the rejection of predetermined notions of style, of what Adorno calls 'conventions'. Leavis' attack on *The Oxford Book of Victorian Verse* exemplifies how the 'practical criticism' of the Cambridge school of critics emerged as a direct consequence of the modernist agenda to 'make it new'. Poetic style, in Leavis' polemical account of the

Victorian era, was simply a case of belonging to a particular school, of perpetuating the same tired diction. Leavis, like Empson, turns to Graves as an authority, citing his views on Hardy's reactionary poetics:

> 'In [Hardy's] opinion', reports Mr Robert Graves in his superb autobiography *Goodbye to All That*, '*vers libre* could come to nothing in England. All we can do is to write on the old themes in the old styles, but to try to do a little better than those who went before us.'[59]

Against this Victorian view of 'styles' as predetermined, Leavis sees his modernist notion of 'style' as integrating the rhythms of modern life into the very movements of the verse. Far from simply picking a ready-made style off the shelf in order to provide the seemliest register for a 'poetic' subject, the modernist poet according to Leavis seeks rather to make his style reflect – and indeed enact – the rhythms of everyday life:

> Mr T.S. Eliot suggests [...] that probably the modern's perception of rhythm has been affected by the internal combustion engine. All that we can fairly ask of the poet is that he shall show himself to have been fully alive in our time. The evidence will be in the very texture of his poetry.[60]

Leavis' closing phrase here contrasts with Hardy's insistence on the 'old themes in the old styles'. Leavis clearly thinks that the 'texture' of poetry is all-important, since he then immediately repeats the term when dismissing Alfred Noyes' long poem *The Torch-Bearers*, about the great astronomers, as 'completely' insignificant, since 'such an undertaking would have to justify itself in the texture of the verse, by an unmistakable newness of tone, rhythm, and imagery, by an utterly unfamiliar "feel"'.[61] Leavis' attack on Victorian verse may be polemically overstated, but its very ferocity proves how keen he was to distinguish modernist 'textures' from Victorian 'styles'. 'Newness', modernity, is to be determined by the incorporation of topic into texture, of subject matter into style.

This becomes particularly apparent in the last of the main chapters of *New Bearings in English Poetry*, on Gerard Manley Hopkins. Leavis takes Eliot, Pound and Hopkins as representative of 'a decisive reordering of the tradition of English poetry'.[62] Although Hopkins died in 1889, Leavis claims that 'had he received the attention that was his due the history of English poetry from the nineties onward would have been very different'.[63] Leavis uses Hopkins as a kind of test case, citing the reaction of the then poet laureate Robert Bridges, a representative Georgian poet, as typical of vestigial nineteenth-century conceptions of style. Bridges writes of Hopkins' poetry that

> there are definite faults of style which a reader must have courage to face, and must in some measure condone before he can discover the great beauties. For these blemishes in the poet's style are of such quality and magnitude as to deny him even a hearing from those who love a continuous literary decorum and are grown to be intolerant of its absence.[64]

The disagreement between Bridges and Hopkins exemplifies the changing conceptions of style. Leavis, as arbitrator of the dispute, claims that adherence to a predetermined notion of 'good' style, of 'literary decorum', becomes a 'cramping absurdity'[65] when applied so unilaterally. Hopkins clearly felt torn between his own poetic instincts and the pressure of his time, since he wrote in a letter of 1879 to Bridges:

> No doubt my poetry errs on the side of oddness. I hope in time to have a more balanced and Miltonic style. But as air, melody, is what strikes me most of all in music and design in painting, so design, pattern, or what I am in the habit of calling *inscape*, is what I above all aim at in poetry.[66]

Thankfully, Hopkins never did iron out his 'oddness' into Miltonic smoothness. Leavis' comment on Bridges' objections to the awkwardnesses of Hopkins' style is telling, since it locates the latter's 'inscape' within the Modernist moment: 'one is reminded of *les jeunes* who discuss whether Mr Eliot's methods in *The Waste Land* are "legitimate" or not, when the only question worth discussing is, Do they work?'[67] Indeed, Leavis goes on to defend Hopkins from attacks on the 'ambiguity' of his syntax ('He had positive uses for ambiguity')[68] in ways that are obviously reminiscent of Empson. Leavis even has a little fun at the expense of Sturge Moore, 'a critic and verse-writer formed in the last century': writing in his book *Style and Beauty in Literature*, Moore offers to 'improve' Hopkins by turning him into something like sub-Tennyson. Hopkins' poem opens:

How to kéep – is there ány any, is there none such,
   nowhere known some, bow or brooch or braid or
   brace, láce, latch or catch or key to keep
Back beauty, keep it, beauty, beauty, beauty, ... from
   vanishing away?

Moore, as Leavis quotes him, offers the following
'improved' version:

   How to keep beauty? is there any way?
   Is there nowhere any means to have it stay?
   Will no bow or brooch or braid,
   Brace or lace
   Latch or catch
   Or key to lock the door lend aid
   Before beauty vanishes away?[69]

Moore reduces Hopkins' poetry to paraphrase, blithely
disregarding the essential sinews of his verse, what
Hopkins himself called 'the feeling of physical
constraint'.[70]

   Leavis' comments on the reactions to Hopkins'
poetry of Bridges, Moore and other such writers
'formed in the last century' exemplify the incorporation of style into sense, of 'texture' into text, that
the Modernist movement had brought about. In the
manner of Eliot's essay 'Tradition and the Individual
Talent' (1919), one could say that it was no longer
a case of the later poet adapting his style to fit a
preconceived template, but rather the template having to be revised in the light of the later poet. This
is, of course, one of the great legacies of modernism:
time-honoured forms such as the elegy, the sonnet

and the novel were retrospectively revised, 'made new', through sheer force of stylistic innovation.

In 1922, John Middleton Murry published his Oxford lecture series *The Problem of Style*. In his introduction, Murry distinguishes between what he sees as three different models of style, taking Buffon, Stendhal and Flaubert as the respective avatars. Buffon is famously associated with the position that 'le style, c'est l'homme même'. Stendhal, for his part, represents for Murry a kind of self-consciousness about the circumstances of a given style: 'Le style, c'est ajouter à une pensée donnée toutes les circonstances propres à produire tout l'effet que doit produire cette pensée' (in French in the original).[71] Flaubert, meanwhile, is the emblematic 'martyr' of literary style, in Walter Pater's famous term, seeking to reduce all thought to its stylistic expression.

Murry takes what one could term an anti-symbolist[72] view of style, rejecting the 'notion that style is applied ornament' as 'the most popular of all delusions about style'.[73] He favours rather an organicist perspective:

> It is from the inside that we must approach the question of 'artificiality' of style. If the vital centre of feeling is there, perceptible to us, then we may be sure that what seems artificiality is in reality a triumph of art.[74]

Mere 'ornament' is transformed into true style by a process of internalization, a correlation to the 'vital centre of feeling'. 'Style is organic,' Murry accordingly concludes, 'not the clothes a man wears, but the flesh, bone, and blood of his body.'[75]

Six years after Murry's *The Problem of Style*, Herbert Read published his influential *English Prose Style* (1928, reprinted 1952). Although Read's book is essentially a primer on stylistics, and as such need not detain us here, his nine epigraphs give an interesting insight into what had become the established view of style by this period of high modernism. Read's chosen epigraphs seem designed to promote two key points: the idea that style is essentially a means of imposing order on disparate or inchoate thoughts, and the view that style simply *is* thought. The former point is brought out in quotations from amongst others Hulme and Buffon:

All styles are only means of subduing the reader. (T.E. Hulme, 'Notes on Language and Style')

Style consists in the order and the movement which we introduce into our thought. (Buffon, *Discourse on Style*)[76]

The quotation from Buffon inevitably refers the reader back to his most famous statement, 'le style, c'est l'homme même'. It is worth remarking at this point that the last word, often left off, is important: style is not the man, but the man *himself*, that is, it is nothing external to him. Style is thus turned back against the man, foregrounded as his very quintessence to the point of quasi-tautology, where pure style risks becoming purely style. Some of Read's other epigraphs seem designed to make this post-Flaubertian point:

What does the mind enjoy in books? Either the style or nothing. But, someone says, what about the thought? The thought, that is the style, too. (Charles Maurras, *An Essay on Criticism*)

It is hardly necessary to adduce proof that the identity of style and meaning is today firmly established. (W.K. Wimsatt, *The Prose Style of Samuel Johnson*)[77]

Although critical notions of style within the first three decades of the twentieth century varied across Europe, they can all be broadly said to share this same basic idea. Within the German-speaking world, the *Stilbegriff*, the concept of style, enjoyed particular currency in the years following the First World War owing to an evident desire to escape nationalistic, political readings of art and literature.[78] The conception of style in this period derives in the first instance from two main directions: the visual idiom of art history, and the linguistic preoccupations deriving from the so-called *Sprachkrise*. In 1893, the Austrian art historian Alois Riegl had published *Stilfragen* (translated into English in 1993 as *Problems of Style*),[79] in which he coined the influential idea of *Kunstwollen*, 'artistic volition', as the underlying reason for stylistic shifts from period to period. In 1908, the 26-year-old Wilhelm Worringer published his doctoral dissertation *Abstraction and Empathy: A Contribution to the Psychology of Style*, in which he builds on Riegl's term, understanding it as 'will to form'.[80] Worringer contrasts ability (*Können*) with volition (*Wollen*): 'ability is only a secondary consequence of volition. The stylistic peculiarities of past epochs are, therefore, not to be explained by lack of ability, but by a differently directed volition.'[81] Worringer thus sees artistic style not as the product of particular historical periods, but rather as psychologically determined: the drive to abstraction on the one hand, and to empathy on the other, are the two main impulses that shape the cultivation of style as the means of self-expression. Noting, in the foreword to the 1948 edition, that the success of his dissertation could be explained by 'the fact that a whole period was disposed for a radical reorientation of its standards of aesthetic value',[82] Worringer proceeds to associate 'the concept naturalism with the process of empathy [and] the concept style with the other pole of human artistic experience, namely with the urge to abstraction'.[83]

Seven years later, in 1915, the art critic Heinrich Wölfflin, who had already written important books on the Renaissance, the Baroque, and the concept of 'form' in Italian and German art, published his highly influential *Principles of Art History: The Problem of the Development of Style in Later Art*. Wölfflin posited that the development of artistic style from the Renaissance to the Baroque could be traced through the transition of five 'pairs of concepts':[84] from the linear to the painterly, from plane to recession, from closed to open form, from multiplicity to unity, and from absolute to relative clarity. In outlining these paradigmatic transitions, Wölfflin discerned three distinct forms – 'individual style', 'national style' and 'period style' – which, he claimed, 'illustrated the aims of an art history which conceives style primarily as expression, expression of the temper of an age and a nation as well as expression of the individual temperament'.[85]

If, as René Wellek notes, 'the influence of Heinrich Wölfflin's *Kunstgeschichtliche Grundbegriffe* (1915) on literary studies [was] particularly strong in Germany',[86] this was not only because of the post-war desire to

escape political methodologies, but also because the
notion of artistic style as predominantly a visual concept already had great currency in the wake of the
Jugendstil movement of the 1890s (as well as that of
its related literary counterpart, impressionism). The
recurring topoi of *Jugendstil* – gardens in spring, *jeunes
filles en fleur*, an atmosphere of ethereal otherworldliness – suggest an artistic sphere at one remove from
the everyday existence of modernity; the alternative
French term *Art Nouveau* interestingly highlights by
default the sense, inherent in the German, of a movement predominantly concerned with 'style' – with
presenting style itself, through its conjunction with
'youth', as a response to mass modernity. The title of
the journal *Die Insel* (founded in 1899), perhaps the
most representative organ of the movement, accordingly evokes the search for what the editors of the
first issue called an 'oasis' from the everyday world;[87]
indeed, the illustrator of the journal, the painter
Heinrich Vogeler, succinctly described the aims of
Jugendstil as an 'escape from reality'.[88] This suggests the
possibility of a similar transition to that outlined in the
English-speaking world, namely the subsequent rejection of the perceived preciosity and predetermined
notions of artistic style of their predecessors by the
'high' modernists; in the case of Germany in the war
years, this largely meant the expressionists reacting
against the 'impressionists'.

Yet the situation was not as clear-cut in Germany
as it seemed to be in England. For one thing, the
influence of the fin-de-siècle arguably lingered longer,
in particular through the patronage of Stefan George
and his famous circle. George cultivated an hermetic,

highly stylized form of poetry, more interested in obscure mythological figures than in the issues of the modern world (his poems have been described as 'counter-images to modernity');[89] his celebrated declaration that 'no thing may be where the word breaks off' (*kein ding sei wo das wort gebricht*)[90] gives a fair indication of his symbolist view of the primacy of language over object, of signifier over signified. George also carefully maintained a personality cult around his own image. Through the disciples he gathered around him in his *Kreis*, he exerted a considerable influence on German poetry around the turn of the century, an influence which extended to the critical establishment of the day.[91] Friedrich Gundolf, arguably the best-known German literary critic of the post-war Weimar Republic, can be taken as the leading example. Gundolf had joined the George circle in 1899, and his subsequent criticism reflected this: in his books on Shakespeare, Goethe, Kleist and other canonical figures he sought to depict the individual poetic work not as a self-sufficient literary text, but as a kind of pseudo-autobiographical embodiment of the existential philosophies of the great men behind it (as embodied by his famous dictum 'Experience determines method' [*Methode ist Erlebnis*]). Although style is central to Gundolf's criticism, it is something closer to Buffon's position that 'le style, c'est l'homme même' than to the style of the literary work itself. Jean-Yves Tadié summarizes Gundolf's approach in the following terms: '[His] great lesson remains that of the unity of experience and of a vision which is not to be found in the supposed subjects or problems, but in the *style*, in the manner of seeing and speaking.'[92]

One of the most noteworthy stylistic events to come out of the George circle, at least indirectly, was the rediscovery of Friedrich Hölderlin. In 1912, Norbert von Hellingrath, a young scholar and member of the *Kreis* who was to die in the trenches in 1916, published an historical-critical edition of Hölderlin's poetry. The immediate impact of this edition in the 1910s can be measured by its effect on Rilke, who knew Hellingrath personally and took a great interest in his work.[93] Hölderlin's idiosyncratic, Greek-inflected syntax and rhythms, defined by Adorno as a kind of 'parataxis',[94] had a lasting influence on Rilke's own poetry, culminating in the complex, elegiac structures of his *Duino Elegies* (finally finished in 1922). Hölderlin's rediscovery and reception in the early twentieth century are based to a large extent on his idiosyncratic style and its possibilities: his so-called 'harte Fügung' (severe joining) would have an enduring influence on subsequent thinkers and poets such as Heidegger and Celan.

Another significant factor contributing to the arguably greater continuity of artistic and critical discourse between the Germany of the 1880s and that of the 1920s than in English literature of the same period was the influence of Friedrich Nietzsche. Nowhere was this influence more obvious than in the rapid acceleration of *Sprachskepsis* across literature and philosophy. Nietzsche's essay 'On Truth and Lying in a Nonmoral Sense' (written 1873, unpublished in his lifetime) famously defined truth as 'a mobile army of metaphors, metonyms, anthropomorphisms',[95] thus founding a scepticism as to the epistemological status of language that would underlie much twentieth-century thought and literature. In this essay, Nietzsche develops an essentially Kantian argument over ends and means: just as the astrologer sees the stars through a necessarily anthropomorphic and anthropocentric telescope, so the user of language tends to forget that words are mere metaphors, mere signifiers, confusing them rather with the things they are supposed to signify. 'Forgetting that the original metaphors of perception were indeed metaphors, he takes them for the things themselves.'[96]

The modernist writers associated with the concept of *Sprachskepsis* respond to this by problematizing their own use of language: language should not seek to be the transparent window onto external things which it patently cannot be, but rather should seek meaning in its own opacity, in its 'inscape', to use Hopkins' term. Hofmannsthal's 'Ein Brief' (1902), perhaps the single most significant document of turn-of-the-century *Sprachskepsis*, argues extravagantly against its own existence, using the elaborate conceit of an early seventeenth-century letter in order to bemoan the limitations of language. Yet it can be read historically not just in its own fictional sense, but also within the chronological context of its genesis. Interpreted synchronically as well as diachronically, it can be read as analogous to the subsequent attacks of the English modernists on their Victorian predecessors: just as Eliot and Pound, Leavis and Empson rejected the stilted notions of 'literary decorum' and predetermined 'styles', so Hofmannsthal's Lord Chandos rejects 'rhetoric, which is good for women or for the House of Commons, whose power, however, so overrated by our time, is not sufficient to penetrate into the core of things'.[97] In place of this rhetoric,

Chandos prefers rather 'gay and stimulating moments' which are filled with an 'overflowing flood of higher life' – thus inaugurating one of the key topoi of modernism, namely the search for what James Joyce called 'epiphanies' and Virginia Woolf described as 'alcoves of silence where we can shelter under the wing of beauty'.[98] Characteristic of the many modernist writers who pursued this search is the fact that they structured their writing around it.[99] The quest for such moments was built into the very fabric of their style: Marcel Proust's concept of art in *In Search of Lost Time* (1913–27), Robert Musil's notion of 'essayism' in *The Man without Qualities* (1930–42) and the obsession with rhythm in Woolf's *The Waves* (1931) – to take just three well-known examples from French, German and English literature – can all be said to be concerned with the relationship between their own stylistic processes and the essential provisionality of time, inasmuch as they turn back against themselves, constantly biting their own tails in a never-ending attempt to locate truth and meaning in their own descriptive power. '"Like" and "like" and "like" – but what is the thing that lies beneath the semblance of the thing?' asks Woolf in *The Waves*.[100]

Rhoda
p. 118

Fritz Mauthner, whose *Beiträge zu einer Kritik der Sprache* (1901–2) form one of the key documents of post-Nietzschean language scepticism, undertook to conceptualize this line of reasoning explicitly. In his estimation, language could be a means of communication, even of expression, but not a means of ultimate knowledge. For the philosopher, words are 'unusable tools'. Yet the paradox is that the writer, despite the inevitable insufficiency of language, is defined by his idiosyncratic use of it, as Mauthner argues:

> Every distinctive writer can be recognized by his characteristic, individual language, at every step of the way. As with the images of a distinctive painter. Whoever does not have his own style is not a born writer.[101]

In the same year, 1902, Rémy de Gourmont published *Le Problème du style*. Whilst Gourmont does not develop a philosophy of language à la Mauthner, he views style in similar terms as a distinctive marker of individuality, describing the 'real problem of style [as] a question of physiology. [...] We write, as we feel, as we think, with our entire body.'[102] Gourmont repeatedly mentions Schopenhauer and Nietzsche as the key philosophers of the modern age; although he does not quote him directly, his conception of style as physiology seems to recall Schopenhauer's famous definition of style in his *Parerga and Paralipomena* (1851) as 'the physiognomy of the mind [*des Geistes*]'.[103] Gourmont set the terms of subsequent debate: in his 1929 essay on Proust, for instance, Walter Benjamin picked up on this discourse, claiming that 'a physiology of style would take us into the innermost core of this creativeness'.[104] Benjamin's essay systematically develops a notion of style as physiological, defining it as the embodiment in language of certain physical characteristics: 'Proust's syntax rhythmically and step by step reproduces his fear of suffocating [...]. His sentences are the entire muscular activity of the intelligible body.'[105] Proust's style has sometimes been read as a reflection of his asthma, where the long sentences, dependent on a preponderance of relative clauses, can be understood as enacting the self-consciousness of the asthmatic's respiratory rhythm. Benjamin returns again and again in his essay to this view of style as something like the body language of language: he reads Proust's work as the 'highest physiognomic expression which the irresistibly growing discrepancy between literature and life was able to assume'.[106] Striking here is the conceptualization of Proust's 'physiology of style' as a response to the 'growing discrepancy between literature and life', since Albert Thibaudet, amongst other critics, claims that *In Search of Lost Time* represents precisely the opposite: for Proust, 'the life of man and the life of style are merely the vibration and aftershock of the same experience'.[107] Proust's 'physiological' style has thus been read both as affirmative and as critical, as both a retreat from, and an assertion of, life itself: modernist style is once again located at the crossroads between pure poetry and *Sprachskepsis*, between absolute faith in language and absolute scepticism.

Around the same time as Benjamin was writing on Proust's style, Leo Spitzer published the two volumes of his *Stilstudien* (1928). From his first book onwards, *Die Wortbildung als stilistisches Mittel exemplifiziert an Rabelais* (1910), Spitzer was obsessed with the question of literary style. Jean Starobinski, in the foreword to the influential French version of *Etudes de style* which appeared in 1970, summarizes his technique as follows: 'To perceive a stylistic difference [*écart*] compared to usual usage; to evaluate this difference, to identify its expressive significance; to reconcile this discovery with the tone and general spirit of the work [...]: such is the initial movement of Spitzer's criticism.'[108] Hans-Jörg Neuschäfer suggests that Spitzer defines style as 'the unity of expression (*Ausdruck*) and meaning (*Sinn*) which must be re-experienced in every text; as the *unmistakeable* unity of expression and meaning' (his italics).[109] Yet he also adds that Spitzer understands style as 'the mediation between a norm and its deviations. [...] In this respect, style is no longer merely the *expression* of meaning, but rather a *process* that makes meaning possible in the first place.'[110] If Spitzer's *werkimmanent* methodology is thus broadly analogous to the close reading advocated by Richards, Empson and Leavis, it also implies that one should not neglect the socio-historical context: 'In order to be able to make a balanced judgement about the difference of a given style, in order to appreciate its tension, we need to pose a further question: does the cultural environment allow this difference, does it condemn it or encourage it?'[111]

The shift in critical discourse identified in England as a reaction against the Victorian sense of style as 'literary decorum', and in the German-speaking world as a response to influential voices in art history as well as to the post-Nietzschean devaluation of language, can perhaps be characterized most easily in France by a single phrase: *Contre Sainte-Beuve*. Starobinski uses Proust's essay collection as shorthand for a paradigm shift in his foreword to Spitzer's *Etudes de style*: 'Does it not suffice to show with accuracy how the text is organized? Is the *why* not implicit in the *how*? As we know, this is the thesis of the enemies of biography and psychologism, the thesis of Proust in *Contre Sainte-Beuve*.'[112] Proust anticipated the anti-intentionalist, formalist critics of the later twentieth century by criticizing Sainte-Beuve for his biographical approach to literature, insisting in his chapter on 'The Method of Sainte-Beuve' that 'a book is the product of a different *self* from the self we manifest in our habits, in our social life, in our vices'.[113] Proust recalls how Sainte-Beuve patronized Baudelaire, for instance, referring to *The Flowers of Evil* as 'the Baudelaire Folly'[114] whilst calling the man himself 'a nice fellow' with 'perfectly correct manners'.[115] Yet what distinguishes one genuine artist from another, insists Proust *pace* Sainte-Beuve, is 'the particular amplification [*la broderie particulière*] which can proceed only from him'.[116] And it is for this reason, he continues, that 'I make no distinction between High Art, which deals only with love and lofty conceptions [...] and the art which has no morality or purpose about it.'[117] Just like Leavis and Empson, in other words, Proust rejects what he sees as an outdated, 'nineteenth-century' notion of predetermined 'styles' and registers, preferring to see the power of language to transcend the given moment as the subject of modern art, rather than the 'real' world outside:

> The stuff of our books, the substance of our sentences, should be drawn from our imaginations, not taken just as it comes from real life; but our actual style, and the episodes too, should be made out of the transparent substance of our best moments, those in which we transcend reality and the present. It is from those consolidated drops of light that the style and the story of a book are made.[118]

Proust's position here seems to echo Mallarmé's famous rebuke to Degas that 'one does not make poetry with ideas, but with *words*'. This statement is quoted by Paul Valéry in a lecture given in 1939 in Oxford entitled 'Poetry and Abstract Thought',[119] in which he discourses on a term that will become familiar when we turn to look at his poetry in Chapter 4, namely *la voix*. Valéry conceives 'voice' as central to poetry and *a fortiori* to all self-consciously 'literary' use of language, which oscillates as he understands it between the two extremes of sound and sense: 'Between Voice and Thought, between Thought and Voice, between Presence and Absence, oscillates the poetic pendulum.'[120] Valéry's notion of 'voice', whilst essentially classical in its foregrounding of the Orphic poet, is also typically modernist in its refusal of any attempt to separate *forme* and *fond*:

> To distinguish between form and content in poetry; between a subject and its treatment; between sound and sense; to consider rhythm, meter, and prosody as naturally and easily separable from the *verbal expression* itself, from the *words* themselves, and from the *syntax*; these are so many symptoms of noncomprehension or insensibility in poetic matters.[121]

Valéry advocates here an understanding of poetry that considers style and substance to be one and the same thing. His particular inflection, proper to his vision of his own calling as poet, tends to take the form of an insistence on the contrast between poetry and prose: quoting Malherbe, Valéry memorably defines the relationship between poetry and prose as analogous to that between dancing and walking. Interestingly, he uses the same term as Proust and Benjamin – 'physiology' – to make this distinction: 'the difference between the action of a poem and of an ordinary narrative is physiological'.[122] Valéry's vision of 'poetic' language as one that is charged with a certain kind of 'muscular organization' is in this sense strikingly similar to Benjamin's definition of Proust's sentences as 'the entire muscular activity of the intelligible body'.

Valéry's summary of the essence of the transition from realism to early modernism is worth briefly dwelling on:

> When one looks back to the youth of that epoch [...] there reigned at that moment a kind of disillusion with philosophic theories, a contempt for the promises of science, that had been very ill interpreted by our predecessors and elders, the realist and naturalist writers. [...] Before us was a white, blank page, and we could inscribe on it only a single affirmation. [...] Our certainty was in our emotion and our feeling for beauty.[123]

Valéry is describing here the aestheticism of the fin-de-siècle, their turn away from scientistic positivism towards questions of aesthetic beauty and 'pure' style. One of the aphorisms collected in *Tel Quel*, first published in 1926, takes a broader historical perspective to make the same point: whilst the style of Racine and La Fontaine always stayed close to the 'living person', the early modernists started to look to language itself as the driving-force:

> With Mallarmé and certain others, a sort of tendency to non-human, *absolute* language emerges – language which evokes some kind of independent entity – a god of language – illuminated by the Omnipotence of the Harmony of Words. It is the faculty of speech which speaks; and speaking, becomes intoxicated; and intoxicated, dances.[124]

Adapting Valéry himself, then, one could say that the transition to a modernist conception of style that he sketches out is broadly analogous to his distinction between prose and poetry: where previously style 'walked', as a process of communication with a particular destination in mind, in the second half of the nineteenth century it began to dance, intoxicated by linguistic movement for its own sake.

Yet the distinction between the realists/naturalists and the subsequent early modernists which Valéry discerns is not as clear-cut as this might suggest. Flaubert, to take just one instance, is on the one hand an emblematic realist of the mid-nineteenth century, and on the other hand an acknowledged forefather of European modernism. How is one to square this circle? Part of the answer lies in the obvious but important fact that artistic movements are never discrete entities – as Roman Jakobson rightly insisted, a 'simultaneous preservation of tradition and breaking away from tradition form the essence of every new work of art'.[125] In any case, 'realism' is not confined to the mid-nineteenth-century movement of that name, as Jakobson also pointed out:

> Classicists, sentimentalists, the romanticists to a certain extent, even the 'realists' of the nineteenth

century, the modernists to a large degree, and finally the futurists, expressionists, and their like, have more than once steadfastly proclaimed faithfulness to reality, maximum verisimilitude – in other words, realism – as the guiding motto of their artistic program.[126]

The key distinction here is that realism is an aim, but also a style, just as modernism is also both aim (an attempt to encompass modernity) and style (stream of consciousness, montage, fragmentation, etc.). If modernism is to be understood as an aesthetic reaction against the conditions of modernity, then this reaction crucially takes the form of a foregrounding not only of various different kinds of style, but of the very *concept* of style. As we shall see in Chapter 2, this is arguably what makes a 'realist' such as Flaubert an early modernist: he is ultimately as interested in his own literary style as in the external world he happens to depict. If, as Roman Jakobson famously claimed, romanticism depends essentially on metaphor, whereas realism tends to metonymy,[127] is it perhaps possible to claim that modernism subsumes both tropes into a preoccupation with the surfaces of language – in short, with style?

'Saturated with style'

This study argues that the modernist conception of aesthetic style has its roots in the mid-nineteenth century, but only slowly comes to full fruition as the subsequent generations of artists unfold. The seminal decade for modernist conceptions of style is taken to be the 1850s, when notions of style that would become crucial for subsequent writers were being hatched in Germany and in France. In 1851, Schopenhauer published his essay 'On Style', which would soon be trumpeted by English critics; in 1857, Baudelaire published *The Flowers of Evil* and Flaubert *Madame Bovary*. Just as this study traces what we have called the double movement of modernism, so it also has a double beginning: whilst the first chapter retraces the conceptual legacy of Schopenhauer and Nietzsche, the second chapter turns explicitly to the literary legacy of the two French writers. Two key years will be taken as representing the dawning and the zenith of modernism: 1857 and 1922. For Fredric Jameson, 1857 represents the 'crucial year' for modernism ('the art of Baudelaire and Flaubert [is] a response to the temporal crisis of modernity'),[128] whilst Henri Meschonnic writes that 'literary modernity begins with what Sartre called the generation of 1850', and cites Charles Russell to the effect that 1857 represents 'the moment when the artist became aware of his alienation from the dominant values of bourgeois culture'.[129] Although one could go back further than 1857 – and modernism obviously extends beyond 1922 – these two years nevertheless provide useful milestones within which to trace the modernist trajectory.[130]

Two questions require initial answers at this point. Why concentrate on the modernist period, and why privilege the literary? If the concept of style remains central to successive waves of modernists from Flaubert and Baudelaire onwards, it is because one of the defining characteristics of the various artistic movements of this whole period, despite their many differences, is an increased self-consciousness about their own processes of creation. Roland Barthes' reflections on 'Style and its Image' (1969) suggest some of the reasons why style came to the fore in the modernist period. Texts are not to be understood as a fruit with outer flesh and an inner kernel, writes Barthes, but rather as 'an onion, a construction of layers [with] no irreducible principle, nothing except the infinity of its own envelopes – which envelop nothing other than the unity of its own surfaces'.[131] Although such a comment says as much about the time in which it was made – with its emphasis on structures and its nod to the Derridean 'il n'y a pas de hors-texte' – as it does about the pre-war period, Barthes' striking repetition of the term 'nothing' echoes Flaubert's stated desire of more than a century previously to write 'a book dependent on nothing external'. Important here is also the notion of 'surface', a term that Barthes makes synonymous with 'envelopes'. Barthes implies that meaning is infinitely deferred, so that such meaning as there is comes to reside in this very process of deferral. 'Style is essentially a citational process, a body of formulae, a memory', states Barthes.[132]

Such an understanding of style suggests why we find it foregrounded so self-consciously in modernist literature, as Barthes implies when he claims that 'modern poetry is saturated with style'.[133] High modernism is famously characterized by its allusive intertextuality, by the weight of classical culture which can be felt constantly pressing on its textual surfaces. 'Style is a distance, a difference; but in reference to what?' asks Barthes.[134] Modernism answers this question through its self-conscious *modernity*: it is defined by a constant recalibration of its relationship to the past. This relationship is at times recuperative or conservative – looking to classical models in an effort to rejuvenate modern life – at times aggressive or even oedipal (in Harold Bloom's sense of an 'anxiety of influence'). Either way, style becomes of necessity a central preoccupation. Indeed, one could argue that this ambivalence of conservation/aggression is built not only into the concept, but also into the very etymology of 'style': the *OED* defines style as deriving from *stylus*, meaning a 'writing-implement', but adds that it can be 'used as a weapon of offence, for stabbing etc.', since the Latin *stilus* comes from the root *stig*, stigma, stick, German *stechen*.[135] Flaubert himself plays on this, writing of his quest for a 'style which would pierce your mind like the point of a stiletto'.[136] Style can thus be used both to conserve and commemorate *and* to attack and destroy: it is both 'stylus' and 'stiletto'.[137]

This etymology suggests, moreover, a possible answer to our second question, namely why privilege the literary? If the concept of style derives from writing, one must start by considering its home territory. 'Style is the quintessence of all language in art,' we have seen Adorno claim;[138] 'literature is the domain of style', writes Barthes.[139] Pursued back as far as the *dolce stil nuovo* of Cavalcanti and Dante, it is clear that (in contrast to the painterly *maniera*) '*stilo* or *stile* was initially strictly reserved for the field of writing'.[140] An examination of modernist style, whilst it must point to a wider cultural and political context, is thus necessarily rooted in literary aesthetics; the central chapters of this study accordingly trace its conceptualizations from the 1850s of Flaubert and Baudelaire, via the 'decadent style' of the 1880s, to the 1920s of high modernism. Yet the brief overview of contemporary criticism offered in this Introduction suggests equally that style in the modernist period must be understood as an aesthetic term that tends to self-consciousness, that foregrounds its own discussion: Chapter 5 thus investigates the phenomenon of self-stylization in the manifestos characteristic of the time.

Modernist style also has a pre-history, however, in the philosophy of the nineteenth century. A study of style in modernism must begin with the history of this preoccupation in its earliest avatars. The first chapter accordingly focuses on the philosophical legacy of Schopenhauer and Nietzsche, the two nineteenth-century philosophers who would have the greatest influence – through both their 'form' and their 'content'[141] – on the development of modernist style.

1
Philosophical Beginnings

Arthur Schopenhauer and the symbolist 'will to style'

In 1851, Arthur Schopenhauer published two volumes of essays, *Parerga and Paralipomena*. Schopenhauer's main body of philosophical work, begun in 1818 with the first volume of *The World as Will and Representation*, had slumbered unread for decades. Yet it was the incidental essays that would provide his breakthrough: they came to the attention of the English dramatist John Oxenford, who reviewed them in 1852 for George Eliot's *Westminster Review*.[1] Oxenford then read *The World as Will and Representation*, and in 1853 he published a more substantial essay, also in the *Westminster Review*, entitled 'Iconoclasm in German Philosophy', which was then translated into German and published in the *Vossische Zeitung*. Schopenhauer's immense influence on European art over the next century had begun.

Christopher Janaway gives an initial idea of the extent of this posthumous influence: 'In the 1850s Wagner fell under the Schopenhauerian spell [...].

In the 1860s something similar happened to Nietzsche, and to Tolstoy; in the 1880s and 1890s he was read by Thomas Hardy, Thomas Mann, and Marcel Proust, and in the 1900s by the young Wittgenstein.'² To this distinguished list one could add many more of the best-known cultural figures of the modernist period.³ Yet what is striking about this reception history is that it was based in the first instance not on Schopenhauer's main body of thought, but on his marginal work. As Bryan Magee writes in his biography, 'for the rest of Schopenhauer's life, and for some years after his death, his essays were more widely read than his philosophy [. . .], and it is clear that many readers of the philosophy came to it, as John Oxenford had, via the essays'.⁴ In his summary of the main qualities of Schopenhauer's philosophy of the will, Janaway concludes that it was its incidental implications that found the widest resonance:

> It [his conception of will] enables him to explain thought-processes as having an organic, survival-related function, to show the influence of unconscious drives and feelings on the intellect, to suggest that our picture of ourselves as rational individual thinkers is in some sense an illusion, to place sexuality at the core of human psychology, to account for the power of music and the value of aesthetic experience, to argue that ordinary life is inevitably unfulfilled, and to advocate the renunciation of individual desires as the route to reconcilation with our existence. It has been these applications, rather than the bald metaphysical statement that the thing in itself is will, that have had

the most influence on philosophers, psychologists, and artists of later generations.[5]

If the bass note of Schopenhauer's influence on subsequent generations of artists was his underlying pessimism, its higher melody was his celebration of aesthetic experience. Whilst this chapter will necessarily concentrate on the latter, one can only understand it in the context of the former: it is the pessimistic view of life defined as suffering that elicits the idea of art as a temporary respite from the drives of the will. It is thus no accident that, as Janaway suggests, Schopenhauer's philosophy of the will reserved a special place for aesthetic experience.

The World as Will and Representation is divided into four books. The first two volumes define the concepts of 'representation' and 'will', as something broadly akin to the Kantian distinction between the *Ding für sich* and the *Ding an sich*: the individual subject represents to himself the phenomena of everyday existence, and it is only through these that he can hope to access the world of the will. 'Only the will is thing in itself [...]. It is that of which all representation, every object, is the phenomenon, the visibility, the objectivity. It is the innermost essence, the kernel, of every particular thing and also of the whole.'[6] We will see that this metaphysical distinction will be rejected by Nietzsche, but embraced by the symbolists, for whom 'symbols' play the role of Schopenhauer's phenomena in representing the world of the Platonic Ideas.

The focus of the third volume on aesthetic experience, however, reverses the thrust of Schopenhauer's philosophy. Rather than representing the individual subject as constantly striving to assert and access the will, aesthetic disinterest can suspend the will, since 'it considers things without interest, without subjectivity, purely objectively'.[7] Not without straining, Schopenhauer seeks to relate the Platonic Idea to the Kantian *Ding an sich*; he suggests that artists (as well as, in a different way, saints) can approach the Platonic Idea through what amounts to the Kantian disinterest of their renunciation of the will. It is not that they can obtain direct access to the will – as Bryan Magee rightly insists, for Schopenhauer, no one can;[8] but they can at least temporarily obviate it through a kind of *via negativa*. Since the will by definition cannot be accessed, progress can only be achieved through renouncing it. 'Art ends by presenting the free self-abolition of the will.'[9] This is reflected in Schopenhauer's understanding of the true province of genius as 'imaginative perception, and not conceptual thinking':[10] the genius is in fact *less* controlled by the will than the ordinary man, not more. It is also reflected in the hierarchy of the arts which Schopenhauer famously constructs, from the instrumentalized art-forms such as architecture and landscape gardening at the bottom, to music as the purest of all arts at the top. The common factor to both Schopenhauer's understanding of genius and his prioritization of music is their a-conceptual nature: through flattening out the distance between conceptualization and concept, between signifier and signified, the will and its representation get as close as they are likely to get. Since 'inner knowledge is a knowledge of surfaces only, of appearances only',[11] this places a particular emphasis on these surfaces, since it is they that are to provide the 'copy of the will'.

One of the incidental essays collected in *Parerga and Paralipomena* bears the title 'On Style'. Schopenhauer's thoughts on style can essentially be divided into two separate, but interlocking areas: an evaluative, normative notion of style as 'good practice', and a much broader sense of style as a way of seeing the world as mediated through aesthetic experience. In order to understand the second, broader category, we need to take a brief look at the narrower first category.

Schopenhauer uses the notion of 'good' style as a stick with which to beat his preferred enemies: the iconoclasm to which Oxenford refers in the title of his pioneering essay 'was Schopenhauer's attempt to destroy the reputations of all three of what were then [...] the most imposing names in German philosophy: Hegel, Schelling and Fichte'.[12] Schopenhauer accordingly attacks the idealists at the level of their language, which he dismisses as unnecessarily complex and obscurantist, an attempt 'to sell words for thoughts'. This 'mask of unintelligibility' is particularly acute in Germany,[13] Schopenhauer claims, 'introduced by Fichte, perfected by Schelling, and carried to its highest pitch in Hegel'.

What, in Schopenhauer's eyes, constitutes good style? 'Style receives its beauty from the thought it expresses; but with sham-thinkers the thoughts are supposed to be fine because of the style. Style is nothing but the mere silhouette of thought.'[14] Schopenhauer pleads for style to follow the thought, rather than thought the style, since 'a man's style shows the *formal* nature of all his thoughts'.[15] This contrasts notably with his nemesis Hegel's definition of style, in the subsection of his *Aesthetics* dedicated to 'Manner, Style, and Originality',[16] as 'a mode of representation which complies with the conditions of its material as well as corresponding throughout with the demands of definite species of art and the laws originating in their essence':[17] where Hegel inherits the classical sense of achieved style as the subordination of individuality to the conventions of pre-established genres, Schopenhauer inaugurates the modernist 'invention of a personal, private style', in Jameson's terms. This should not be confused with mere individual subjectivity, Schopenhauer warns: 'Style should [...] never be subjective, but *objective*.'[18] Nonetheless, he claims that 'to be naïve is to be attractive',[19] and that 'Goethe's naïve poetry is incomparably greater than Schiller's rhetoric'.[20]

What thus emerges from these stylistic prescriptions, even allowing for a degree of polemical disingenuity, is Schopenhauer's vision of good style as a kind of naïve objectivity. This seeming paradox anticipates the modernist ideal of personal impersonality that runs from Flaubert to Eliot, summarized by John Middleton Murry's declaration in 1922 that the greatest style is 'a combination of the maximum of personality with the maximum of impersonality'.[21] Whilst style is the 'physiognomy of the mind'[22] – to quote the famous opening sentence of Schopenhauer's essay – it should also seek at all times to reach beyond the individual mind, to 'force the reader to think precisely the same thing as the author thought when he wrote'.[23] Schopenhauer sees style as a way of mediating between creation and reception, writer and reader, and this in turn places an obligation on the writer to take great care in the composition of his texts. The Schopenhauer who writes approvingly of Plato that he 'is said to have written the introduction to his *Republic* seven times over in different ways'[24] resonates in the legendary pains taken by Flaubert or Kafka over their manuscripts.

It should be stressed, however, that Schopenhauer is dealing in this essay mainly with thinkers, and not with creative artists or writers. Indeed, it is only when we turn to the second, broader category of style, namely as a way of seeing the world as mediated through aesthetic experience, that the real force of Schopenhauer's subsequent influence in the modernist period becomes apparent. In his *New History of German Literature*, David. E. Wellbery defines three main reasons for Schopenhauer's 'prodigious literary influence', the third of which he lists as 'the extravagant significance he attributed to aesthetic experience'.[25] This significance rests, as we have seen, on Schopenhauer's fundamental distinction between the 'will' and its 'representation'. We have suggested that this is similar to the Kantian distinction between the 'thing for itself' and the 'thing in itself'; yet although Schopenhauer requests of his reader that s/he be fully conversant with Kant's philosophy before beginning to read his own book, he distances himself in a crucial way from his predecessor. Although the 'will' or 'thing in itself' is in Kantian terms 'unknowable', it is, for Schopenhauer, crucially not 'unexperienceable' (*unerfahrbar*) – and one of the most important means of experiencing it is the aesthetic.

Art, according to Schopenhauer, can function as a 'palliative of the will' (*Quietiv des Willens*). Wellbery summarizes this position in the following terms:

> In Schopenhauer's account, to view the world aesthetically is to become detached from all particulars of individual identity and to assume the disinterested standpoint of a 'pure subject of representation'. [...] Aesthetic contemplation offers a unique vehicle of redemption from the unrelenting suffering that is life.[26]

The appeal of Schopenhauer's thought to generations of subsequent artists and thinkers, from Wagner and Nietzsche, through late nineteenth-century French symbolists and Freudian psychoanalysts, to high modernists such as Thomas Mann, Hermann Hesse and Marcel Proust, is thus not hard to discern. Schopenhauer offers a nihilistic world-view, in tune with a secular, pessimistic age, that privileges the redemptive force of art. 'Aesthetic experience', as Wellbery writes, 'has genuine metaphysical content.'[27] Schopenhauer can thus be said to inaugurate the privileging of the aesthetic that is characteristic of modernism, the doctrine that Nietzsche will encapsulate in his statement that 'only as an aesthetic phenomenon is existence and the world eternally justified'.[28]

In defining aesthetic experience as one of the key ways of mediating between the will and its representation, Schopenhauer implicitly places issues of style at the heart of the debate: the will can be 'experienced' by the *how* of style, even if the *what* of content cannot be 'known'. Central to this distinction is Schopenhauer's use of the adjective 'pure' (*rein*): time and again he expresses successful aesthetic contemplation in terms of purity. The highest form of the artist, the genius, is held to reject concepts and conceptualization in favour of 'pure perception',[29] a 'pure knowing' which is 'entirely devoid of relation to will';[30] genius is consequently 'precisely the opposite of that method of thought which seeks merely the content of the phenomenon'.[31] Schopenhauer's rhetoric of purity suggests a rejection of this phenomenal 'content' in favour of a neutral state of contemplation: what matters is not matter ('Matter as such cannot be the expression of an Idea'),[32] but *manner*, the aesthetic surfaces which convey this state of grace. The modernist concept of purity, of 'pure poetry' and intransitive style, descends directly from Schopenhauer's conceptualization of 'pure' aesthetic experience.

This belief finds its fullest expression in his view of music. Music, as Schopenhauer sees it, is the universal, autonomous art *par excellence*: it is alinguistic and thus unrepresentative of any particular aspect of the will, and its use of melody, of minor and major keys, means that it can directly mirror the emotions. It provides, in short, 'a copy of the will itself'.[33] This view of music as the crowning art set a paradigm for the next 50 years: music became the aspirational art-form not only of literature, but of the arts in general. Walter Pater's famous statement of 1873 is worth pausing over:

All art constantly aspires towards the condition of music. For while in all other works of art it is possible to distinguish the matter from the form, and the understanding can always make this distinction, yet it is the constant effort of art to obliterate it. That the mere matter of a poem, for instance, its subject, namely, its given incidents or situation – that the mere matter of a picture, the actual circumstances of an event, the actual topography of a landscape – should be nothing without the form, the spirit, of the handling, that this form, this mode of handling, should become an end in itself, should penetrate every part of the matter: this is what all art constantly strives after, and achieves in different degrees.[34]

Whilst Pater is writing here in the context of a book on Renaissance art, his programmatic insistence on the 'form, the spirit, of the handling' anticipates in its way the formalist turn of modernism. His Schopenhauerian privileging of music, the most purely formal of all the art-forms, brings with it an inevitable self-consciousness about artistic style: in Pater's account, 'the mere matter' of the artwork is made to seem almost secondary to the 'mode of handling', which 'become[s] an end in itself'.

Whilst this view of art as what one might term with Adorno a 'will to style'[35] reaches its apogee in the symbolist movement of the late nineteenth century, the influence of the Schopenhauerian view of music as the paradigm for all art endures well into the high modernist period. This can be illustrated through the example of Edouard Dujardin's *Les Lauriers sont coupés* (first rendered in English, by Joyce's translator Stuart Gilbert, as *We'll to the Woods No More* [1938], retranslated by Anthony Suter in 1991 as *The Bays are Sere*).

Although first published at the height of symbolism in 1888, *Les Lauriers sont coupés* – to which we shall return in more detail in Chapter 3 – was famously cited by Joyce as the key precursor of the stream of consciousness technique used in *Ulysses* (1922). As such its influence reached well into the 1920s and 1930s. Dujardin's novel describes a day in the life of the protagonist Daniel Prince, as he prepares for an evening out in Paris with the actress he is currently courting. The prose follows the internal thoughts of Prince, essentially inventing the 'interior monologue' for the modernist era. Looking back in 1931 at what he and the other symbolists were trying to do in the last two decades of the nineteenth century, Dujardin made it clear that Schopenhauer's influence was key to the development of this new technique, since it encouraged the cultivation of a certain self-conscious musicality in the use of language:

> We deliberately placed poetry on the Schopenhauer level of music. And that is what is meant by saying that Symbolism, liberating poetry from the servitude of intellectualism, restored to it its musical value.[36]

The novel's status as a symbolist work in these terms can be established from its opening paragraphs:

> An evening of setting sun, remote air, deep skies; and of obscure crowds; sounds, shades, multitudes; infinite vastnesses of space; an ill-defined evening...
> For from the chaos of appearances, amid periods and sites, in the illusion of things being begotten

and born, one among the others, distinct from the others, yet similar to the others, one the same and yet another, from the infinity of possible existences, I appear; and this is time and space being defined; it is the Now; it is the Here; the clock striking; and, around me, life; the time, the place, an April evening. Paris, on a bright evening of setting sun, the monotonous noises, the pale houses, the foliage of shadows; a milder evening; and the joy of being someone, of walking; the streets and multitudes, and, stretching far in the air, the sky; all around, Paris sings, and, in the haze of shapes perceived, softly it frames the idea.[37]

If one sets this opening passage against Dujardin's own definition of interior monologue, then a sense of how the symbolists sought to place poetry on the 'Schopenhauer level of music' emerges. Dujardin states in his study of 1931 that 'interior monologue must not render thought "raw", but give the impression of it. And in this way it proves itself to be a work of art much more than the logical analysis of the psychological novel.'[38] In stressing that he does not seek to convey thought as it actually occurs, but rather simply to give this 'impression', Dujardin foregrounds the stylistic surface of the novel as a work of art, rather than as a psychological treatise, in a manner reminiscent of Schopenhauer's insistence on 'perception' rather than conception. Antoine Baillot's description in 1927 of Mallarmé's stylistic aims typifies the symbolist agenda:

> With his collections of words which are more 'incantatory' formulas than verses, he avoids the

concrete and 'commercial' meaning of language in order to be better able to transport the reader away from any 'articulated' idea into the world of pure thought and pure sensation, 'where life and spirit [*esprit*] mysteriously find form'.[39]

Baillot uses a familiar rhetoric of purity to justify the rejection of a vulgar world of commerce in favour of the stylized world of art. Through foregrounding stylistic surface, the symbolists sought to recalibrate the balance of power between word and world: 'pure' poetry, where the Mallarméan 'esprit' or the Schopenhauerian Will 'forms itself', is one in which art is both signifier and signified.

In composing his text in this way, Dujardin had one other major model alongside Schopenhauer, namely Wagner. Looking back in 1931, Dujardin explicitly claimed that the aim of his novel had been Wagnerian:

> I am going to divulge a secret: *Les Lauriers sont coupés* was undertaken with the wild ambition of transposing into the literary field Wagnerian procedures which I defined for myself as follows: the life of the soul expressed through the incessant eruption of musical motifs, coming up to speak, one after the other, undefined and in succession, the 'states' of thought, in no logical order, in the form of bursts of thought rising from the depths of the self, from what we today would call the unconscious or the subconscious.[40]

Les Lauriers sont coupés thus combines a Wagnerian use of leitmotifs with the Schopenhauerian attempt to access the will through music, 'from the chaos of appearances'. Indeed, Baillot noted that Schopenhauer's influence on the symbolists was essentially mediated through Wagner: 'In the eyes of the major symbolists, Wagner, the disciple of Schopenhauer, always remained the master of concordance [*concordances*], since one of the characteristics of symbolist "poetry" was the search for melody rather than rhythm.'[41]

If Schopenhauer's influence on symbolism, and by extension on the subsequent developments in modernism that grew out of symbolism, was thus considerable, it is important to note its less purely affirmative flipside. The double movement of modernism manifests itself in the self-destructive nature of symbolism: when pushed to its logical extreme, the symbolist aesthetic starts to forgo any notion of an organic, necessary relationship between signifier and signified, and simply imposes a particular motif as an arbitrary symbol of something else. Schopenhauer, interestingly, already recognized this danger, strikingly using the term 'symbolism' *avant la lettre* (even if he was obviously not referring directly to the literary movement):

> If there is absolutely no connection between the representation and the conception signified by it, founded on subsumption under the concept, or association of Ideas; but the signs and the things signified are combined in a purely conventional manner, by positive, accidentally introduced laws; then I call this degenerate kind of allegory *Symbolism*.[42]

The transition from the habitual term of praise 'pure' to the dismissive 'purely conventional' is telling. What

Schopenhauer outlines here is a kind of language scepticism *avant la lettre*: language becomes suspect where its arbitrary nature implies a lack of organic, epistemologically justified connection between signifier and signified. Schopenhauer can thus be seen as the philosophical precursor not only of the self-conscious aestheticism of modernism (pure style), but also of its crisis of representation (purely style).

This double legacy quickly found an heir in the 1870s. For if Schopenhauer's influence arrives in the period of high modernism via the symbolist appropriation of music as the aesthetic paradigm *par excellence* (culminating in the 'decadent style' to which we shall return in the following chapters), it also takes another, equally scenic route. It is stating the obvious to say that modernist notions of style are unthinkable without the man who was both Schopenhauer's most influential disciple and his most vociferous critic.

Friedrich Nietzsche and 'the art of style'

Nietzsche's views on style go to the heart of his philosophy. Partly this is because his conceptualization of style relates to his own style in interesting ways; partly it is because his views change, whilst essentially remaining the same. His stylistic influence on modernism, through both his theory and his practice, is in any case immense. Why is this?

All contingencies of reception and dissemination aside, the short answer is that Nietzsche brought the relationship between what the philosopher writes about, and the way he writes about it, to an unprecedented pitch. Style, remarks Douglas Thomas, 'is a uniquely rhetorical aspect of his work'.[43] Nietzsche, it has often been noted, is as much a writer as a thinker;[44] the style of his books matters as much as their content. This is not to say that his style remains consistent or homogeneous: Walter Kaufmann writes of 'the variety of styles that distinguish Nietzsche's literary output', defining early works such as *The Birth of Tragedy* and *Untimely Meditations* as 'diverse forms of the essay', middle-period works such as *Human, All Too Human, Dawn* and *The Gay Science* as 'various treatments of an aphoristic style', and later works from the mid-1880s such as *Thus Spake Zarathustra* and *Beyond Good and Evil* as respectively 'an experiment in dithyrambs' and a 'turning away from his previous aphoristic style'.[45] Yet what unites these changing styles is precisely their restless inconstancy, their incessant need to keep experimenting with differing means of expression. Indeed, Nietzsche argues in 1873 that it is only the 'cultural philistine' who seeks 'unity of style', since this is 'above all a negative quality: the absence of anything offensive – *but anything truly productive is offensive*'.[46]

Nietzsche's virulently anti-systemic thinking has stylistic as well as conceptual resonance for the modernist era, as Kaufmann neatly summarizes:

Nietzsche's ceaseless experimenting with different styles seems to conform to the *Zeitgeist* which was generally marked by a growing dissatisfaction with traditional modes of expression. Wagner, the Impressionists and the Expressionists, Picasso and the Surrealists, Joyce, Pound, and Eliot all show a similar tendency. Nietzsche's experiments, however, are remarkable for the lack of any deliberateness, even in the face of their extreme diversity. Thus Ludwig Klages, the characterologist who began his literary career as a George disciple, can speak of 'the almost peerless uniformity of Nietzsche's style'. What is perhaps really peerless is the concomitance of uniformity and diversity. [...] Involuntarily almost, Nietzsche is driven from style to style in his ceaseless striving for an adequate medium of expression.[47]

It is indeed the very fact that Nietzsche is constantly looking to express himself in different ways that suggests his preoccupation with the issue of style. Underlying this preoccupation is the recurring claim of *The Birth of Tragedy* that 'only as an aesthetic phenomenon is existence and the world eternally justified'.[48] Two things are worth noting straightaway about this statement, perhaps too well known for its own good. First, it is not just that the world is to be justified aesthetically, but that it is to be justified as an aesthetic *phenomenon*: life is understood as surface and *Schein*, there is no noumenal sphere beyond the phenomenal. (That an 'aesthetic phenomenon' is a quasi-tautology for Nietzsche is, we shall see, one of the abiding lessons of his concept of style.) Secondly, this statement does not simply mean that the ostensibly non-aesthetic must be understood in terms of the aesthetic, but also, conversely, that the aesthetic determines the non-aesthetic, that is to say the cultural, political and moral. Whilst Nietzsche's foregrounding of the aesthetic derives directly from Schopenhauer's privileging of 'aesthetic contemplation', his concept of style encompasses a much broader sense of culture and character.

In order to understand Nietzsche's theories of style, one has to trace their development (the very fact that one has to use the plural 'theories' is telling). In his early work, the young Nietzsche sought to elevate style to the level of a national precept. In an 1872 fragment he writes that he is advocating 'not education on a national basis, but the education of German style through living knowing creating talking walking etc.' (KSA 7, 510). His first book, *The Birth of Tragedy*, published in the same year, is a plea for the rejuvenation of Germanic culture through music. Nietzsche would have contemporary Germany look back to 'the Greeks as stylists' (KSA 7, 407); he notes, in 1873, that 'German as an artistic quality of style is still to be discovered, just as the Greeks only discovered their style belatedly' (KSA 7, 645–6). The desiderated reconciliation of Dionysian drives and Apolline form, famously at the heart of the book, is at this stage to be found in the *Gesamtkunst* of Wagner – who, as Nietzsche writes four years later in the fourth of the *Untimely Meditations*, thus becomes the founder of a new 'stylistic tradition'. Given that this 'invented tradition' (to use Eric Hobsbawm's term)[49] is inscribed 'not in signs on paper, but in effects upon the souls of men',[50] style is to be understood not as a purely literary or aesthetic construct, but as a psychological and cultural concept. For, as Nietzsche declares near the beginning of the first of the *Untimely Meditations* in 1873, 'culture is, above all, unity of artistic style in all the expressions of the life of a people'[51] – whereas 'barbarism' is tellingly defined as its exact opposite, 'a lack of style'.[52]

For the Nietzsche of the early 1870s, then, the very notion of culture is a function of style. Yet it is defined, from a German perspective, *ex negativo*: German *Kultur* lags a long way behind French *civilisation* ('we are still dependent on Paris in all matters of form'),[53] since 'public speech has in Germany not yet attained to a national style or even to the desire for a style'.[54] Whilst the inferiority complex towards French *civilisation* was a standard topos of German cultural criticism of the time, it is notable that Nietzsche frames it in terms of style and form: Germans, he argues in 1874 in the second of the *Untimely Meditations*, reject any sense of form and possess only 'the sense of the content'.[55] Nietzsche thus implicitly elides the Germanic with what he terms, in *The Birth of Tragedy*, the Socratic: in both instances an overemphasis on the theoretical or conceptual occludes the aesthetic or the 'desire for a style'. Nietzsche's notes of the period make clear that his criticism of Socrates in *The Birth of Tragedy* is based on a similar insistence on art as form; as early as 1869 he bemoans 'the destruction of form through content', since 'Socratism destroyed form in Plato, as well as the very distinctions in style [*Stilgattungen*] of the Cynics' (KSA 7, 17).

Although in the 1880s Nietzsche came to reject much of his earlier thought, *The Birth of Tragedy* and its associated fragments nevertheless inaugurate what is arguably his most enduring obsession, namely the relationship between aesthetic surface and metaphysical depth. Indeed, one way of tracing Nietzsche's development is to chart the oscillations in this relationship. Through the opposition of Apollo and Dionysus, *The Birth of Tragedy* attempts a reconciliation of tragic 'knowledge' (*Erkenntnis*) and aesthetic 'semblance' (*Schein*). Nietzsche's *Nachlass* notes make clear that he

understood the relationship between the two dialectically. He develops a series of related terms: tragedy is
the 'victory of beauty over knowledge' (KSA 7, 73); he
sees 'the terrible in the mask of the beautiful' (KSA 7,
80); he notes that there can be 'no beautiful surface
without a terrible depth' (KSA 7, 159); and he asks himself rhetorically 'How does art emerge? As the antidote
[*Heilmittel*] to knowledge' (KSA 7, 198). These statements can all be understood as variations on a theme.
They fall largely into two groups: either they imply
that aesthetic beauty derives from the 'overcoming'
(the key Nietzschean term which lurks behind both
'victory' and 'antidote') of tragic insight; or they suggest that 'the terrible' (*das Schreckliche*) is hidden, viti-
ated – but not vanquished – by the dazzle of superficial
beauty.

We must pause here over the terms 'mask' and
'surface', for the rhetoric of surface and depth that
finds expression in them will resonate not only in
Nietzsche's own work, but also in the subsequent
development of modernism more generally. The open-
ing lines of Rilke's first 'Duino Elegy' – 'beauty | is
really nothing but the first stirrings of a terror | we
are just able to endure' – are merely the best-known
example of this definition of beauty as balanced pre-
cariously on the knife-edge of terror. If we understand
modernism (as outlined in the Introduction) as a reaction against the conditions of modernity, then the
definition holds true more generally, both in an historical sense for the post-war high modernist period,
and in a broader sense for a whole epoch torn between
competing tendencies to fragmentation and monu-
mentality. For 'the terrible in the mask of the beautiful', one could substitute 'chaos in the mask of order';

the tension, the pressure placed on aesthetic stylization remains the same. Nietzsche's dictum inaugurates
the sense of stylization in the modernist era as necessary dissimulation, as a 'mask' for mere anarchy,
for the Dionysian forces threatening to tear apart a
centre which cannot hold. It marks the specifically
modernist twist to Roland Barthes' claim that all literature states 'larvatus prodeo':[56] in Max Weber's secular,
'disenchanted' age, modernist art points to its own
stylistic mask not out of choice, but out of necessity.
'The path to style must be followed, not skipped over'
(KSA 7, 685), notes Nietzsche in 1874. In Flaubert's
dream of a book about nothing, style becomes metaphysics, 'just as the earth, suspended in the void,
depends on nothing external for its support'.

Alongside the image of the mask, Nietzsche also
speaks repeatedly of the 'surface' (*Fläche*). Arguably a
more neutral term (since it does not suggest dissimulation or performance), it resonates equally in the visual
idiom of modernism: painters such as Cézanne and
Picasso, sculptors such as Rodin and Gaudier-Brzeska,
and poets such as Rilke and Pound all repeatedly speak
of 'planes' and 'surfaces'. The importance of the term
to Nietzsche is twofold: it locates meaning in aesthetic
surface, and yet at the same time it dialectically evokes
the depth beneath this surface. Indeed, Nietzsche's
love of the ancient Greeks was based on precisely their
recognition of this dialectic; at the end of one of his
very last works, *Nietzsche contra Wagner*, he comes back
to the topic:

They knew how to *live*: what is needed for that is
to stop bravely at the surface, the fold, the skin;
to worship appearance, to believe in shapes, tones,

> words, in the whole *Olympus of appearance*! Those
> Greeks were superficial – *out of profundity.*[57]

The term 'surface' functions, in other words, as a microcosm of the early Nietzsche's Schopenhauerian drive to raise aesthetics to ethics: 'The purpose of the world is painless perception, pure aesthetic pleasure' (KSA 7, 207).

Nietzsche's aesthetics of the 'surface' can only be understood in the context of his engagement with previous thinkers. As Douglas Thomas writes, 'coming to terms with Nietzsche's style means confronting Nietzsche's relationship with the philosophical tradition'.[58] The key lies in his rejection of Platonism, of the conventional hierarchy of essences and appearances. In a move that would have far-reaching consequences for philosophy and the arts in the early twentieth century, Nietzsche formulated what one could call with Gilles Deleuze an 'overturning'[59] of the prioritization of essences over appearances; 'essence, for Nietzsche, is abstracted from appearance'[60] – and not, as in the Platonic tradition, the other way around. Nietzsche thus rejected what he came to see as philosophies of essence, be they the Platonic 'forms', the Schopenhauerian 'Will' or the Kantian '*Ding an sich*'; 'there is *only* a perspective seeing, *only* a perspective "knowing"', as he notes in *On the Genealogy of Morals.*[61]

If Nietzsche seeks to rehabilitate the concept of style through this insistence on aesthetic surface, it is only possible because 'style and content are not binary opposites, but [rather] indistinguishable. Style, for Nietzsche, is that which gives meaning to life through representation.'[62] Yet this foregrounding of appearances over essences cuts both ways, affirming the primacy of 'surfaces', whilst at the same time acknowledging their illusoriness. What Nietzsche offers with the one hand, he withdraws with the other: in contrast to the 'truth' claims of Platonic philosophies, the truth of art lies in its very 'untruth'. 'Truth returns as illusion, or at least as truth about its own illusion.'[63] It is this second kind of truth that will come to define modernist attitudes towards aesthetic 'surface'. In the secular, post-Darwinian age of the early twentieth century, man is condemned to the world of representation, since the metaphysical consolations of transcendental essences are no longer available. After Nietzsche, in other words, style replaces (Platonic) substance, even though – indeed because – it is illusory: art, as he famously writes in *The Birth of Tragedy*, is a 'necessary illusion' ('We *live* only by means of the illusions of art,' he notes in 1873).[64] Wittgensteinian language games, modernist *Sprachskepsis*, the various forms of abstract visual art: in their ambiguity towards both the possibilities and the limitations of representation, they can all be said to descend from Nietzsche's inversion of the Platonic order.[65] Adorno implies as much in his *Aesthetic Theory*:

> Art's illusoriness progressively became absolute; this is concealed by Hegel's term 'art-religion', which was taken literally by the œuvre of the Schopenhauerian Wagner. Modernism subsequently rebelled against the semblance of a semblance which denied it is such.[66]

This transition from a view of art as offering an alternative to transcendental philosophy (i.e. 'truth') to a view of art as offering only a second-order truth (i.e. aesthetic 'untruth') makes Nietzsche's move beyond the 'Schopenhauerian Wagner' the key to the subsequent modernist 'rebellion'. Rather than denying that art is the 'semblance of a semblance', Nietzsche acknowledged this as its cardinal virtue, raising style into an aesthetics of immanence. 'Art treats illusion as illusion; therefore it does not wish to deceive; therefore it is true' (KSA 7, 632). Where Hegel had famously celebrated art as the sensuous representation of the Idea, Nietzsche saw the Idea as essentially an artistic construct, defining truth, in the early essay 'On Truth and Lying in a Nonmoral Sense' (1873), as simply a 'mobile army of metaphors, metonymies, anthropomorphisms'.[67] If aesthetic surfaces became scratched to opacity by the mid-twentieth century, if whole schools of philosophy became essentially exercises in rhetoric, then the original sin lies largely with Nietzsche.

Having established the primacy of aesthetics over metaphysics, the next step in Nietzsche's development was to broaden this out into ethics. The pedagogical aspect of his thought is often underestimated: education (*Erziehung*) was from early on a key part of his 'revaluation of all values'. Nietzsche saw himself as *praeceptor germaniae*, and one of his main goals was to develop a pedagogy of style; we have seen how he sought to define the very notion of culture itself as a function of style. One of the principal tasks of his middle period was to refine this sense of culture as the pursuit of 'greatness': 'The aesthetic concept of the great and the sublime: the task is to educate for this. Culture depends on how one defines "the great".'[68] Nietzsche defined this 'greatness' notably in terms of style – and in terms, moreover, that echo his earlier insistence on the relationship between the 'beautiful' and the 'terrible': 'Grand style originates when the beautiful carries off victory over the monstrous.'[69]

Nietzsche makes this statement in the second half of *Human, All Too Human* ('The Wanderer and his Shadow', published in 1880), which contains arguably the most sustained exposition of his views on style. Building on his earlier view of culture as the 'unity of artistic style in all the expressions of the life of a people', his pedagogical instinct pushes him to develop a normative ideal of the 'best style':

> *Teaching of the best style.* – The teaching of style can on the one hand be the teaching that one ought to discover the means of expression by virtue of which every state of mind can be conveyed to the reader or auditor; on the other hand, it can be the teaching that one ought to discover the means of expression for the most desirable state of mind, the state, that is to say, which it is most desirable should be communicated and conveyed: that of the spiritually joyful, luminous and honest man who has overcome his passions. This will be the teaching that there exists a best style: the style corresponding to the good man.[70]

Nietzsche here aligns aesthetics with ethics into a vision of style as a moral index: 'To improve one's style – means to improve one's thoughts.'[71] The 'good

European' is to be identified by his refined style, he proclaims, echoing his earlier observations about the inferiority of German compared to French. Variant terms for this refined style recur throughout this section of *Human, All Too Human*: within the space of just a few pages, Nietzsche speaks of 'high style', 'fine style', 'the style of immortality' and 'grandiloquent style'.[72] The definition of this 'grand style' as the moment 'when the beautiful carries off victory over the monstrous' suggests a vision of style as barely contained tension, as a struggle that has always only just been won. Without the monstrous Dionysus, the beautiful Apollo cannot aspire to sublimity; the grandeur is precisely in the overcoming. As Nietzsche notes in a later fragment, grand style is the 'expression of the "will to power" itself'.[73]

Style is thus to be imposed on the crude matter of reality through an act of supreme artistic will; it is a kind of ethical *Kunstwollen*, one might say with Alois Riegl. All around him, the Nietzsche of the late 1870s sees a tired naturalism that seeks to flatten aesthetic experience into an attempt at mere mimesis, an etiolated version of 'reality'. In reaction against this, Nietzsche advocates rather a self-conscious stylization, an insistence on aesthetic surface and semblance. Yet this aesthetic project nonetheless derives its pathos from its ethical dimension: 'Intellectual style emerges belatedly, always on the basis of ethical style' (*des Ethos-Stils*) (KSA 8, 285). By the time of his next book, *The Gay Science* (1882), Nietzsche makes the ethical nature of his anti-naturalism explicit:

One thing is needful. – To 'give style' to one's character – a great and rare art! It is practised by those
who survey all the strengths and weaknesses that
their nature has to offer and then fit them into an
artistic plan until each appears as art and reason and
even weakness delight the eye. Here a great mass of
second nature has been added; there a piece of first
nature removed: both times through long practice
and daily work at it. Here the ugly that could not be
removed is concealed; there it is reinterpreted into
sublimity.[74]

Nietzsche aligns the realm of the aesthetic with
strength of character, where the cultivation of style
becomes comparable to the discipline of artistic
training; 'conversely', he continues, 'it is the weak
characters with no power over themselves who *hate*
the constraint of style' (*die Gebundenheit des Stils*).
The 'artistic plan' that imposes order, that mediates
between 'original nature' (*erste Natur*) and 'second
nature' (*zweite Natur*), transforms self-fashioning into
an aesthetic process – which in turn is configured as
an ethical, existential doctrine.

Amongst the work Nietzsche produced in the summer of 1882 under the spell of the young Lou Andreas-
Salomé (the so-called 'Tautenburger Aufzeichnungen'),
the ten points of the short text 'Zur Lehre vom Stil'
('On the Lessons of Style') elaborate an alternative ten
commandments, the very form of which suggests that
Nietzsche saw style in quasi-religious terms. Despite
the fact that 'Nietzsche is interested here only in

writing', and that 'style – in accordance with its etymology – is understood here as a way of writing',[75] his
vision of style resonates with implicit erotic energy:
the very first point, the leitmotif, is that 'style must
live' (KSA 10, 38). The italicized emphasis on *living*
suggests that style is foregrounded as a means of overcoming the Cartesian duality of mind and body: 'Style
must prove that one *believes* in one's thoughts, and
that one does not merely think them, but *feels* them'
(KSA 10, 39). Indeed, if one gazes along the gallery
of Nietzsche's favoured figures – Sophocles, Caesar,
Goethe, Wagner, Zarathustra – it becomes clear that
they all function at given moments as variations on
'the man who overcomes himself, sublimating his
impulses, consecrating his passions, and giving style
to his character, [who] becomes truly human or – as
Zarathustra would say, enraptured by the word *über –
super*human'.[76]

Striking in this desire 'to give style to character' is
Nietzsche's characteristic emphasis on activity, on the
necessary *poeisis* of self-stylization. Nietzsche abhors
what he sees as the passivity of Christian culture, its
reification of suffering as a moral virtue. Accordingly,
he celebrates the transfiguration of nature through art.
The desideration of a process of 'giving style' echoes
Apollo's function in *The Birth of Tragedy* ten years earlier as what Kaufmann calls the 'form-giving force',[77]
just as Nietzsche's preference for 'second nature' over
'original nature' echoes the 'second mirror-image' of
the Apolline dream.[78] For Nietzsche, aesthetic semblance, style, *untruth*, offers the only truth that there is.

Whilst the young Nietzsche already prefers the aesthetic to the moral – this is one of the constants of

his work, despite his shifting allegiances – if anything his position hardens over time: where he writes in 1872 that 'art represents the highest task and the truly metaphysical activity of this life', by the time of his 'Attempt at a Self-Criticism' 14 years later he spells out the implicit opposition explicitly: 'art – and *not* morality – is the true *metaphysical* activity of man'.[79] His fundamental 'counter-doctrine', he writes in 1886, is 'a purely artistic, an anti-Christian one'.[80] Yet despite this strengthening of his aesthetic world-view, by 1886 Nietzsche had long since rejected his early enthusiasm for the aesthetic models of Wagner and Schopenhauer. What lay behind this transition?

Wagner and Schopenhauer, one might suggest by way of a provisional answer, represented for Nietzsche something like Wittgenstein's ladder of thought: once he had climbed up them, he threw them away. Despite recording in his letters how important the discovery of *The World as Will and Representation* was for him as a 21-year-old in 1865, and how delighted he was to learn that Wagner was also a devotee of Schopenhauer,[81] as early as 1868 Nietzsche was in fact already taking issue with the Schopenhauerian notion of the 'knowledge-less will' and its mediation to the world through representation.[82] Yet it is clear from his early work, from both *The Birth of Tragedy* and *Schopenhauer as Educator* (the third of the *Untimely Meditations*), that it was this concept of the will that had helped him establish the distinction between Apollo and Dionysus, between the *principium individuationis* on the one hand and the notion of intoxication (*Rausch*) on the other. By 1877, however, he was claiming that Schopenhauer's metaphysics was simply false,[83] rejecting the idea that one could conceive of any kind of *Ding an sich* or unknowable will. The kind of pure, knowing subject that Schopenhauer posited had become, for Nietzsche, impossible, since he felt that the subject would always interpose his own interpretations. One should not seek to get beyond aesthetic representation, but rather celebrate it as an end in its own right. Nietzsche's 'solution to the Schopenhauer problem' was thus the 'self-dissolution of the will' (*Selbstaufhebung des Willens*), since 'the will itself is nothing but semblance' (KSA 7, 207). If Schopenhauer's 'will to life' became Nietzsche's 'will to power', it was an aesthetically inflected reconfiguration. As Christopher Janaway notes, Nietzsche felt 'there are only interpretations, but there is no I that is the subject of the interpretation'.[84] The best one could do, according to Nietzsche, was thus to learn 'how to utilise [...] the difference in the perspective and in the emotional interpretations'.[85]

Nietzsche's move beyond Schopenhauer was also a move beyond Wagner. Characteristically, he framed the development of his thought in terms that pointed beyond the aesthetic to the ethical – his aim, he wrote looking back in 1888, had been 'to take sides against everything sick in myself, including Wagner, including Schopenhauer, including the whole of modern "humaneness"'.[86] Yet his key term of objection insists on its aesthetic provenance nonetheless: 'the thing I have been most deeply preoccupied with is the problem of decadence'.[87] If the concept of the 'decadent' is the main stick with which Nietzsche beats both Wagner and the early modernist period more generally – it is the central term of *The Case of*

Wagner (1888) – then this is because he sees himself as having been infected by it. It is the term that links his rejection of both Schopenhauer and Wagner: 'It took the philosopher of decadence to give the artist of decadence *himself*.'[88] Striking for our purposes is that Nietzsche conceives of decadence in terms of style, as the stylistic counterpart to what he diagnoses as the modern 'total sickness, this maturity and over-excitement of the neurological mechanism, which is why Wagner is the modern artist par excellence, the Cagliostro of modernity':[89]

> For the moment I am going to look at the question of style. What is the hallmark of all literary decadence? The fact that life does not reside in the totality any more. The word becomes sovereign and jumps out of the sentence, the sentence reaches out and blots out the meaning of the page, and the page comes to life at the expense of the whole – the whole is not whole any more. But this is the image of every decadent style: there is always an anarchy of the atom, disintegration of the will, 'freedom of the individual', morally speaking, – or, expanded into a political theory, 'equal rights for all'.[90]

Nietzsche's concept of style in *The Case of Wagner* is central to his analysis of modernity: the political and ethical sphere has become – on the model of decadent style – an atomized realm of individuality, with no hope of laying claim to a coherent totality. The description of the stylistic fragmentation, the disintegration of any claim to a systemic whole, is notoriously stolen from Paul Bourget's *Essays in Contemporary Psychology* (1883 and 1885):

> A decadent style is one in which the unity of a book decomposes to leave room for the independence of the page, the page decomposes to leave room for the independence of the phrase, and the phrase to leave room for the independence of the word.[91]

Nietzsche's key move is to broaden this purely literary analysis – which would become a *locus classicus* of modernist discussions of style – into a critique of modernity more generally. His suspicion of Wagnerian bombast and attempts to manipulate 'das Volk' would of course prove prescient for his subsequent appropriation by the Nazis;[92] tellingly, it is once again his concept of style that underscores this. In keeping with his stated preference for surface over depth, at the start of *The Case of Wagner* he proposes Bizet as a counter-example of French 'lightness' and 'cheerfulness' (*Heiterkeit*); Wagnerian music is simply too Germanic, too heavy. Nietzsche satirizes the Wagnerian–Schopenhauerian concept of style in the following terms:

> What it means to give people vague presentiments: our notion of 'style' takes this as its point of departure. Above all, no thinking! Nothing is more compromising than a thought! Instead, the state prior to thinking, the throng of unborn thoughts, the promise of future thoughts, the world as it was before God's creation, – a recrudescence of chaos...Chaos gives rise to vague presentiments...[93]

This location of style in a pre-conceptual world of becoming is here inflected negatively, as part of Nietzsche's ongoing *agon* with Wagner: 'I am afraid that the ugly truth is only too obvious under my cheerful lines,' continues Nietzsche.[94] He even goes so far as to claim that 'any music today that claims to be in the "grand style" is either false to us or false to itself'.[95] By 1888, then, Nietzsche had become the Cassandra of chaos, presciently identifying the fragmentary forces of modernity that would gather pace in the years leading up to the First World War. His concept of style had become a prime tool in this analysis, diagnosing Wagnerian 'grand style' as just another version of decadent thought, as a way of papering over the lack of conceptual clarity underneath the surface of its bombast.

Yet there remains a counter-narrative. In the same year in which he stated that any claim to the 'grand style' in music had become axiomatically false, Nietzsche also wrote in *Twilight of the Idols* that 'The highest feelings of power and self-assurance achieve expression in a grand style.'[96] What sense can one make of this apparent contradiction? Undoubtedly Nietzsche's pronouncements in the frenzied year of 1888, his last year of sanity, do contain contradictions and confusions. But was there method to his incipient madness?

Nietzsche's simultaneous celebration and condemnation of 'grand style' are two sides of the same coin. The common cause behind both is his insistence on what we would now, after Saussure, call the primacy of the signifier. His very contradictions suggest the importance of the concept of style to his analysis of modernity, and indeed this is where we can see the crucial role he played for the development of the double movement of modernism: on the one hand, linguistic and visual surface is foregrounded as its own subject matter; on the other hand, this brings with it the suspicion of *mere* surface conceptualized by the *Sprachskepsis* of the turn of the century. In his critique of decadence, Nietzsche gives the concept what Peter Nicholls terms 'a definitive twist [...], seeing it not as summation and aporia, but as the ashes from which a new, regenerative culture might rise',[97] whilst his anti-naturalism, his insistence on what Karl Heinz Bohrer calls the 'art-pathos of modernism',[98] is a way of insisting on aesthetic surface, on artificiality and semblance as a means of giving form to inchoate experience. Style becomes, in essence, a version of the will-to-power, a means of self-assertion that renders moral or epistemological considerations of 'truth' or 'falsity' irrelevant. As Bohrer writes, 'this pre-moral, purely aesthetic-rhetorical form of pathos remained Nietzsche's leitmotif, however much he distanced himself from the main example of it, namely Wagnerian music'.[99] Nietzsche's final substantial statement about style, in the autobiography *Ecce Homo* (also written in the frantic year of 1888), suggests the relationship between *poeisis* and pathos that runs through all his pronouncements on the subject:

> I will say a general word about my art of style. To communicate a state, an inner tension of pathos, with signs, including the tempo of these signs – that is the meaning of every style; and considering that

I have an extraordinary number of inner states, I also have a lot of stylistic possibilities – the most multifarious art of style that anyone has ever had at his disposal. Every style that really communicates an inner state is good.[100]

Nietzsche's typically hyperbolic claim to possess the 'most multifarious art of style' ever conceived pivots on the primacy of the signifier, on the 'tempo of these signs'. Once again, one can discern the characteristic double movement that will come to define modernist conceptions of style: on the one hand, good style is that which 'really communicates an inner state'; on the other hand, the success of this style depends on its ability to mask and 'overcome' the inner pathos, as we saw earlier. In the words of Karl Heinz Bohrer, style must 'effect a gesture of concealment'.[101] Jacques Derrida's image of style as a 'spur' marks a similar double movement:

Style would seem to advance in the manner of a *spur* of sorts. Like the prow, for example, of a sailing vessel, its *rostrum*, the projection of the ship which surges ahead to meet the sea's attack and cleave its hostile surface. [...] [Yet] style also uses its spur as a means of protection against the terrifying, blinding, mortal threat (of that) which *presents* itself, which obstinately thrusts itself into view. And style thereby protects the presence, the content, the thing itself, meaning, truth – on the condition that it should not already be that gaping chasm which has been deflowered in the unveiling of the difference.[102]

Nietzsche thus inaugurates what we have called the double movement of modernism, developing a model of style that both reveals and conceals. If modernism foregrounds style, both as theory and as practice, it is also this very act of foregrounding that brings it into question, rendering it suspicious. Nietzsche's stylistic legacy is the notion that style must become a kind of opaque surface, one which implies depth – 'the presence, the content', in Derrida's words – yet also 'protects' and 'veils' it.

That this double movement is both aesthetic and ethical is clear from Nietzsche's many attempts to understand the concept of style as a pedagogical principle. As this chapter has sought to show, the development of his thought illustrates what Bohrer describes as the 'establishment of the aesthetic as the yardstick of modernism':[103] where Nietzsche's early conception of Dionysus celebrated the chthonic and irrational, his late conceptualization of Dionysus (what has been called 'Dionysus II') transforms his theory of tragedy into a school of style.[104] If Nietzsche 'single-handedly created [...] a new language of art, which opposed the rise of naturalism, but anticipated the aesthetic absolutism of the later avant-gardes',[105] this is because his concept of style raised aesthetics to ethics, whilst at the same time turning ethics into aesthetics. The manner in which modernism, for better and for worse, sought to aestheticize every aspect of modernity from the political to the poetic, is unthinkable without Nietzsche's 'art of style'.

2
1857: Literary Beginnings

The development of a stylistic self-consciousness in modernism can be traced in the first instance by comparing the 1850s – the period of the genesis of *Madame Bovary* and *The Flowers of Evil* – with their subsequent reception in the 1920s. After the failed revolutions of 1848, the literary landscape across Europe underwent something of an inward turn. Since politics, it seemed, did not have the answers, perhaps poetics did. Emblematic of this would become Baudelaire's figure of the dandy or 'flâneur', dawdling defiantly at the margins of modern capitalism. The dandy's sense of self-consciousness – the dandy 'should live and sleep in front of the mirror'[1] – cultivated the aesthetic to the exclusion of the political or moral; 'the figure of the leisured dandy thus aligned style with the refusal to compromise'.[2] The 'ivory tower' became a common metaphor to writers such as Gérard de Nerval and Flaubert, in retreat from what they saw as the philistinism of modern life. 'I have always tried to live in an ivory tower,' the latter memorably wrote, 'but a tide of shit is beating at its walls, threatening to undermine it.'[3]

This inward turn marked a paradigm shift from the public to the poetic. 'This is not to suggest that writers suddenly ceased to be oppositional,' notes Peter Nicholls, 'but rather that the ground of opposition shifted from political rhetoric and polemic to literary "style".'[4] Indeed, one can say that aesthetic modernism was in a sense sparked into being by the 'assiduous cultivation of style'[5] as a quasi-political reaction against modern life, a kind of inner exile. The ambivalent relationship between modernists and modernity is apparent from the start.

At the other end of modernism, at its height in 1920, Marcel Proust returned to the question of Flaubert's style. 'A propos du style de Flaubert' – the last of several pieces by Proust on his predecessor[6] – is a curious essay, inasmuch as Proust repeatedly claims on the one hand that he does not particularly like Flaubert's style, and yet on the other hand that he 'changed our way of seeing things'. This is more than a mere expression for Proust: Flaubert 'has renewed our way of seeing things almost as much as Kant', he writes.[7] 'That which before Flaubert was action became impression. Things have as much life as people.'[8] Proust hints here at one of the underlying tensions of early modernism. On the one hand, he suggests, Flaubert anticipated impressionism in both literature and visual art: action and plot give way to impression and perception. On the other hand, Proust's insistence on 'things' suggests the realism of which Flaubert is emblematic – and yet it too anticipates later developments in modernism, for instance the *Dingdichtung* of Rilke or the *chosisme* of Francis

Ponge. Proust, as we shall see, was not the only critic to see Flaubert as equal parts aestheticist and naturalist.

Despite his protestations to the contrary, Proust characterizes Flaubert's achievement as fundamentally stylistic: 'it is only the beauty of his style that alerts us to Flaubert's genius'.[9] Proust objects to Flaubert's perceived lack of metaphors – but, as he concedes, 'metaphor is not everything in style',[10] and the mastery of tenses and temporal shifts more than compensates. Proust is particularly taken with Flaubert's use of the imperfect, writing that 'this imperfect, so new in literature, completely changes how we look at things and people' (*l'aspect des choses et des êtres*).[11] These shifts in tense produce a 'kind of sadness',[12] according to Proust, a melancholy that is driven by an 'hermetic continuity of style'.[13] 'Since he gave so much care to his syntax', Proust wrote in another (unpublished) essay on Flaubert, 'it is here that his enduring originality is to be found. He is a grammatical genius.'[14]

This reception of Flaubert as a stylist, a stubborn perfectionist, was widespread by the time of high modernism in which Proust was writing. In the same year in which Proust wrote his essay on Flaubert's style, Ezra Pound wrote of Hugh Selwyn Mauberley that

> His true Penelope was Flaubert,
> He fished by obstinate isles;
> Observed the elegance of Circe's hair
> Rather than the mottoes on sun-dials.[15]

Mauberley, like Eliot's J. Alfred Prufrock and Rilke's Malte Laurids Brigge, both caricatures and captures the essence of the modernist poet, torn between the brutality of contemporary life and the temptation to retreat into aestheticism. In Pound's poem this is immediately determined by his characterization of Mauberley's style and register: his attempts to 'maintain the "sublime" | In the old sense' were 'wrong from the start'. Yet a vestigial aestheticism persists, despite the post-war excoriation of a 'botched civilization', and the guiding star for this craftmanship, *il miglior fabbro*, remains Flaubert. Pound's juxtaposition of Homer and Flaubert is quintessentially modernist, as we know from *Ulysses* or *The Waste Land*: common to both Penelope and Flaubert, as Pound understands them here, is their untiring perfectionism, the 'obstinate' weaving of their texts (the etymology of *textere* – 'to weave' – suggesting the common link). For the poet at the zenith of high modernism, Flaubert, the indefatigable stylist, represents the link between classical ideals and contemporary art.

In *The Notebooks of Malte Laurids Brigge* (1910), one of the central novels of European modernism, Rilke similarly turns to two key figures in his search for stylistic forebears.

Do you remember Baudelaire's incredible poem 'Une Charogne'? It may be that now I understand it. Except for the last stanza, he was in the right. What was he to do, once he encountered that? It was his task to see in this horrible form that exists, repulsive only in appearance, its validity amidst all that exists. There can be no selecting out or rejecting. Do you think it an accident that Flaubert wrote his *Saint Julien l'Hospitalier*? It seems to me as if that was the decisive thing: whether one can summon up the strength to lie down beside the leper and warm him with the heat of the heart in nights of love; that can turn out no other way but well.[16]

Baudelaire and Flaubert are both adduced here as models of the modern, as the main avatars in the genres of poetry and prose. In its refusal to reject the 'ugly' in favour of traditionally 'beautiful' subjects, Baudelaire's poem 'Une Charogne' ('A Carcass') is taken as an emblem of artistic integrity: 'There can be no selecting out or rejecting.' Flaubert, too, is singled out for the way in which he embraces the ugly, embodied by the figure of St Julian the Hospitaller in the second of his *Three Tales* (1877), who disregarded his own safety by getting into bed with a leper in order to warm him up, and was accordingly rewarded (when the leper turned out to be an angel) by being taken up into heaven. Importantly, Malte's citation of Flaubert's story constitutes both an aesthetic and a moral judgement: both the man and the writing lie down with lepers. Indeed, the striking lesson of both Baudelaire and Flaubert for the modernist poet Malte is that aesthetic appreciation, even – or perhaps especially – in a doctrine of *l'art pour l'art*, comports a moral element: just as St Julian was prepared to give the whole of his body to the unappealing stranger, so the artist must be prepared to give his full attention even to the most unassuming of objects.

This subsuming of ethical concerns into the sphere of the aesthetic is characteristic of the modernist notion of style: through its very aestheticism, style paradoxically comes to represent an ethical position. Preconceived notions of traditional style are

self-consciously turned against unconventional subject matter in differing, but related ways. Rilke's Malte
sees Baudelaire's poem as emblematic of this self-
conscious break with the traditional idea of matching
a given style to an appropriate content. The first four
stanzas of 'A Carcass' set the template:

> Remember, my love, the object we saw
> That beautiful morning in June:
> By a bend in the path a carcass reclined
> On a bed sown with pebbles and stones;
>
> Her legs were spread out like a lecherous whore,
> Sweating out poisonous fumes,
> Who opened in slick invitational style
> Her stinking and festering womb.
>
> The sun on this rottenness focused its rays
> To cook the cadaver till done,
> And render to Nature a hundredfold gift
> Of all she'd united in one.
>
> And the sky cast an eye on this marvellous meat
> As over the flowers in bloom.
> The stench was so wretched that there on the grass
> You nearly collapsed in a swoon.[17]

Baudelaire's idiom lures the reader into expecting traditional invocations of beauty on a glorious summer
morning, in order to subvert these expectations the
more thoroughly. Just as the carcass is 'opened in slick
invitational style', so the poem too is proud of its
own subversion of the relationship between style and

content: its alternating alexandrines and rhyming couplets establish a stylistic expectation which Baudelaire deliberately disappoints by concentrating on the 'rottenness' of the carcass.

There is, however, an important difference between the relative positions of Baudelaire and Rilke, between what we can take as representative of early and high modernism. Why does Malte pointedly reject 'the last stanza' of the poem?

> Ah then, o my beauty, explain to the worms
> Who cherish your body so fine,
> That I am the keeper for corpses of love
> Of the form, and the essence divine![18]

The fact that Malte refuses this vestigial notion of Platonic 'form' is characteristic of the development of European modernism in the early twentieth century. Where Baudelaire could console himself in 1857 by extracting a 'divine essence' from the rotting carcass of modernity, Rilke in 1910 seeks no such solace. This can also be seen at the literal level of artistic 'form': the classical model of form as a kind of frame, a container which holds and gives shape to its content (however disparate or chaotic that content may be), can still be seen to obtain in the mid-nineteenth century; by the early twentieth century, Mallarmé and subsequent modernists have broken this contract, reinterpreting form as the enactment, rather than the mere occasion, of its content.

'Little Aster', the opening poem of Gottfried Benn's highly influential collection *Morgue* (1912), can be read as an updating of Baudelaire's poem to the mortuary slab. It too notably refuses any such Platonic consolations of form:

> A drowned truck driver was propped on the slab.
> Someone had stuck a lavender aster
> between his teeth.
> As I cut out the tongue and the palate
> through the chest
> under the skin
> with a long knife,
> I must have touched the flower, for it slid
> into the brain lying next.
> I packed it into the cavity of the chest
> among the excelsior
> as it was sewn up.
> Drink yourself full in your vase!
> Rest softly,
> little aster![19]

The 'lavender aster' clamped between the dead man's teeth seems to echo the way in which Baudelaire's 'superb cadaver' is said to 'blossom like a flower'. Yet the 'vase' of Benn's poem does not even offer this ironic solace: whilst the closing exclamation marks mimic (or mock?) the Baudelairean sense of a transcendent conclusion, for the expressionist Benn no 'form' or 'divine essence' endures beyond the rotting body. In Benn's poem the aster, the flower itself, is apostrophized, rather than the cadaver: to the eye of the professional mortician Dr Benn, the dead man is simply dead matter, a physical object foreclosing metaphysical abstraction. No Platonic 'form' is thus to be extracted from the object in question – and neither, *a fortiori*, is it to be extracted from the work of art, the poem or 'vase'. The work of art *is* the form: Benn's 'vase' is Keats' 'well-wrought urn', famously raised into the emblem of New Criticism in 1947 by Cleanth Brooks. The poem or work of art is all surface, inasmuch as there is nothing beyond that surface: as Benn wrote *à propos* the late work of Alfred Döblin, 'God is a bad rule of style.'[20]

What are the implications of this distinction between differing notions of form for the modernist notion of 'style'? Can a transition be discerned from Flaubert and Baudelaire to the later modernists? Proust in French, Pound in English, Rilke in German: at the zenith of high modernism in all three of these major European languages, Flaubert and Baudelaire are explicitly taken as the key stylistic forebears. Having established the importance of these early avatars, we must take a closer look at what was so influential about their stylistic positions.

Gustave Flaubert and 'les affres du style'

Flaubert, claimed Rémy de Gourmont in *Le Problème du style*, is 'one of the most profoundly personal writers that ever existed, one of those who may be read most clearly through the lace of style'.[21] Twenty years later in his book of the same name, John Middleton Murry claimed that Flaubert 'has had perhaps a greater influence than any other single person on the ideas of writers during the last thirty years'.[22] Foremost among these ideas is his conception of style.

It was in a letter of January 1852 to his lover Louise Colet that Flaubert made his famous statement that he would like to write 'a book [...] which would be held together by the strength of its style'. As a key document not only of Flaubert's artistic aims, but also of early modernism more broadly, the letter is worth quoting at length:

> There are in me, literarily speaking, two distinct persons: one who is infatuated with bombast, lyricism, eagle flights, sonorities of phrase and the high points of ideas; and another who digs and burrows into the truth as deeply as he can, one who likes to treat a humble fact as respectfully as a big one, who would like to make you feel almost *physically* the things he reproduces [...]
>
> What seems beautiful to me, what I should like to write, is a book about nothing, a book dependent on nothing external, which would be held together by the strength of its style, just as the earth, suspended in the void, depends on nothing external for its support; a book which would have almost no subject, or at least in which the subject would be almost invisible, if such a thing is possible. The finest works are those that contain the least matter; the closer expression comes to thought, the closer language comes to coinciding and merging with it, the finer the result. I believe that the future of Art lies in this direction. [...] This emancipation from matter can be observed everywhere: governments have gone through similar evolution, from the oriental despotisms to the socialisms of the future.

It is for this reason that there are no noble subjects or ignoble subjects; from the standpoint of pure Art one might almost establish the axiom that there is no such thing as subject, style in itself being an absolute manner of seeing things.[23]

What is so striking about this letter, aside from its explicit establishment of the goal of modern art – and indeed, of modern life and politics – as a kind of intransitive 'style' without a subject, is that Flaubert positions himself halfway between the extremes of romanticism and realism, 'lyricism' and 'humble fact'. This is indeed an accurate description of his method: time and again Flaubert is torn between his twin gods of fidelity and flair, accuracy and aesthetics, gods who can only be propitiated by incessant sacrifices. 'Style is achieved only by dint of atrocious labour, fanatical and unremitting stubbornness,' he wrote in another letter to Louise Colet.[24] Flaubert's letters are thus seminal documents of the beginnings of modernism not only because they so often revolve around his obsession with style, but more specifically because they give an insight into the stylistic tension between realism and aestheticism that is at the heart of modernist aesthetics. As Maurice Bardèche writes, 'Flaubert's meditation on *style*, on *rhythm*, is very new in the technique of the novel.'[25]

The declaration that 'from the standpoint of *pure* Art' one can define style as an '*absolute* manner of seeing things' echoes Schopenhauer's use of the adjective 'pure' as discussed in Chapter 1,[26] and anticipates the rhetoric of purity of the later modernists, in particular that of the aestheticists of the fin-de-siècle.

Flaubert's friend Théophile Gautier's doctrine of 'L'art pour l'art', expounded most famously in the preface to *Mademoiselle de Maupin* (1835), had already found currency by the mid-nineteenth century, although *Madame Bovary* can hardly be classed in this category.[27] Indeed, there seems to be a striking disparity between Flaubert's artistic aims as stated in his letters of the early 1850s and the novel that he was writing at this time. *Madame Bovary* of course *does* have a subject matter, namely the boredom of bourgeois marriage and the fleeting escape offered by the excitement of adultery. Yet even this very subject matter can be seen as a product of the tension between romanticism and realism identified by Flaubert: 'the book attacks both the romantic and the bourgeois values – those two antitheses which together defined the intellectual and social climate of the France of his day', writes Francis Steegmuller;[28] 'every word transfixes an element of reality and is at the same time a plate in his armour against it. Flaubert's preoccupation with form is anything but formalistic.'[29] 'I wrote *Madame Bovary* to annoy Champfleury,' Flaubert claimed. 'I wanted to show that bourgeois *tristesses* and mediocre emotions can support beautiful language.'[30] In both its style and its subject matter, *Madame Bovary* is thus emblematic of an early modernist aesthetic that oscillates between the two extremes of realism and romanticism, seeking their reconciliation in the foregrounding of aesthetic style. After Flaubert's death in 1880, critics soon started to see him in these terms: J.-K. Huysmans, writing in 1880, insisted that one had to distinguish between the aesthete and the naturalist;[31] Paul Bourget, writing in 1882, saw Flaubert as defined by 'two opposing personalities: a romantic poet and a savant';[32] Arthur Symons, writing in 1901, claimed that 'in *Madame Bovary* we find the analyst and the lyric poet in perfect equilibrium'.[33]

Flaubert's position halfway between these two stylistic tendencies can be taken as representative of the origins of modernism, which derives from the tension between the drive to an increasingly personal self-expression on the one hand and the drive to an impersonal aestheticization of the world on the other. Looking back from the late modernist vantage point of the 1940s, Paul Valéry identified the logical conclusion of this tension as an increased preoccupation with style:

> This tension between realist dogma – attention to the banal – and the wish to be an exception, an admired personality, had the effect of encouraging the realists to attend very carefully to style. They created the artistic style [*style artiste*]. They employed an admirable refinement, care, labour and virtue in order to describe the most ordinary objects, sometimes the most base; but without realising that in doing this, they were betraying their own principle, they were inventing another level of 'reality', a truth of their own fantasy and fabrication.[34]

Valéry thus makes Flaubert not only the origin of the modernist preoccupation with style in general, but more specifically the origin of 'le style artiste' that would culminate in the decadent style of the symbolists of the 1880s (which will be examined in more detail in the following chapter). In taking his realist ambition to reproduce the empirical world to such an aesthetic extreme, Flaubert paradoxically ends up at a greater distance from this world, since he creates an alternative realm of language that *rivals*, rather than reproduces, the world it describes. Flaubert's dream of writing a book 'about nothing [...], held together by the strength of its style', thus marks both the beginning, and the beginning of the end, of the decadent style that is at the heart of modernism, since it signals the death-drive inherent in the fetishization of style: the reification of words comes at the cost of the things they are describing. Language becomes a parasite that slowly strangles its host, supplanting the empirical world it is supposedly describing in favour of 'another level of reality' (*un autre vrai*).

One can argue, then, that two opposing currents spring from Flaubert: on the one hand the extreme realism of the naturalists and their ambition to chronicle the conditions of modern life as accurately as possible; on the other hand the extreme aestheticism of the symbolists and their ambition to *stylize* modern life as ornately as possible.[35] Where the former sought to place signifying language in the service of the signified world it seeks to describe, the latter took the opposite view, marginalizing the signified in favour of an overdeveloped, hypertrophied signifier. The shared ancestry of these opposing movements is not surprising if one recalls that when the realist movement started to establish itself in France in the 1850s – in particular through Champfleury and his journal *Le Réalisme* – the two tendencies were initially not seen as competing, but rather as complementary: 'Le Réalisme' was as it were placed alongside romanticism, their common cause being an interest in the 'modern' and a rejection of classicism. Through the course of the second half of the nineteenth century, however, they were driven ever further apart by the competing impulses to describe (naturalism) and to decry (aestheticism) the brutality of post-industrial modernity. Flaubert arguably marks the point of divergence of these two approaches, as his letters from the time when he was writing *Madame Bovary* confirm. 'The entire value of my book', he writes, 'will consist in my having known how to walk straight ahead on a hair, balanced above the two abysses of lyricism and vulgarity (which I seek to fuse in analytical narrative).'[36] Flaubert sees Style – with a capital 'S' – as the agent of this reconciliation: in coining the doctrine of impersonality that will become so important to later modernists such as Eliot and Pound, he seeks to sublimate emotion into style:

> Passion does not make poetry, and the more personal you are, the weaker. [...] That is why I detest so-called poetic language. When there are no words, a glance is enough. Soulful effusions, lyricism, descriptions – I want all these embodied in Style. To put them elsewhere is to prostitute art and feeling itself.[37]

Achieved art for Flaubert lies not in the suppression of emotion and personality *per se*, but rather in their sublimation into the textures of the work itself, into 'Style': 'It is wrong to think that feeling is everything. In the arts, it is nothing without form.' This is the position that we shall see, mediated via Gourmont, emerge as modernist orthodoxy with T.S. Eliot. In his lecture notes on *Madame Bovary*, no less an authority than Vladimir Nabokov repeatedly emphasizes this defining credo, claiming that Flaubert manages to transform 'a sordid world' into 'one of the most perfect pieces of poetical fiction known', simply through

> the inner force of style. [...] Without Flaubert there would have been no Marcel Proust in France, no James Joyce in Ireland. Chekhov in Russia would not have been quite Chekhov. So much for Flaubert's literary influence.[38]

To this list, of course, one can add Nabokov himself, who claimed that 'style and structure are the essence of a book; great ideas are hogwash'.[39]

Yet despite his seemingly settled position, one can nonetheless trace contradictions in Flaubert's aesthetics as they develop. Whilst writing *Madame Bovary* in the early 1850s, he rejects effusive aestheticism, claiming that 'the time for Beauty is over. [...] The more Art develops, the more scientific it will be.'[40] Later in the 1870s, however, he comes to reject 'scientific' realism:

> I am wrecking my health trying not to have a school. *A priori*, I reject all schools. Those writers whom I often see [the naturalists] admire everything that I despise and worry but little about the things that torment me. Technical detail, factual data, historical truth, and accuracy of portrayal I look upon as very secondary. I aim at *beauty* above all else.[41]

What seems to happen, in other words, is that Flaubert reacts against what he perceives to be prevailing dogma. In the early 1850s, he advocates a move away from the post-romanticism of *l'art pour l'art* and the cult of beauty; by the mid-1870s, he recoils from the rise of the naturalists – not unlike Nietzsche – and returns to an insistence on the centrality of beauty.

What unites these two positions is the enduring emphasis on style. 'I am convinced that everything is a question of style, or rather of form, of presentation,' he writes in 1853.[42] And again, in 1857: 'For me, the capital difficulty remains style, form, that indefinable Beauty implicit in the conception and representing, as Plato said, the splendour of Truth.'[43] Almost 20 years later, in December 1876, he continues to think in the same terms when criticizing Zola and his doctrine of naturalism: 'As for poetry and style, the two elements that are eternal, he never mentions them!'[44] Flaubert's obsession with style can thus be read as a kind of *Aufhebung* of the antitheses of romanticism and realism. It is precisely this that makes him a key proto-modernist. For Flaubert, style *is* art, surface *is* depth, as he indicates as early as 1846: 'you cannot remove the form from the Idea, because the Idea exists only by virtue of its form. [...] Good stylists are reproached for neglecting the Idea, the moral goal [...] as though the goal of Art were not, first and foremost, Beauty!'[45] By 1852, this has been reduced to the basic statement that 'distinctions between thought and style are a sophism'.[46] Of course, this obsession leads at times to crippling self-doubt: 'I am afraid of everything having to do with style,'[47] he writes in 1851; 'I foresee terrifying difficulties of style,'[48] again in 1851; 'Oh, what a rascally thing style is!' in 1852.[49] 'Ah! how I will have suffered from them [...], *les affres du style.*'[50]

It thus seems valid to wonder about the psychological motivation for this preoccupation with style, as Bourget did in 1882:

> The unquenchable desire to extinguish a solid reality in the midst of the ruins scattered across his soul led [Flaubert] to an idiosyncratic theory of style. This nihilist thirsted for the absolute [*était un affamé de l'absolu*]. Since he could find this absolute neither outside nor inside himself [...] he placed it both outside of himself and outside of things, in the work of art; since he was a writer, this work of art was for him the Written Sentence.[51]

Bourget's speculations suggest why we can see Flaubert's interest in style as emblematic of early modernism. If Flaubert is a nihilist, it is only in his *content*, argues Bourget; through his *style*, he finds a means of resisting and countering this nihilism.[52] The Balzacian *recherche de l'absolu* that is so characteristic of a modernity yearning to replace discredited metaphysical certainties is thus turned inwards onto the work of art itself, culminating almost inevitably in a cult of the aesthetic, a quasi-idolatrous quest for the perfect sentence. 'A writer should be in his work like God in creation, invisible and all-powerful: he should be everywhere felt, but nowhere seen,'[53] to quote one of the most famous of Flaubert's comments in his letters. Style is invested with the weight of meaning previously invested in a (supposedly) well-ordered empirical and metaphysical reality. The artist becomes his own God, *faute de mieux*.

Bourget's description of the 'ruins scattered across his soul' (*ruines dont son âme était jonchée*) anticipates Eliot's 'fragments shored against my ruin', and suggests the dialectic out of which this preoccupation with style would grow. Insisting on the particularities of style is a way of giving order to an increasingly chaotic and disordered world: modernism, when understood as an aesthetic that foregrounds style, constitutes a reaction against the conditions of modernity – a way, in a sense, of *resisting* modernity. As Jonathan Culler observes:

> Inexpressibility [...] becomes part of a creative linguistic act and a source of agony – the agony of the unending search for *le mot juste*. This agony has been an extremely important feature of modern literature, and to pay homage to Flaubert is one way of expressing solidarity with the writer in his battle with language and obsessive exploration of its possibilities.[54]

Culler notes that some subsequent writers – he gives the example of Gide – would willingly have traded Flaubert's novels for his correspondence, which 'records this nobler and more poignant struggle'.[55] Yet he also rightly insists that without the novels, without *Madame Bovary*, *L'Education sentimentale* (1869), or *Bouvard et Pécuchet* (1881), the letters would be little more than a sterile mockery of the artistic process: it is the ends of the novels that justify the means of the creative struggle.

This struggle amounts to the hope that an insistence on stylistic surface will give the novel the density of a poem. Flaubert wanted 'to give prose the rhythm of verse',[56] since he viewed 'cadence as the foremost quality of style', as Bourget puts it.[57] Nabokov echoes this view, stating that 'stylistically [*Madame Bovary*] is prose doing what poetry is supposed to do',[58] whilst Culler notes that Flaubert wanted 'to make the novel an aesthetic object rather than a communicative act, in which he would have only to construct sentences, whose polished surfaces might aspire to the condition of sculpture'.[59] Flaubert's aim in doing this was to make the formal, expressive qualities of language central to its epistemological content: 'what I love above all else, is form, provided it be beautiful, and nothing beyond it', he wrote as early as 1846.[60] Thirty years later, he maintained the same position: 'what seems to be outward form is actually essence', he wrote to George Sand in 1876. Guy de Maupassant endorsed this from the perspective of a friend and junior colleague, writing in the same year in an article in *La République des Lettres* that 'the foremost quality of M. Flaubert is form',[61] whilst from a critical perspective Bourget established this view of Flaubert in the 1880s:

> Flaubert's doctrine of style is captured in a sentence of Buffon's, which he approvingly cites somewhere: 'All the intellectual beauty which is to be found in a beautiful style, all the links of which it is composed, are also practical truths, and they are perhaps more valuable to the public spirit than those which form the content of a subject ...' This boils down to saying

that the usual distinction between form and content [*le fond et la forme*] is an analytical error.[62]

In specific terms, Flaubert's enduring stylistic innovation, according to Bourget, was to establish the *style indirect libre* as one of the key narrative mechanisms of modernity. 'It is probably here, in the continuous and involuntary notation of interior speech, that resides the secret of this still mysterious magic: Style.'[63] This narrative perspective manages to combine the internal viewpoint of the protagonist with that of external reality; it can as such be read as proto-modernist, inasmuch as it conveys the subjective individual's response to modernity (anticipating, amongst other developments, the stream of consciousness writing which we will consider in the following chapter). What Bourget states of Flaubert – that 'his example has delayed by many years the triumph of barbarism which nowadays threatens to invade our language. He has established the precedent of an attention to style [*un souci du style*] which will not disappear any time soon'[64] – can be traced in the first instance in subsequent attempts to push the novel towards the stylistic density of poetry, as well as in the development of 'le style artiste'. Before we turn to these developments, however, we need to take a step sideways to Flaubert's contemporary Baudelaire.

Charles Baudelaire and 'le style nerveux'

Taken alongside the genesis of *Madame Bovary*, Baudelaire's *The Flowers of Evil* – the first edition of which was also published in 1857 – marks the start of European literary modernism. As with Flaubert on prose, Baudelaire's influence on modernist verse was decisive: he was 'the poet who lingered at the crossroads of modernity',[65] whose post-romantic concepts of *spleen* and *ennui* set the tone for the self-reflexive melancholy of the modernist era. This proto-modernist melancholia marks Baudelaire out as a pivotal figure in the dissemination of Schopenhauerian pessimism: what Baillot terms the 'wave of Schopenhauerian pessimism'[66] around 1880 was owing in no small part to the centrality of Baudelaire's work for the symbolist generation. As explored in the previous chapter, the counterpart to this Schopenhauerian pessimism was a heightened sense of the aesthetic: Baudelaire consoled himself 'by contemplating plastic forms. And even this ecstasy is perhaps for him simply the stylisation of his desires.'[67]

Flaubert himself immediately recognized the importance of Baudelaire's achievement, writing to him in July 1857 to express his enthusiasm:

> You have managed to give romanticism a new lease of life. You resemble no one – the highest of all virtues. The originality of your style springs from the conception; each sentence is crammed to the bursting-point with the refinements of language which set it off, like the ornaments on a Damascus blade.[68]

What is nonetheless striking about *The Flowers of Evil*, despite the book's position as a founding document of modernism, is just how traditional the poems are formally. Rimbaud, who idolized Baudelaire, criticized his formal conventionality, providing an interesting insight into the differences between what one could call the first- and second-generation modernists. In the second of his so-called *Lettres du voyant*, written in 1871, Rimbaud first declares that 'form' is the decisive criterion for the true poet (who must 'see to it that his inventions can be smelt, felt, heard. If what he brings back from *down there* has form, he brings forth form; if it is formless, he brings forth formlessness. A language has to be found'),[69] then, surprisingly, criticizes Baudelaire in these terms:

> Baudelaire is the first *seer*, king of poets, *a real god!* Unluckily he lived in too artistic a circle; and the form which is so much praised in him is trivial. Inventions from the unknown demand new forms.[70]

The 'modern' element of *The Flowers of Evil*, as Rimbaud implies, is not 'the form which is much praised', but rather the stories and sentiments the collection expresses. Time and again Baudelaire uses alexandrines and sonnets, two of the most classical forms of French literature, yet presses them into the service of decidedly unclassical subject matter. The poem 'The Frame', itself a sonnet, can be read as an ironic comment on this relationship:

> Just as the frame adds to the painter's art,
> Although the brush itself be highly praised,
> A something that is captivating, strange,
> Setting it off from all in nature else,

So jewels and metals, gildings, furnishings
Exactly fit her rich and rare appeal;
Nothing offends her perfect clarity,
And all would seem a frame for her display.

And one could say at times that she believed
Everything loved her, in that she would bathe
Freely, voluptuously, her nudity

In kisses of the linen and the silk,
And with each charming movement, slow or quick,
Display a cunning monkey's childlike grace.[71]

Read in poetological terms, the frame of the paint-ing can be compared to the form of the poem, which 'isolates' or contains the content, the 'rare beauty' of the painting. The first two stanzas which describe the painting are themselves framed by the word 'frame' (although in French Baudelaire uses two different words, *cadre* and *bordure*), and by opening the poem directly with a simile, the poet creates a further frame, inasmuch as the poem thus becomes an image of an image. Form and content are thus in unison in this poem, but in a classical manner: the frame/form may 'add' to the painting/poem, but it 'isolates' it, it delimits it.

If Baudelaire's poetic style is proto-modernist, it is thus not through its formal innovation. Baudelaire's modernism rests rather on his sense of modernity as belated and chaotic: modernist art must give form to this formlessness. Writing in 1924, Valéry suggests that Baudelaire should be understood not as giving 'roman-ticism a new lease of life', as Flaubert saw him, but rather as classical, in reaction to the romanticism with which he grew up in the 1840s:

> *The essence of classicism is to come afterwards. Order* presupposes a certain disorder which it seeks to master. *Composition*, artifice, succeeds a primitive chaos of intuitions and natural developments. *Purity* is the result of infinite operations on language, and attention to *form* is nothing other than the considered reorganisation of the means of expression.[72]

Valéry implies that Baudelaire's respect for form suggests another kind of 'purity': not an absolute style à la Flaubert, but rather a classical purity of form. T.S. Eliot sees Baudelaire in the same terms, praising him as 'a classicist, born out of his due time'[73] – although, tellingly, two years later he adds that Baudelaire's poems

> seem to me to have the external but not the internal form of classic art. One might even hazard the conjecture that the care for perfection of form, even among some of the romantic poets of the nineteenth century, was an effort to support, or to conceal from view, an inner disorder.[74]

The modernity of Baudelaire's poetry derives from this tension between external order and 'inner disorder', between the classical forms and their shockingly candid content. Adorno makes the point when he contrasts Baudelaire's aesthetics with those of the later *Jugendstil*:

> The [*Jugendstil*] idea of beauty is limited because it sets itself up as directly antithetical to a society rejected as ugly rather than, as Baudelaire and Rimbaud did, extracting this antithesis from the content – from the imagery of Paris, in Baudelaire's instance – and putting it to the test.[75]

This tension creates a kind of shock effect, as we saw with 'A Carcass': time and again the reader is lulled into expecting conventional assertions of beauty, only to have the rug precipitously ripped from under her feet. Baudelaire delights in subverting expectations, as for instance in the poem 'A Martyr', where he devotes the first two stanzas to establishing a typically romantic *mise-en-scène*, in order then to shock the reader with the visceral brutality of 'a decapitated corpse' at the start of the third. Even in his public readings, Baudelaire is recorded as having cultivated a disparity between the shocking content of his poems and their cool, carefully stylized delivery: 'The contrast between the violence of the images and the perfect placidity, the suave and emphatic accentuation, of the delivery was truly striking.'[76] Flaubert implicitly recognizes this technique of juxtaposing form and content: although he praises 'the originality of [Baudelaire's] style', he adds that it 'springs from the conception', as though it were the thoughts, and not the manner in which they are expressed, that define his originality. In the same short letter, Flaubert moves from speaking of Baudelaire's 'style' to speaking of his 'tone' (Baudelaire's 'tone is so right') and finally of his 'manner':

> To sum up, what I love above all in your book is that in it Art occupies first place. Furthermore, you write of the flesh without loving it, in a melancholy, detached manner that I find sympathetic.[77]

If we follow Flaubert and divide the notion of 'style' into 'conception', 'tone' and 'manner', we start perhaps to understand why Baudelaire was so seminal for subsequent modernists. What is stylistically innovative in his poetry is not its formal structure, but Baudelaire's angle of observation on the world, 'the matter-of-factness of his way of looking' (*diese Sachlichkeit seines Anschauens*), to use Rilke's phrase about Cézanne.[78] Flaubert's description of Baudelaire's 'melancholy, detached manner' anticipates Rilke's other great passage on Baudelaire, in his so-called *Letters on Cézanne*, written to his wife in 1907 after visiting an exhibition of the painter's work in Paris. Rilke reminds his wife of what he has already written about Baudelaire's poem 'A Carcass' in his (at that stage unpublished) novel *Malte*, and then broadens the artistic perspective:

> I was thinking that without this poem, the whole trend toward plainspoken fact [*zum sachlichen Sagen*] which we now seem to recognize in Cézanne could not have started; first it had to be there in all its inexorability. First, artistic perception had to overcome itself to the point of realizing that even something horrible, something that seems no more than

disgusting, *is*, and shares the truth of its being with everything else that exists.[79]

Rilke here holds Baudelaire responsible not only for the modern artist's belief that there can be no 'selecting out or rejecting', but also for the stylistic *expression* of this doctrine, *das sachliche Sagen* as he terms it. Moreover, Rilke also makes the claim that modern visual art – such as that of Cézanne – would have been impossible without Baudelaire, thus placing the poet at the source not only of literary modernism, but of aesthetic modernism more generally.

Whatever the truth of Rilke's claims for Baudelaire's transdisciplinary influence, the very fact that he repeatedly makes them is telling. Baudelaire was in many ways a very inconsistent writer, full of self-contradictions about the social role of the aesthetic. Yet what the later modernists picked up on was almost always his zealous defence of the self-sufficiency of art, seeing him as the high priest of Art with a capital 'A', a view established by Flaubert in 1857. 'It was Baudelaire the aesthete, the dandy and the Satanist who was acclaimed in the decades that followed his death,' suggests Michael Hamburger.[80] The reason for Baudelaire's enduring reception as an aesthete can be located in his 'melancholy, detached manner', his *sachliches Sagen*. His essay on *Madame Bovary* (written in October 1857) gives an insight into his view of style in the early modernist period. Just as Flaubert identified Baudelaire's style as central to his achievement, so Baudelaire returns the favour. Imagining Flaubert's own justification of his work, Baudelaire undertakes a curious act of ventriloquism, speaking on the novelist's

behalf. First, he writes that he is sketching out 'a nervous style [*un style nerveux*], picturesque, subtle, exact,
on a banal canvas'. Just a few lines later, however, he
seems to contradict himself, having Flaubert state that:

> I have no need to worry about style, about pic-
> turesque arrangement, about the description of
> scenes; I possess all these qualities in overwhelm-
> ing abundance. I am determined rather to advance
> through analysis and logic, and in doing so to prove
> that all subjects are equally good or bad, depending
> on the manner in which they are treated, and that
> even the most vulgar may become the best.[81]

Baudelaire flags up Flaubert's style in order to claim
that if he does not need to think about it, it is precisely because he possesses such an 'overwhelming
abundance' of style. What matters for both Flaubert
and Baudelaire are not the given stories or 'subjects'
related, but 'the manner in which they are treated', a
position echoed 50 years later by Rilke's statement that
'there can be no selecting out or rejecting': if the modern artist is required to embrace all facets of existence,
then what comes to distinguish a given artist is not
the events s/he chooses to depict (s/he is precisely
not allowed simply to pick the most seemly subjects),
but the style in which s/he depicts them.

Baudelaire's insistence on Flaubert's 'style nerveux'
resonates, of course, in his own poetry. The general
critical consensus, writes J.B. Ratermanis in his *Etude
sur le style de Baudelaire*, is that 'the essential character of Baudelaire's style is the way it fuses, the way it
elides the physical and the psychological, the sensual

and the intellectual, all, moreover, in the service of a spiritual element'.[82] Neurasthenia, a 'constant affective tension',[83] is the default setting for modernist art: the 'style nerveux' of both Flaubert[84] and Baudelaire prefigures the Europe-wide reaction against naturalism in the 1890s that the literary critic Hermann Bahr would call a 'mysticism of the nerves'.[85] 'Baudelaire is perhaps the first to portray the modern and decadent artist as someone with an overdeveloped nervous system,'[86] writes Clive Scott. The language of the 'nervous system' would go on to define the modernist era: from Freudian psychoanalysis, through Prufrock's 'magic lantern [which] threw the nerves in pattern on a screen',[87] to the frazzled wife in *The Waste Land* whose 'nerves are bad tonight';[88] from the 'abnormal nervous system' of Hofmannsthal's 'Zurückgekehrten'[89] to Antonin Artaud's prose pieces *Les Pèse-Nerfs* (1925). This 'nervousness' depends upon the precondition of extreme self-consciousness so characteristic of modernity. Although self-consciousness as the driving force of modern thought and literature can be traced back through the romanticism of Wordsworth, Coleridge, Rousseau or Hölderlin to Montaigne's *Essais* and the Cartesian *cogito*, the particular inflection of the modernist period derives most immediately from the legacy of French symbolism, which in turn looks back to Baudelaire. In *The Symbolist Movement in Literature* (1899), the work which T.S. Eliot remembered 'as an introduction to wholly new feelings',[90] Arthur Symons claimed that 'what distinguishes the Symbolism of our day from the Symbolism of the past is that it has now become conscious of itself'.[91] Symons identified Stendhal as the first writer to have 'substituted the brain for the heart': 'we have been intellectualising upon Stendhal ever since'.[92] This is equally true of Flaubert and Baudelaire, to whom Symons dedicated essays in the revised edition of his study published in 1919: Baudelaire's work is said to be 'made out of his whole intellect and all his nerves'.[93] This 'style nerveux' is in essence a doctrine of linguistic self-consciousness, as Clive Scott concisely concludes: 'What then did the Symbolist revolution achieve? Most fundamentally, it awakened an acute consciousness of language.'[94] (As we shall see in Chapters 4 and 5, one of the most influential consequences of this for later modernism would be a concomitant suspicion of rhetoric: early on in his study, Symons introduces symbolism as a 'revolt against exteriority, against rhetoric', quoting Verlaine's advice to 'take eloquence, and wring its neck!')[95]

If *The Flowers of Evil* was perceived by the symbolist generation as a paradigm of their decadent, neurasthenic style (Jean Moréas wrote in his symbolist manifesto of 1886 that 'Baudelaire must be considered the true precursor of the present movement in poetry'),[96] clearly this could be seen as an insult as well as a compliment. The critic Edmond Scherer, for instance, wrote of Baudelaire in 1886 that 'like many another author of his day, he was not a writer but a stylist. His images are almost always inappropriate.'[97] The implied criticism here, one which we will repeatedly re-encounter in the following chapter, is that style has taken over and perverted meaning: the contagious 'virus' of modernism has been contracted. Théophile Gautier expressed similar sentiments, but in much more positive terms. In his influential preface to the 1868 edition, which quickly took on the status of a manifesto, he wrote that Baudelaire's achievement will be 'to have brought within the possibilities of style numbers of objects, sensations, and effects unnamed by Adam, the great nomenclator'.[98] Gautier sees Baudelaire's poetry as one of contrasts, noting 'the woof and warp of the style [*la trame du style*]. Baudelaire weaves in it threads of silk and gold with strong, rough threads of hemp, as in those stuffs of the East, at once superb and coarse.'[99] In a manner that anticipates Valéry's view of *The Flowers of Evil* as 'classical', Gautier notes that Baudelaire 'has reached the extreme point of maturity which marks the setting of ancient civilisations', producing an 'ingenious, complex, learned style, full of shades and refinements of meaning'.[100] Baudelaire's 'decadent style' is defined by these chiaroscuro nuances: 'contrary to the classic style, it admits of the introduction of shadows'.[101]

These 'shades and refinements of meaning' manifest themselves through the intensely poetological nature of Baudelaire's poetry. Time and again in *The Flowers of Evil* the poet reflects on his own status as poet and builds this into the ostensible subject matter of the verse. He speaks for instance of his 'polished verses, metal deftly twined, | Learnedly spangled with my crystal rhymes' ('To a Madonna');[102] he suggests the relationship between prosody and physiology by comparing the rhythms of his own blood to 'a fountain's pulsing sobs' ('The Fountain of Blood').[103] Allied to the basic stylistic principle of juxtaposing opposites (as in the very title of the collection) and the famous doctrine of 'correspondances' (according to which the world is composed of 'forests of symbols' in which one sense corresponds to another), this self-reflexive 'reversibility' – to borrow the title of one of the poems – suggests the stylistic self-consciousness with which Baudelaire initiated the characteristically modernist tendency to turn writing back on itself. In describing, in *Artificial Paradise*, the heightened sense of language brought about by opium and hashish, Baudelaire is also describing his own sense of poetry:

> Even grammar – sterile grammar, itself – becomes something like a sort of evocative witchcraft; words come to life, wrapped in flesh and bone – the noun, in all its substantative majesty; the adjective, transparent garb that dresses and colours it like glaze; and the verb, angel of motion, that sets the sentence moving.[104]

The stylistic implications of this proto-symbolist self-consciousness would become central to high modernism: there is no need to rehearse how much the likes of Eliot, Pound, Valéry and Rilke all owed in their different ways to Rimbaud, Laforgue, Verlaine, Mallarmé and the rest of the generation that wrote in the shadow of Baudelaire and Flaubert.[105] In his introduction to the movement, Symons adopts the definition of the symbol developed by Comte Goblet d'Alviella in his book on *The Migration of Symbols* (1891): 'a symbol might be defined as a representation which does not aim at being a reproduction'.[106] In linguistic terms one might understand this as suggesting that the symbol is a signifier which insists on its self-sufficient status, which does not seek a mere transparency of 'reproduction', but rather foregrounds itself as an essential component of the work of art. Symons notes that from the Greeks onwards the term 'symbol' gradually 'extended its meaning, until it came to denote every conventional representation of idea by form'. With the advent of the French symbolists, he writes,

> form aimed above all things at being precise, at saying rather than suggesting, at saying what they had to say so completely that nothing remained over, which it might be the business of the reader to divine. And so they have expressed, finally, a certain aspect of the world; and some of them have carried style to a point beyond which the style that says, rather than suggests, cannot go.[107]

It is thus not surprising that language scepticism should have developed out of the post-symbolist era: the symbol, the signifier, became so overburdened that it collapsed (Schopenhauer, as we have seen, anticipated this). 'The style that says' could go no further. The historical avant-garde of surrealism and Dada can be understood as attempts to break out of the impasse.[108]

For Symons, it is this foregrounding of style that makes Flaubert and Baudelaire the precursors of symbolism, and by extension the founding fathers of modernism. He allows, however, that there are differences between them:

> Compare the style of Flaubert in each of his books, and you will find that each book has its

own rhythm, perfectly appropriate to its subject-matter. The style, which has almost every merit and hardly a fault, becomes what it is by a process very different from that of most writers careful of form. Read Chateaubriand, Gautier, even Baudelaire, and you will find that the aim of these writers has been to construct a style which shall be adaptable to every occasion, but without structural change; the cadence is always the same. [...] [Flaubert] invents the rhythm of every sentence, he changes his cadence with every mood or for the convenience of every fact. He has no theory of beauty in form apart from what it expresses. For him form is a living thing, the physical body of thought.[109]

The claim that Flaubert has 'no theory of beauty in form apart from what it expresses' is disingenuous, since, as we have seen, this itself is Flaubert's theory of form: it *is* what it expresses. 'Modern ways of thought', as Symons notes, 'in *Madame Bovary* bring with them an instinctively modern cadence';[110] if the cadence changes, it is because the thought changes. Baudelaire's cadence, on the other hand, remains the same in each of his works: he imposes his style on differing occasions 'without structural change'.

Despite their common concern with the propriety of Art, then, despite their mutual cultivation of aesthetic autonomy, Flaubert and Baudelaire ultimately offer two differing models for modernist style. Whilst Flaubert's legacy is the quasi-nihilistic dream of reducing modernity to nothing but style, Baudelaire urges modernity 'to fathom the Unknown, and find the *new'*.[111] To put it polemically: where Flaubert fled from modernity into pure style, Baudelaire fled from pure style into modernity. The following chapter will trace this double legacy in the development of modernist prose.

3
The 'Virus of Prose': Decadent Style and the Modernist Novel

Prose poetry, stream of consciousness, interior monologue

Twelve years after *The Flowers of Evil*, and two years after his death in 1867, a work of Baudelaire's was published that in its own way would be just as important as its predecessor for the development of modernist notions of style. *Le Spleen de Paris* (1869) not only reinforced the idea, established in *The Flowers of Evil*, that the locus of modern life was the big city – of which Paris was the exemplar *par excellence* – it also sought to bring together the two competing forms of poetry and prose (as its alternative name, *Petits poèmes en prose*, suggests). Through his brief, lyrical vignettes of modern life in the streets of Paris, Baudelaire took a decisive step towards the Flaubertian dream of giving 'prose the rhythm of verse'. His aim, as stated in the preface to the collection, was this miracle, a poetic prose, musical without rhythm or rhyme, supple and choppy enough to accommodate the lyrical movement of the soul, the undulations of reverie, the bump and lurch of consciousness [*soubresauts de la conscience*].[1]

Alongside Flaubert's dream of an intransitive style, Baudelaire's notion of a 'poetic prose' inaugurates the turn towards stylistic self-consciousness that would characterize modernist prose. For the best part of the next hundred years – as far, perhaps, as the Beckett of the great trilogy (*Molloy, Malone Dies, The Unnamable,* 1951–53) – the 'soubresauts de la conscience' would become the defining theme of modern literature.

The forms this theme took can be summarized initially under three related, but differing terms: prose poetry, stream of consciousness and interior monologue. Between them, these forms define much of modernist prose. The prose poem as established by Baudelaire can be said to represent a *kind* of prose, a way of writing rather than a specific genre. It is a stylistic term, defined by the rhythmical and syntactical characteristics outlined above by Baudelaire. At the height of modernism in 1926, Virginia Woolf defined it as 'impassioned prose', a style epitomized, she claimed, by De Quincey: 'With immense elaboration and art he formed a style in which to express these "visionary scenes derived from the world of dreams".'[2] A year later, Woolf elaborated on the idea that 'prose is going to take over – has, indeed, already taken over – some of the duties which were once discharged by poetry'. Prose, she continues in the same essay, will show itself capable of rising high from the ground, not in one dart, but in sweeps and circles, and of keeping at the same time in touch with the amusements and idiosyncracies of human character in daily life.[3]

One can contrast this optimistic vision of the possibilities of poetic prose with E.M. Cioran's typically acerbic perspective on modernist prose in his 1956 essay 'Style as Risk': 'Virus of prose, a poetic style dislocates and wrecks it: poetic prose is sick prose [*une prose malade*].'[4] Technically speaking, Cioran is right: stylistic self-consciousness does indeed tend to take over and foreground itself in the manner of a virus.

Yet one can give another term to this 'prose malade', namely decadent style, the germ of which can be traced back beyond the 'decadents' themselves to the early modernists of the 1850s. The combination of Schopenhauer's influence on the self-consciously 'musical' style of the decadents of the 1880s and 1890s (the first issue of Anatole Baju's magazine *Le Décadent*, launched in 1886, declared that 'excessive Schopenhauerism' was one of the symptoms of modern decadence),[5] of Flaubert's dream of giving prose the density of verse, and of Baudelaire's subsequent attempt to build the 'soubresauts de la conscience' into the stylistic texture of his poetic prose, laid the foundations for the form of writing that would become known as stream of consciousness, the second of our three related terms. The term itself was established by William James in his *Principles of Psychology* (1890); the technique, as it was later conceptualized, owed much to the subsequent developments of psychoanalysis and impressionism,[6] although Baudelaire's doctrine of 'synaesthesia' – the simultaneous apprehension and *correspondance* of sensory impulses by more than one sense – arguably anticipated it.

The stream of consciousness novel famously reached its apogee in Joyce's *Ulysses* (1922), in Virginia Woolf's *Mrs Dalloway* (1925) and *The Waves* (1931). Yet we saw in Chapter 1 how Joyce himself insisted that he owed his technique to Edouard Dujardin's *Les Lauriers sont coupés*, which was published as early as 1888–89, only 20 years after Baudelaire's *Le Spleen de Paris*. Dujardin's novel played a key – if only belatedly acknowledged – role in the development of modernist prose style, since it essentially invented what later became known as interior monologue, the third of the related terms often used of modernist prose. Given this historical importance, our analysis of representative forms of modernist prose style must start with *Les Lauriers sont coupés*.[7]

'Une écriture blanche'? Edouard Dujardin, *Les Lauriers sont coupés*

Although the terms 'interior monologue' and 'stream of consciousness' are sometimes used interchangeably, one can arguably distinguish between the former as 'technique' and the latter as 'genre' (or at least as the psychological phenomenon identified by James that then gave rise to a genre).[8] Perhaps one of the most basic differences is that streams of consciousness, such as the narratives of Woolf, are often written in the third person, whilst interior monologues tend to be by definition interior, that is, written in the first person. Dujardin defined the interior monologue in the following terms:

> Interior monologue is, like poetry, unheard, unspoken speech, through which a character expresses his most intimate thoughts, closest to the unconscious, prior to all logical organization, that is to say as it comes into being, by means of sentences in direct speech reduced to their syntactic minimum, in order to give the impression of raw experience [*l'impression 'tout venant'*].[9]

Dujardin's novel is astonishingly modern for its time, reading like the Virginia Woolf of the 1920s transposed to the Paris of the 1880s. Stylistically, it provides the missing link between symbolism and later stream of consciousness writers such as Joyce and Woolf: as Melvin J. Friedman writes, 'the novels of James, Proust, Joyce, Conrad, Faulkner and Virginia Woolf are in some sense fictional inheritances from French Symbolist poetry'.[10] *Les Lauriers sont coupés* luxuriates in the symbols, repetitions and overwritten language of fin-de-siècle 'aestheticists' such as J.-K. Huysmans and his *A Rebours* (1884); its use of long sentences, sudden changes of emphasis and – in particular – semi-colons, constructs a syntax that not only reflects, but also *enacts* the thought processes of the protagonist Daniel Prince, by means of 'syntactic devices intended to reproduce his most intimate thought-emotive patterns'.[11] 'When I begin to think about something, my mind wanders off at a tangent,'[12] Prince says to himself; this is reflected in a style that is both ornament and epistemology, symbolist and 'stream of consciousness'.[13]

Two stylistic examples will suffice here. First, Dujardin uses adverbs in a manner analogous to the technique used in symbolist poetry described by Clive Scott as the 'suggestive adverb'.[14] In the following, not atypical passage, the protagonist is preparing himself in his flat to go out to meet Léa, the actress he is courting, when he falls into a reverie about the cosiness of his rooms:

> One feels absolutely confident, very content, full of energy, the white light of the candles, whitened gold; the softness of the carpets and hangings; it is well-being, sweetness, happiness. I'm going happily to prepare myself, here, in the peace of this narrow room [...] undisturbed here, quite undisturbed and enviably so.[15]

Dujardin's idiosyncratic use of adverbs here foregrounds the *manner* in which his protagonist perceives his environment, alongside the adjectival qualities of the room being perceived ('white', 'whitened gold'). The awkward construction 'I'm going happily to prepare myself, here' (*je vais être heureusement pour me préparer, ici*) can be read either as an inversion of the usual word order (one might imagine it rewritten in more standard French as something like 'heureusement, je vais être ici pour me préparer'), or as a substitution of an adverb for an adjective ('je vais être heureux pour me préparer, ici'): in either case, Dujardin pointedly foregrounds the adverb. The way in which he then sandwiches the adjective 'undisturbed' between two adverbs – 'quite undisturbed and enviably so' (*tout à fait tranquille et enviablement*) – serves equally to highlight the manner in which one is 'undisturbed' (i.e. completely and in a way that is to be envied), rather than the state.

A slightly different example of Dujardin's deployment of adverbs occurs when Prince is walking along the Parisian streets:

> slow horses; stairways; the sky dimmed by thicker growing trees; my steps monotonously on the asphalt; the song of a barrel-organ, a dance tune, a sort of waltz, the rhythm of a slow waltz [...][16]

Here the verb is suppressed in order, through the adverb, to foreground the manner in which Prince's steps resonate (one might imagine that it would normally read something like 'my steps *resonate* monotonously on the asphalt'). Strikingly, this then leads into the language of music (indeed, immediately following this quotation Dujardin even includes two bars of musical notation), as though the monotone sound of his steps were keeping time to the 'rhythm' of the song. The 'suggestive adverb' is designed to draw attention to the 'musical value' of the language, and can thus be said not only to contribute to Dujardin's style, but to 'symbolize' it in both senses of the verb: it typifies his style, but it also defines it as symbolist.[17]

The second aspect of Dujardin's style that can be understood as typically symbolist is his use of colour, in particular his repeated preference for white, as in the passage quoted above where he speaks of 'the white light of the candles, whitened gold'. A further example pits the blackness of the street against the pale whites of the pavement and sky to create an evocative chiaroscuro:

> Up the dark street, the double row of gas-lamps seeming smaller and smaller; no passers-by in the street; the pavement resounding, pale under the pallor of the clear sky and the moon; in the background, the moon in the sky; the pale, elongated crescent of the pale moon; and on each side, the houses ever the same.[18]

The repeated insistence on the colour white in this passage (rendered here in English as 'pale', but given in the original French as 'blanc'), together with its evident synaesthesia – the pale/white moonlight corresponding to the pale/white sound of the pavement underneath Prince's feet – suggests that one might usefully adapt Roland Barthes' notion of an 'écriture blanche'. Barthes famously wrote in 1953 that an 'écriture blanche' would be 'neutral' or 'innocent': 'freed from all bondage to a pre-ordained state of language', it would become 'writing at the zero degree'.[19] Given his symbolist insistence on the particularities of the colour white, one might plausibly apply the term to Dujardin's prose, but with a crucial dialectical twist. For Dujardin's 'écriture blanche' is the polar opposite of the Barthesian model: it is not the cultivated absence of style (the 'style of absence which is almost an ideal absence of style' which Barthes ascribes to *L'Etranger*),[20] but rather its absolute *presence*. Dujardin's 'deformed syntax' serves to render the transparency of realist language opaque, so that the weight of attention falls not on what is being described, but rather on *how* it is being described. In his *Esthétique de la langue française*, first published ten years after *Les Lauriers sont coupés* in 1898–99, Rémy de Gourmont describes the notion of 'déformation' as in fact 'a precision, in the sense that it appropriates, determines, directs and stigmatizes':[21] this idea of deformation as precision is precisely what Dujardin seeks to effect with his paratactic syntax and catachrestic adverbs.[22]

Decadent style and the death-drive

Barthes' notion of 'neutral' style forms an instructive contrast to the symbolist style which Paul Bourget termed 'décadent' in his *Essays in Contemporary Psychology*. Bourget, as Matei Calinescu notes, is the first writer 'to accept unwaveringly (unlike Baudelaire or even Gautier) both the term and the fact of decadence, and to articulate this acceptance in a full-blown, philosophic and aesthetic theory of decadence as a style'.[23] As we saw in Chapter 1, Nietzsche applied Bourget's definition to modernity more broadly:

> A decadent style is one in which the unity of a book decomposes to leave room for the independence of the page, the page decomposes to leave room for the independence of the phrase, and the phrase to leave room for the independence of the word.[24]

The fracturing of style into its constituent parts that Bourget identifies here is exemplified by Dujardin's typically symbolist use of the adverb analysed above. If the 'independence of the word' finds its ultimate expression in a part of speech fetishized into exemplary status, it is no accident that in Dujardin's case this part of speech should serve to convey the manner and style of an action, not the action itself.

Moreover, if the style of *Les Lauriers sont coupés* can be identified as decadent in Bourget's sense, this underlines its importance as a pivotal work for the development of modernism more broadly, since decadent style offers a microcosm of modernist style. 'In order to express the modern soul, as complicated as it is,' wrote the Belgian symbolist Emile Verhaeren, 'a rhythmical language [*une langue rhythmée*] is necessary, one that is free and subtle, malleable.'[25] Prose poetry, stream of consciousness and interior monologue – arguably the major forms of modernist prose – can all be understood as versions of a decadent style which foregrounds its own 'rhythmical language' as part of a quasi-narcissistic love affair with itself. Henri Mitterand suggests that decadent style is essentially a more hermetic, introverted version of 'l'écriture artiste':

> Incapable of inventing a new style, [decadent style] adapted the most pronounced anomalies of *l'écriture artiste*, diverting them from their initial purpose – which was to analyse sensation ever more precisely – to create a language for initiates, a sort of code for disabused, dilettantish aesthetes.[26]

Mitterand's analysis captures nicely the double movement of decadent style: on the one hand, it seeks to evoke 'sensation' as accurately as possible; on the other hand, it threatens constantly to lose sight of this purpose by becoming too inward, too self-obsessed.

As Rémy de Gourmont wrote in 1902, 'the style of the pure[ly] visual, a style composed of nothing but completely original images, would be absolutely incomprehensible. Something of the banal and vulgar is needed as common bond, as cement serves the shaped stones.'[27] Bourget's famous definition suggests that decadent style is by nature self-destructive, since the process of self-decomposition, when taken to its logical extreme, must ultimately undo language altogether. Where does the inward regression – from book to page to sentence to word – finally stop? As Peter Nicholls notes, 'the decadent aesthetic projects a literal desire for death and dismemberment into the style itself',[28] producing a narcissistic style of glittering surfaces that threaten to suffocate under their own weight. Examples of this abound in the literature of the 1880s and 1890s: Verlaine writes of the 'golden style' of decadence; Wilde's Dorian Gray identifies the 'curious jewelled style' of Aubrey Beardsley's 'yellow book' (linking it explicitly to 'the French school of *Symbolistes*'); Huysmans' Des Esseintes diagnoses Mallarmé's 'adhesive style, a unique, hermetic language, full of contracted phrases, elliptical constructions, audacious tropes'.[29] Language is overloaded, in other words, to the point of collapse. Already in his 1868 essay on Baudelaire, Gautier seems to sense the tipping-point which decadent style would inevitably reach, when he notes that 'decadent style is the final expression of the word which is called upon to express everything, and which is worked for all it is worth'.[30] Nicholls suggests that Gautier's view of decadence 'expresses the inner logic of a modernity which has reached the terminal point in a cultural parabola', since the search for ever greater sophistication must ultimately collapse under its own weight:

> Gautier understands the decadent style not as just one style among many, but as the expression of a deeper logic in all cultural production: for in so far as the arts seem to develop towards ever greater formal complexity, so style is at once supplementary – it adds nuance and detail to its object – and destructive – it 'decomposes' the matter upon which it 'works'.[31]

It is this constant negotiation between foregrounding language and undermining it, between what we have termed 'pure style' and 'purely style', that makes decadent style a microcosm of modernist style more broadly. Nicholls makes the point:

> If the principal qualities of decadent style – its sceptical view of representation and linguistic transparency, its mixed registers, its analytic intelligence – seem somehow familiar, it is because they would reappear in different guises in modernist style.[32]

This notion of decadent style as the kernel of modernist style more broadly can be seen not only in terms of the 'musical' style typical both of symbolism and of the highly composed, 'symphonic' narrative structures of high modernism (John Middleton Murry writes in 1922 that 'when the musical suggestion is allowed to predominate, decadence of style has begun'),[33] but also in the context of contemporary theories of sexuality.[34] Whilst 'Bourget's idea of decomposition confirms our understanding of the death-drive within the decadent style,'[35] *thanatos* also evokes *eros*. And if *eros* is omnipresent, if often only implicitly, in decadent style, then by Nicholls' logic it is also *pars pro toto* central to modernist style more generally. *Les Lauriers sont coupés* anticipates both the theory of the Freudian sex-drive and the practice of, say, Thomas Mann's *Death in Venice*, where the ageing writer Gustav von Aschenbach 'yearns' (to use a key term) for the youthful beauty of the Polish boy Tadzio. Indeed, Dujardin's novel builds up to an anti-climax in the specifically sexual sense: Prince spends the day lusting after the actress Léa, hoping that tonight she will allow him to sleep with her, only to be rebuffed yet again. This sexual tension is the conceptual and stylistic motor of Dujardin's prose: the oscillation between hope and frustration, the constant 'tangents' of his thoughts, are driven by Prince's pursuit of his desire.[36]

In the Freudian era of the turn of the century, *eros* and *thanatos* provide the two stylistic poles of the interior monologue. Arthur Schnitzler's *Lieutenant Gustl*, first published on Christmas Day 1900, is arguably the first stream of consciousness text in German;[37] Freud famously claimed that Schnitzler was his 'Doppelgänger',[38] exploring through prose what he himself was attempting to achieve through psychoanalysis, namely the uncovering of the repressed unconscious. The plot is quickly summarized: the eponymous Lieutenant Gustl overreacts to an altercation at the opera with a baker, and challenges him to a duel in order to satisfy his honour. Yet if *eros* is frustrated in *Les Lauriers sont coupés*, then *thanatos* is frustrated in *Lieutenant Gustl*:[39] the duel never actually happens, since the baker dies before their dawn appointment. Schnitzler's story, just like Dujardin's, is more interested in the psychological tension leading up to the act than in the act itself. This is reflected in their style: where Dujardin uses semi-colons to suggest the insatiable restlessness and impatience of thought, Schnitzler uses dashes and ellipses to convey the skittish paranoia of the self-important lieutenant. The jumps in tense are also characteristic of interior monologue, where past and future are conflated into the present tense of solipsistic self-consciousness. Just as Daniel Prince's thoughts all turn around his desire for Léa, so the threat of imminent death concentrates Gustl's mind: 'Yes, I know: I must die, so it is all irrelevant – I must die ...'[40] The simultaneous attraction and repulsion of death are thus inscribed in both the plot and the style.

Thomas Mann and 'stylistic and formal talent'

Decadence and its death-drive are a determining presence in Thomas Mann's great early novel *Buddenbrooks*, first published in 1901, around the same time as *Lieutenant Gustl*. Mann's story of the 'Decline of a Family' traces the degeneration of a robust family of senators and businessmen to the sensitive, sickly Hanno Buddenbrook, whose death is emblematic of Mann's view of the artist as axiomatically ill, marginalized from healthy society. Mann's early fiction abounds with variations on this idea of the artist as decadent: in the 70 pages of the short story *Tonio Kröger* (1903) alone, the artist is depicted as by turns a sick man, an actor, a conman, a homosexual, a thief and a madman, whilst the best-known subsequent works such as *Death in Venice* (1912), *The Magic Mountain* (1924) and *Doctor Faustus* (1947) reinforce this view of the artist as necessarily alienated from the ordinary citizen. These are the words in which *Tonio Kröger* establishes the terms of the debate: the artist ('Künstler') is to be distinguished from the citizen ('Bürger'), indeed, he is in a sense defined through this distinction.

Mann's understanding of this distinction places great emphasis on the stylistic and formal aspects of art. Chapter 4 of *Tonio Kröger*, in which the eponymous young writer visits the Russian painter Lisaweta Iwanowna in her atelier, functions essentially as an exposition of Mann's views on art at the time, which can be seen both in the context of late nineteenth-century theories of decadence (physical as well as stylistic)[41] and in the broader context of what would become modernist orthodoxies of 'impersonality'. Kröger insists that the true artist does not seek to express emotion or feeling, which he dismisses as a 'naïve amateur illusion';[42] rather, the artist must cultivate a cool distance from his material. The way he does this is through emphasizing the aesthetic aspects of his style:

Because, of course, *what* one says must never be one's main concern. It must merely be the raw material, quite indifferent in itself, out of which the work of art is made; and the act of making must be a game, aloof and detached, performed in tranquility.[43]

Mann prioritizes here the 'how' over the 'what', the form over the content. If the latter is understood as the main current of daily life as experienced by the normal 'citizen', this inevitably leads to the distancing of the artist, to an alienation from ordinary life that is expressed both stylistically as well as existentially. Mann has Kröger state apodictically:

> Our stylistic and formal talent, our gift of expression [*die Begabung für Stil, Form und Ausdruck*], itself presupposes this cold-blooded, fastidious attitude to mankind, indeed it presupposes a certain human impoverishment and stagnation. For the fact is: all healthy emotion, all strong emotion lacks taste.[44]

Decadence thus becomes not simply a stylistic principle, but rather a stylistic *prerequisite*: it is not that decadence implies a certain style, à la Bourget, but that style implies a certain decadence. This is the basis for Mann's famous irony: the artist's 'over-stimulated consciousness of himself' (*sein überreiztes Ichgefühl*) leads to a 'gulf of irony'[45] between himself and the rest of the world. Mann even goes so far as to suggest a parallel between literary and sartorial style, claiming that 'so far as outward appearances are concerned one should dress decently [...] and behave like a respectable citizen'.[46] Just as the cool, classical style of Mann is designed both to conceal and to reveal the passion (in the etymological as well as the emotional sense) of the artist behind it, so Kröger would have the artist dress his body up like his text, taking refuge behind a certain style of respectability.

If one defines irony as saying the opposite of what one actually means, then its use as a stylistic principle calls into question the sincerity of the artist, and indeed more broadly the ability of style to convey meaning. Mann's term 'outward appearances' (*Äußerlich*) implies that Kröger's bourgeois respectability is only skin-deep (only *style-deep*, one might say). Equally, however, his self-appointed status as the marginalized, decadent artist is also only a mask, indeed it is of its very essence that it must be a mask. For, crucially, Kröger is fully aware of his dual status both as bourgeois citizen and alienated artist. He suffers from what one could call the self-hatred of the bourgeois artist; the painter Iwanowna concludes their discussion by characterizing him as a 'bourgeois *manqué*',[47] and, by the end of the story in the final short chapter, Kröger is lucid enough to define himself as caught 'between the two worlds'. As he confesses, he simply loves life and people too much (Mann writes of this 'bourgeois love of mine for the human')[48] in order to be able to embrace fully the necessary 'human impoverishment and stagnation' of the single-minded artist. Mann's implication, in other words, is that the pure stylist would have to shut out all ethical or moral concerns. The derivation from – the reaction *against* – theories of decadence and *l'art pour l'art* is clear, long before Mann makes it explicit in the penultimate chapter of his *Reflections of a Nonpolitical Man* (1918), where he writes that he 'despised the aesthetic, renaissance-Nietzscheanism that was all around me and that seemed to me to be a boyishly mistaken imitation of Nietzsche'.[49] Aestheticism, for Mann, is a 'gesture-rich, highly talented impotence in life and love';[50] even though 'the inner essence' of art 'has always been style, form and selection, reinforcement, elevation, a rising above the material',[51] aestheticism that is only aestheticism is in fact 'anti-aestheticism', since it is irresponsible and doomed to decadence.

Indeed, this is arguably Mann's great subject, his lifelong obsession: what is the ethical cost of the aesthetic? Beyond Tonio Kröger, through Aschenbach in *Death in Venice*, Adrian Leverkühn in *Doctor Faustus* and the conman Felix Krull (to name but three of his major figures), Mann is constantly worried – in an obviously self-reflexive way – by the dangers of uncurbed aestheticism. 'The magisterial poise of our style is a lie and a farce,' he quotes from Plato's *Phaedrus* in *Death in Venice*.[52] The essay 'The Artist and the Man of Letters' ('Der Künstler und der Literat', 1913) expands on this relationship between aesthetic style and ethical integrity. The artist is defined as 'ethically indifferent, as irresponsible and innocent as nature',[53] whereas the man of letters is 'fundamentally respectable' (*wesentlich anständig*).[54] Yet the latter's ethical engagement passes through his 'stylistic and formal talent'. In a move that recalls Schiller's *Letters on Aesthetic Education* (1794), Mann states that 'to write well essentially means to think well, and from there it is not far to acting well'.[55] The man of letters is a moralist, but only 'artistically' (*aus Künstlertum*);[56] his moral views express themselves 'through *words*',[57] as Mann emphasizes in italics, recalling, not for the first time in the narrative of modernist style, Mallarmé's comment to Degas that poetry is made out of words and not ideas. The exact calibration of the relationship between ethics and aesthetics is crucial:

His ethical passion derives from his talent. The purity and nobility of his style is reflected (and it is probably not the other way around) in his perception of the human, social, and political spheres.[58]

Mann is at pains to point out (as his somewhat awkward parenthesis suggests) that for the 'man of letters' the ethical dimension derives from the stylistic, not the other way around. For the 'artist', this distinction does not even apply, since he is amoral, 'ethically indifferent'. The fact that much of Mann's fiction warns against such a reduction of the ethical to the aesthetic can itself be read as the logical consequence of the decadent impulse at the heart of modernist style: Mann's prose, in effect, constitutes an extended warning against the death-drive of decadent style.

Marcel Proust and the 'palimpsest' of style

In an essay of 1919 entitled simply 'Modern Fiction', Virginia Woolf claimed that modernist writers are essentially 'spiritual', whereas old-fashioned authors such as Wells, Bennett and Galsworthy are 'materialist'. It is clear on which side of the barrier Woolf positions herself and her 'moments of being':

Life is not a series of gig-lamps symmetrically arranged; life is a luminous halo, a semi-transparent envelope surrounding us from the beginning of consciousness to the end. Is it not the task of the novelist to convey this varying, this unknown and uncircumscribed spirit?[59]

Nowhere is this task more vividly conveyed than in *In Search of Lost Time* (1913–27). Along with Joyce and Woolf, Proust is the epitome of 'epiphanic' (as opposed to 'programmatic') modernism (I am following Roger Griffin's terms here).[60] Proust's sense of the 'privileged moment'[61] provides both the subject matter and the structure of the whole cycle, namely 'a fragment of time in the pure state'[62] (*un peu de temps à l'état pur*). His views on style are at the heart of his pursuit of 'lost' time. They come to a head in the final volume, *Time Regained*, in the scene where Marcel is waiting in the Guermantes' library while the concert finishes. This is, in a sense, the pivotal scene in the entire cycle, since it is here that the narrator, triggered by the act of stumbling over a paving-stone, is finally able to look back on the experiences described over the course of the cycle and make sense of them within the context of his artistic project. He comes to the realization that 'reality' is not the surface of things, but the 'depth' behind them: 'The reality that he has to express resides, as I now began to understand, not in the superficial appearance of his subject but at a depth at which that appearance matters little.'[63] This realization places a particular emphasis on style as the artist's means of access to this higher reality:

> style for the writer, no less than colour for the painter, is a question not of technique but of vision: it is the revelation, which by direct and conscious methods would be impossible, of the qualitative difference, the uniqueness of the fashion in which the world appears to each one of us, a difference which, if there were no art, would remain for ever the secret

of every individual. Through art alone are we able to emerge from ourselves.[64]

Proust's view of artistic style makes it the vehicle of his quest for the privileged moment of 'pure' time, whether it be manifested by the paving-stone coming loose, the madeleine dipped in tea, or the phrase from Vinteuil's sonata. Accordingly, he rejects 'so-called realist' art, which 'contents itself with describing things, with giving of them merely a miserable abstract of lines and surfaces'.[65] In a celebrated passage, Proust constructs something close to a metaphysics of style:

What we call reality is a certain connexion between these immediate sensations and the memories which envelop us simultaneously with them – a connexion that is suppressed in a simple cinematographic vision, which just because it professes to confine itself to the truth in fact departs widely from it – a unique connexion which the writer has to rediscover in order to link for ever in his phrase the two sets of phenomena which reality joins together. He can describe a scene by describing one after another the innumerable objects which at a given moment were present at a particular place, but truth will be attained by him only when he takes two different objects, states the connexion between them – a connexion analogous in the world of art to the unique connexion which in the world of science is provided by the law of causality – and encloses them in the necessary links of a well-wrought style; truth – and life too – can be attained by us only when, by comparing a quality common to two sensations, we succeed in extracting their common essence and in reuniting them to each other, liberated from the contingencies of time, within a metaphor. Had not nature herself – if one considered the matter from this point of view – placed me on the path of art, was she not herself a beginning of art, she who, often, had allowed me to become aware of the beauty of one thing only in another thing, of the beauty, for instance, of noon at Combray in the sound of its bells, of that of the mornings at Doncières in the hiccups of our central heating? The link may be uninteresting, the objects trivial, the style bad, but unless this process has taken place the description is worthless.[66]

Proust gives full expression here to his view of style as an issue 'not of technique but of vision'. He makes his metaphysics contingent on his poetics: the 'connexions' he is constantly seeking – in 'life' and in 'nature', as well as in art – can only be expressed through the 'necessary links of a well-wrought style'. Style – even 'bad style' – is thus indispensable.

At the heart of this vision of style is Proust's understanding of metaphor. 'Metaphor alone can give style a sort of eternity,' he claims in his essay on Flaubert.[67] For Proust, writes Gérard Genette in his essay 'Proust Palimpsest' (1961),

metaphor is not an ornament, but the necessary instrument for a recovery, through style, of the vision of essences, because it is the stylistic equivalent of the psychological experience of involuntary memory, which alone, by bringing together two sensations separated in time, is able to release their *common essence* through the *miracle of an analogy*.[68]

Where the realist prose Proust rejects would simply stay on the surface of things, endlessly deferring meaning by 'describing one after another the innumerable objects which at a given moment were present at a particular place', so Proust's metaphorical style seeks to penetrate beneath them.[69] As Genette's essay suggests, his style can be compared to a palimpsest, where one layer of meaning is superimposed on another. In a passage describing Mme Swann's clothes, Proust even directly discusses this idea:

> Young men attempting to understand her theory of dress would say: 'Mme Swann is quite a period in herself, isn't she?' As in a fine literary style which superimposes different forms but is strengthened by a tradition that lies concealed behind them, so in Mme Swann's attire those half-tinted memories of waistcoats or ringlets, sometimes a tendency, at once repressed, towards the 'all aboard', or even a distant and vague allusion to the 'follow-me-lad', kept alive beneath the concrete form the unfinished likeness of other, older forms which one would not have been able to find effectively reproduced by the milliner or the dressmaker, but about which one's thoughts incessantly hovered, and enveloped Mme Swann in a sort of nobility – perhaps because the very uselessness of these fripperies made them seem designed to serve some more than utilitarian purpose, perhaps because of the traces they preserved

of vanished years, or else because of a vestimen-
tary personality peculiar to this woman, which gave
to the most dissimilar of her costumes a distinct
familiar likeness. One felt that she did not dress
simply for the comfort or the adornment of her
body; she was surrounded by her garments as by
the delicate and spiritualised machinery of a whole
civilisation.[70]

The passage functions as a *mise-en-abyme* of Proust's
style. Strikingly, the comparison itself is not just an
example *of* his style, it is also directly *about* it. An analogy is constructed between the form/content relationship of a text and the garment/body relationship of
Mme Swann. The passage can be read self-reflexively,
as referring back to Proust's own style, 'which superim-
poses different forms but is strengthened by a tradition
that lies concealed behind them'; moreover, it is also
performative, in the sense that the long, intricate
sentence enacts the layers of style/garment which it
thematizes. Indeed, one could argue that this very performativity is itself in turn thematized, inasmuch as
the layers of clothing 'serve some more than utilitarian
purpose': neither texture nor text is merely an 'adornment' (or 'ornament', in Genette's words), but rather
they both convey their meaning through their form.

The spirals of meaning here are dizzying. Style is
a metaphor (or, in this case, simile) for clothing,
which in turn can be read as a metaphor for style.
Yet Genette goes on to show that this view of style
as akin to metaphor brings with it a new set of problems, problems that place Proust directly within our
broad narrative of the double movement of modernist

style. Genette argues that the passage from Chardin to Rembrandt described by Proust in one of his essays – where Chardin 'has proclaimed the divine equality of all things under the light which beautifies them and to the mind which reflects on them [...]. With Rembrandt, even reality will be left behind. We shall learn that beauty does not lie in objects' – corresponds to 'the passage from Flaubert to Proust himself'.[71] The danger of this is the danger inherent in modernist style more broadly:

> The passage from the ontological to the analogical, from the substantial style to the metaphorical style, would appear to mark [...] a progress not so much in the quality of aesthetic achievement as in the aware-ness of the difficulties, or at least of the conditions, of such an achievement.[72]

We have seen already how modernist style, as it devel-ops 'from Flaubert to Proust', threatens constantly to destroy itself. Genette argues that Proust's 'metaphori-cal style' runs the same risk, since 'how can a descrip-tion based on the "relationship" between two objects avoid destroying the essence of each?' Proust writes in *Time Regained* that 'as Elstir had found with Chardin, you can make a new version of what you love only by first renouncing it',[73] and this is the problem with his metaphorical style: the more one seeks to compare lev-els of reality, the more one runs the risk of strangling them. 'The paradox [of *In Search of Lost Time*] is that its structure devours its substance,' notes Genette, thereby outlining a variation on Cioran's 'virus'.[74] 'Proust's writing falls prey to a singular reversal: having set out to locate essences, it ends up constituting, or reconstituting, mirages. [...] It discovers a level of the real in which reality, by virtue of its plenitude, annihilates *itself*.'[75]

Yet one can, of course, be more generous, and argue that this is the very point of Proust's style. 'This palimpsest of time and space, these discordant views, ceaselessly contradicted and ceaselessly brought together by an untiring movement of painful dissociation and impossible synthesis – this, no doubt, is the Proustian vision.'[76] As we have seen, Proust both discusses style and enacts it, and it is this that ultimately places him within the modernist pantheon of performative self-consciousness. In Proust's vision of the recuperability of time through artistic endeavour, the double movement of his metaphorical style, which imposes layers of meaning on top of reality whilst in the process slowly effacing that reality, functions as the very vehicle of memory: style is both conjunction and dislocation.

Ulysses and 'the English styles'

Alongside Proust and his quest for 'a fragment of time in the pure state', it was Joyce who, in *Stephen Hero* (written 1904–6, published 1944), famously placed the term 'epiphanies' at the heart of modernist discourse. Woolf takes Joyce as the paradigm of the 'spiritual' writer, arguing that 'he is concerned at all costs to reveal the flickerings of that innermost flame which flashes its messages through the brain'.[77] The stylistic implications of this are evident: 'spiritual' writers attempt to come closer to life, and to preserve more sincerely and exactly what interests and moves them, even if to do so they must discard most of the conventions which are commonly observed by the novelist.[78]

Thus is produced a kind of poetic prose, whether in the form of a first-person interior monologue or third-person stream of consciousness. Modernist style is once again characterized by what Cioran would call the 'sickness' of its syntax; 'making it new' means discarding 'most of the conventions' of the novel.

Nowhere is this more evident than in the paradigmatic modernist novel, *Ulysses* (1922), which brings together many of the stylistic aspects discussed in this chapter, with its use of interior monologue, its emphasis on the fluctuations in consciousness between sexuality and mortality, and its self-conscious musicality of language. Joyce's obsession with the nuances of literary style was so strong that when his brother Stanislaus wanted to discuss fascism, he famously replied: 'Don't talk to me about politics, I'm only interested in style.'[79] Although *Ulysses* undertakes the familiar modernist move of foregrounding its own style, it does so in a way that differs from its stylistic predecessor *Les Lauriers sont coupés*. Where Dujardin's novel is characterized by a single, homogeneous style (which one might define as the Wagnerian–Schopenhauerian idiom typical of symbolism), *Ulysses* revels in an exuberance of heterogeneous *styles*. If Dujardin is a stylistic hedgehog, Joyce is every inch the fox.[80] 'I remind myself of the man who used to play several instruments with different parts of the body,' he wrote in 1921.[81] Arthur Power records Joyce as insisting on this catholicity of styles as the very condition of modern literature:

> In writing one must create an endlessly changing surface, dictated by the mood and current impulse in contrast to the fixed mood of the classical style. [...] [E]verything is inclined to flux and change nowadays and modern literature, to be valid, must express that flux.[82]

Yet the fact that 'virtually every chapter of *Ulysses* is written in a different style', notes the theorist Wolfgang Iser, marks 'a basic difference between Joyce and all other modern writers'.[83] Iser can help us get a sense of Joyce's idiosyncratic approach to style, since chapters seven and eight of his volume of essays *The Implied Reader* ('Doing Things in Style' and 'Patterns of Communication in Joyce's *Ulysses*') tackle the question head-on. Iser focuses in particular on the chapter of *Ulysses* which Joyce originally entitled 'The Oxen of the Sun', where Bloom is waiting for Mrs Purefoy to give birth in Dr Horne's maternity hospital. The whole chapter, as Iser writes, is characterized by 'a sequence of historical styles',[84] ranging from mock medieval to courtly epic, from pseudoscientific discourse to theological disquisition. It is undoubtedly a stylistic tour de force – but to what end? What is the point of such virtuoso ventriloquism? Joyce's translator Stuart Gilbert suggested in 1930 that the sequence of styles was meant to parallel the development of Mrs Purefoy's embryo,[85] but subsequent critics have tended to dismiss this interpretation as too rigid and overdetermined. The most important way to understand the chapter is perhaps through its relationship to the rest of the novel; S.L. Goldberg's view of 'The Oxen of the Sun' as Joyce's commentary on his book suggests that one can interpret it *pars pro toto*.[86]

The sequence of styles adopted in the chapter, and in the novel more broadly, can be viewed in two main ways. On the one hand, they represent an attempt to encompass reality from as many different perspectives as possible; on the other hand, they are obviously also meant as a parody of historical literary styles. What is striking about both these interpretations is that they imply a lack of faith in style as the vehicle of truth and meaning, a vision that places *Ulysses* at the heart of the modernist crisis of representation. The first interpretation can be illustrated by Iser's response to the following sentence from 'The Oxen of the Sun': 'For who is there who anything of some significance has apprehended but is conscious that that exterior splendour may be the surface of a downwardtending lutulent reality.'[87] Iser writes:

> [Joyce's] awareness of the danger that he will capture only the surface view of things, makes him approach the object as it were from all linguistic sides, in order to avoid a perspective foreshortening of it. [...] Language is used not to fix an object, but to summon it to the imagination.[88]

Through the critique of language as mere 'surface', Iser implicitly places Joyce in a narrative that stretches back through the symbolists and decadents to Schopenhauer and Flaubert. Where others respond

to this by clinging ever more tightly to one particular stylistic vision, Joyce responds by producing a
plethora of competing styles, as though in the hope
that through throwing enough stylistic perspectives at
reality, a composite truth will emerge.

Inevitably, however, this stylistic excess tips over
into parody. What are the implications of this parody? *Pace* Stuart Gilbert's attempt to yoke style to story,
'The Oxen of the Sun' exhibits a striking 'incongruity
between style and object',[89] since the very heterogene-
ity of the various styles imitated means that, however
one interprets the relationship between style and story,
they can hardly *all* be commensurate with the subject matter (unlike, say, *Les Lauriers sont coupés*, where
the single, consistent style enacts the fluctuations in
the protagonist's consciousness). Iser interprets the
proliferation of styles as an implict admission of the
essential inability of style to grasp reality:

> If style reproduces only aspects of reality and not –
> in contrast to its implicit claims – reality itself, then it
> must be failing in its intention. This idea is worked
> up through the element of parody in the stylistic
> impersonations. […] By parodying the styles, Joyce
> has exposed their essentially manipulative charac-
> ter. The reader gradually becomes conscious of the
> fact that style fails to achieve its ends, in that it
> does not capture reality but imposes upon it an
> historically preconditioned form.[90]

Joyce's deliberately overdetermined styles are meant to
suggest, then, that since language cannot but preju-
dice one's view of the world, the best response is to

tackle this head-on by 'thematizing the capacity of style itself'.[91] Whilst T.S. Eliot felt that this particular chapter of *Ulysses* showed 'the futility of all the English styles',[92] he also wrote that 'Joyce has arrived at a very singular and perhaps unique literary distinction: the distinction of having, not in a negative but a very positive sense, no style at all. [...] Mr. Joyce's work puts an end to the tradition of Walter Pater.'[93] Eliot's argument depends on viewing *Ulysses* as 'not so distinctly a precursor of a new epoch as [...] a gigantic culmination of an old'.[94] In other words, it places Joyce squarely in the European tradition of style that led from Flaubert to Pater and the symbolists, but as its heir *ex negativo*. Joyce takes the 'deformation' of style to its *nec plus ultra*, as Iser suggests:

> The particular point of view [...] determines which individual phenomena out of all those present are, or are not to be presented. And this, for Joyce, is the whole problem of style. Presentability or nonpresentability is not a quality inherent to any observable reality, but has to be imposed on that reality by the observer. This involves a latent deformation of the object perceived.[95]

Iser's term 'deformation' is striking, since it has a particular ancestry in the development of symbolist conceptions of style. Jean Moréas, in his influential 'Manifeste du symbolisme' (1886), used the term to describe the aims of symbolist literature – 'the impressionist-symbolist novel will construct an œuvre of subjective deformation'[96] – whilst we have seen how Rémy de Gourmont described the notion of deformation as in fact 'a precision, in the sense that it appropriates, determines, directs and stigmatizes'.[97] This deformation is thus also, necessarily, a *formation*. Iser captures something of this double movement when, after following John Middleton Murry in defining style as 'a quality of language which communicates [...] a system of emotions or thoughts, peculiar to the author',[98] he notes that 'this function of style is both its strength and its weakness'.[99]

Joyce's technique of parodying a range of styles suggests that he is aware of this problem. On the one hand, *Ulysses* can be viewed as a prime example of aesthetic modernism's response to the pluralism of modernity: 'Lacking any coherent style of its own, modernity degenerates into an age of pastiche,' writes Peter Nicholls.[100] Yet on the other hand, what Nicholls terms a 'loss of style' in turn *becomes* a style, through the stylistic montage that echoes the modernist use of montage embodied most obviously by Walter Benjamin's unfinished *Arcades Project*: 'Method of this project: literary montage. I needn't *say* anything. Merely show.'[101] Similarly, as Beckett famously observed, Joyce's writing 'is not about something; it is that something itself'.[102] Since Iser dismisses the notion that Joyce was 'advocating a purist use of language' as 'an idea that is hardly worth considering',[103] one might thus suggest that what *Ulysses* typifies is in fact a third aspect of the dialectic of 'pure style' and 'purely style' already identified, namely *impure* style. Where modernity 'degenerates' into an age of pastiche, Joycean modernism generates it, foregrounding its mongrel style as its very seal of authenticity.

'Women's writing' and the 'disease' of style

Alongside her distinction between the 'materialist' Edwardians and the 'spiritual' modernists, Virginia Woolf also argues that the modern era threw up another new literary style, namely that of women. Writing in 1929, she claimed that, in the past, women writers found it hard to escape the ghetto of 'resenting the treatment of [their] sex and pleading for its rights'.[104] With the advent of universal suffrage and other contemporary improvements in the condition of women, however, they were starting to overcome this problem: 'The great change that has crept into women's writing is, it would seem, a change of attitude. The woman writer is no longer bitter.' This brings with it, Woolf argues, a broadening of perspective in female fiction: 'the average novel by a woman is far more genuine and far more interesting today than it was a hundred or even fifty years ago'.[105]

This change also brings with it a shift in style. Woolf suggests that the problem for the modern female writer is no longer moral, but stylistic, since

> the very form of the sentence does not fit her. It is a sentence made by men; it is too loose, too heavy, too pompous for a woman's use. Yet in a novel, which covers so wide a stretch of ground, an ordinary and usual type of sentence has to be found to carry the reader on easily and naturally from one end of the book to the other. And this a woman must make for herself, altering and adapting the current sentence until she writes one that takes the natural shape of her thought without crushing or distorting it.[106]

Female modernists such as H.D., Gertrude Stein, Marianne Moore and Mina Loy set out to explore this change of stylistic perspective. As Woolf suggests, their style can be understood in opposition to the male Anglo-American modernists: where Hulme, Pound, Eliot and Lewis advocated a 'hard', masculine syntax, rejecting the legacy of decadent style as 'feminine' and narcissistic, their female counterparts embraced this 'self-sufficiency of language which had seemed decadent to the "Men of 1914"'.[107] As Nicholls notes, for instance, H.D.'s novel *Her* (written 1927–30, published 1981) looks back to Swinburne in its construction of the narcissistic self, whilst Stein's exploration in her poetry of the 'continuous present' is generally taken to derive from her time as a student of William James, who invented the concept of the 'stream of consciousness'.[108] For these women writers, Bernard's statement in Woolf's *The Waves* (1931) can be taken as programmatic: 'The rhythm is the main thing in writing.'[109]

Through this insistence on the necessary relationship between style and story, and in particular on the fluctuations that this relationship inevitably occasions, 'characters are introduced according to the styles in which they write', notes Finn Fordham.[110] Fordham's discussion of the genesis of *The Waves* relates the disparate 'styles of character' to 'styles of composition'. Analysing the opening page of an early draft of 'The Moths', as the novel was originally to be called, he suggests that by the time of *The Waves*, style – or perhaps one should say in the Joycean manner *styles* – had become for Woolf a way of expressing differing aspects of her personality:

Woolf's perception of her many selves and her intense reflection on her range of different writing styles are in this passage reflections of each other. She had already proposed in her diary that different styles could act as counter-balances and pressure-releases for each other. Ten months before starting *The Waves* but while busy projecting it, she developed an idea of how she would write 'books that relieve other books', making 'a variety of styles' out of her writing life.[111]

The passage in Woolf's diary alluded to here provides a striking synthesis of her views on style. On 7 November 1928, she records:

> One reviewer says that I have come to a crisis in the matter of style: it is now so fluent and fluid that it runs through the mind like water.
>
> That disease began in the *Lighthouse*. The first part came fluid – how I wrote and wrote!
>
> Shall I now check and consolidate, more in the *Dalloway* and *Jacob's Room* style?
>
> I rather think the upshot will be books that relieve other books: a variety of styles and subjects: for after all, that is my temperament, I think, to be very little persuaded of the truth of anything.[112]

Modernist style is here once again configured as a 'disease', as a 'virus', to use Cioran's term. The implication which Woolf takes over from the anonymous reviewer, and couches in relation to her previous books, is that she has *too much* style, that she should perhaps now 'check and consolidate' what it is she wants to say, rather than getting too bogged down in how she says it. Style is thus once more understood as impeding truth and meaning, rather than conveying it; the phrase 'books that relieve other books' suggests that Woolf's perceived overemphasis on style leads merely to an epistemological passing of the buck, a constant deferral of meaning. If she is 'very little persuaded of the truth of anything', then perhaps, she seems to fear, this manifests itself in her all too 'fluent' style.

Woolf's concerns about using this 'variety of styles' as a kind of defensive confessional strategy, shielding her lack of faith in 'truth' behind the fluid surfaces of her style, suggests the salient distinction between this 'feminine' writing and its contemporary male counterpart. The work of the former tends to embrace a style that is enamoured of its own surfaces, a style that is 'deformed' in Rémy de Gourmont's sense (it was Gourmont who set the tone for the subsequent gendering of decadent style, writing in his essay 'Women and Language' [1901] that 'the most musical, the most rhythmical parts of speech' were to be designated as feminine).[113] Male high modernists such as Pound and Eliot, on the other hand, sought broadly to suppress the self (the doctrine of 'impersonality') in order to do justice to a perceived 'objective' world. 'Where Pound's Hugh Selwyn Mauberley found in aesthetic style a form of "armour" for the self, Loy discovers in its very fictionality a release from the ideological "truths" of gender,' writes Nicholls, and one could apply this to female modernists more generally; 'style is grasped not as the privileged vehicle of avant-garde authority but rather as witness to its metaphysical pretensions'.[114] Where 'feminine' style (which does not mean texts exclusively written by women) tends to want to reveal the self, its 'masculine' counterpart seeks to conceal it.

'Beyond language': the late modernist novel

If Woolf's own novels of this period – *Mrs Dalloway* (1925), *To the Lighthouse* (1927), *Orlando* (1928), *The Waves* (1931) – manage to give form to this female sentence without 'crushing or distorting' it, the same cannot be said of late modernist male-authored works such as Joyce's *Finnegans Wake* (1939) or Hermann Broch's *The Death of Virgil* (1945), works that can be taken as the *nec plus ultra* of modernist stream of consciousness prose. Cioran's description of prose poetry as 'a sick prose' finds ample evidence in both novels, in the intensely distorted syntax and sentences that flow over many pages. From its earliest reviews onwards, *Finnegans Wake* was interpreted as foregrounding style over substance, signifier over signified:

> In *Finnegans Wake* the style, the essential qualities and movement of the words, their rhythmic and melodic sequences, and the emotional colour of the page are the main representatives of the author's thought and feeling. The accepted significations of the words are secondary.[115]

Where 'the theme is the language and the language the theme', as an anonymous reviewer for the *Guardian* wrote in 1939,[116] then the foregrounding of style that characterizes modernism has reached its apogee. Samuel Beckett, in switching to French and paring his prose down to a spare minimalism, intuited the stylistic dead-end that Joyce had reached.

Similarly, *The Death of Virgil* pushes the language of prose to breaking point, indeed beyond it: 'his thought became greater than the form of his thought',[117] writes Broch at one point of the dying Virgil, whilst the closing words of the densely composed manuscript are 'beyond language'.[118] Broch's monolithic text, composed like a musical score in order to express the 'music of the inside and the outside',[119] and clotted in the modernist manner with allusions to Dante and Virgil, seeks to push language to its limits in order to go beyond it. One can read this late modernist novel not just as the death of Virgil, but also as the death of the decadent style that is at the heart of modernist prose, as its final 'soubresaut de la conscience'. It is not just the style, polished to the point of opacity, which suggests this reading, but the very subject matter of death – and not just any death, but that of Virgil, whom Valéry takes as the model of 'une littérature de décadence' characterized by its ever greater quest for perfection.[120] *The Death of Virgil* accordingly represents something close to the apotheosis of the death-drive of decadent style.

With texts of this complexity, where the hermetic subtlety of the language occludes any notion of a sustained, coherent 'plot', modernist prose attains a kind of absolute style, where pure style threatens once again to become purely style. One could indeed raise the same 'moral' objection to these typically late modernist texts as was raised to the decadent style of the 1880s and 1890s: does the fetishization of the signifier preclude meaningful engagement with what it is signifying? Where does the inward regression stop? The political background against which Broch wrote *The Death of Virgil* makes this a particularly pressing question. To put it polemically: is style a necessary and sufficient response to Nazism? Another late modernist text from around the same time as *The Death of Virgil* can be read as addressing precisely this question: Thomas Mann's *Doctor Faustus* (1947) allegorizes the descent of Germany into Nazism through the figure of the composer Adrian Leverkühn, whose pact with the devil produces music of the utmost formal beauty, but one that is essentially composed of little more than parodies of other forms (in particular, of Schönberg's 12-tone system). That the double movement of modernism, its inflationary tendency to pile up formal styles, can ultimately lead only to bankruptcy is configured in Leverkühn's Nietzschean slide into madness: Cioran's 'virus' is here given literal form through the syphilis Leverkühn is said to have contracted, à la Nietzsche, in a brothel.

At every stage of modernist prose, then – from its Flaubertian beginnings, via the decadent fin-de-siècle and the high modernism of Mann, Proust, Joyce and Woolf, to the late modernism of the Second World War – the question of the ambivalent nature of style recurs. Wherever aesthetic surface is foregrounded as a reaction to the conditions of modernity, modernity starts to ask in return whether it is not being shortchanged or sidelined. For the question implicit in the modernist preoccupation with style is ultimately this: do the self-regarding signifiers do justice to what they are ostensibly signifying? Does modernism do justice to modernity? The next chapter, which focuses on work produced around the key year 1922, will pursue this question into modernist poetry.

4

1922: Style and the Modernist Lyric

Having traced the development of modernist conceptions of prose style from the germ of decadence to the linguistic fever of late modernism, this chapter proposes to focus on poetic manifestations of style around the zenith of modernism in the year 1922. Works by three of the major lyric figures of the modernist age will be taken to represent three different linguistic traditions: Valéry's *Charms*, Rilke's *Duino Elegies* and *Sonnets to Orpheus*, and Eliot's *The Waste Land*. It is not the aim of this chapter to pursue a point by point exposition of these poems, nor to claim common cause between them. The intention is rather to understand them as crystallizations of certain contemporary views of poetic style, where it is precisely the differences – both of conception and of execution – within a common context that render such a comparative approach worthwhile. Through examining three poets with distinct agendas, the chapter seeks to explore the implications of stylistic self-consciousness for lyric poetry in the modernist era. Does style manifest itself differently in the modernist lyric than in modernist prose?

Paul Valéry and 'absolute poetry'

Of all the major poets of the modernist age, Paul Valéry was by far the most rigorously self-conscious. He once wrote that whilst it is sometimes claimed that what distinguishes man from monkey is the opposable thumb, the real distinction lies in our 'opposable souls',[1] our ability to turn our thought back on ourselves. From 1894, when he left Montpellier for Paris, until his death in 1945, Valéry got up every morning at 4 a.m. to record his thoughts and observations in his famous *Cahiers*, the notebooks that run to nearly 30,000 pages. Related to this legendary self-discipline is the other great cliché about Valéry, namely that from the so-called 'nuit de Gênes' of 4 October 1892 until the publication of *La Jeune Parque* (*The Young Fate*) in 1917 he underwent a period of profound 'silence', abandoning the public sphere of poetry in favour of the intimacy of his own rigorous self-appraisal.[2] It was only from this extended period of self-study, recorded in his notebooks, that the major poetry of *La Jeune Parque* and *Charms* could emerge; as Valéry said of the notebooks in 1922 to André Gide, 'My true self is there' (*mon vrai moi est là*).[3] Given that Valéry made this admission in the same year in which he published *Charms*, any consideration of his views on style must start with the *Cahiers*. Their contradictions and inconsistencies notwithstanding, the practice of Valéry's poetry can only be understood against the theory of the notes, which constitute, in the words of his editor Jean Hytier, the 'poetry of the poetry'.[4]

Valéry represents an intriguing test case of the modernist poet not only because of his extreme self-consciousness, and the rigour with which he kept a record of it, but also because of his self-positioning within modernism more broadly. On the one hand he can be seen, like Eliot after Laforgue, as an heir to the symbolist tradition still dominant in the 1890s in which he first came to prominence: Mallarmé, whom he had known personally, remained his great poetic hero. Yet on the other hand, Valéry came to reject the formal and stylistic innovations of modernism, taking refuge instead in a kind of exalted classicism. His views on style reflect this formal ambivalence.

True to his credo of constant self-surveillance, Valéry viewed style in the first instance as a corollary of self-consciousness:

It seems to me that the *originality* of language, its style, depends to a large extent upon the use that the writer or person makes of language *with regard to himself.* ?? Though I'm not entirely sure I'm right about that.

In any case, it is linked to mental activity, and especially to the individual perception of the *distance* that exists between language and *non-verbal* thought.

Someone who thinks above all in words, has little or no real *style.* […] Style is born when clear thinking sets itself against the inadequacy, the inertia, the vague *mediocrity* of language and successfully violates it. It is born from struggle.[5]

Valéry's italics define style as a consequence of the 'opposable soul': style is understood to derive from the turning back of language against the self, a movement which necessarily results in an increased awareness of the epistemological distance between language and the thought it is attempting to express. This view of style situates Valéry within the lineage of modernist language scepticism. Indeed, an entry in the *Notebooks* in 1902 could be read as a commentary on Hofmannsthal's 'Chandos Letter', published in the same year:

> Literary style results – (is made possible) by the inexactitude of words, their non-uniformity – in relation to mental facts. Each word says more, or less, than is necessary. (*Notebooks* II: 93)

Style, for Valéry, derives from a lack, from a *décalage* between word and thought: it is the attempt to compensate for this ultimately unbridgeable gap that leads to the creation of a particular style. In classic modernist fashion, the concept of style is thus predicated on the limitations of language.

If style is born of a 'struggle', this is because it involves constant vigilance against mediocrity, 'violating' ordinary language in a manner that recalls Roman Jakobson's definition of literature as 'organized violence committed on ordinary speech'. It is indeed impossible to understand Valéry's views on style without considering his much-discussed 'formalism'. Whilst no sustained exposition of his philosophy of 'form' can be attempted here (it is one of the words that recurs most frequently in his work, both in the aesthetic theory and in the poetry), it is nonetheless instructive to contrast the two terms. During the years of 'silence', Valéry's attitude towards style is clearly 'formalist'. In 1909–10, he notes that 'the form renders the idea organic' (*Notebooks* II: 96); two pages later, he records the following thoughts:

> No pure and rigorous work is created out of language without a process of rejection, of new, secret definitions, of specifications which form a new language within the old one.
>
> Style is a language (homogenous, complete, ordered) within a language (given and thus disordered in relation to me). [...]
>
> Art arises from the disorder of language as a whole, a disorder both necessary and *statistic* (to which I can oppose a language). (*Notebooks* II: 97)

Valéry comes close here to defining style in Saussure's terms as the conscious opposition of a specific *parole* to a broader *langue* (in the original French, Valéry uses the term *langage* for both). The purity of a style is to be determined by the extent to which it opposes aesthetic 'order' to linguistic 'disorder'. Broadened out beyond aesthetics, this means that Valéry understands style as the (almost tautological) mark of self-assertion, echoing Buffon's view of style as 'l'homme même':

> Style – I take the word in its simplest sense – graphology – writing – the mark of the individual in his language.

The ultimate in style must be that of the most 'original' man – a style like the man himself – (possessed or impulsive to an exceptional degree). [...]

If you want the most unequivocal example of style: it's that of Napoleon. (*Notebooks* II: 263)

Valéry comes close here to affirming style as a means of resisting the modern age of technical reproducibility. For to view style as the signature of the individual is to insist on the primacy of 'originality' or uniqueness: 'Nothing is more devoid of style than that which is imitable or the product of mechanical fabrication,' writes Valéry in a section of his late thoughts entitled 'Style'. 'I thus deplore (although it is too late) the use of the word to designate an epoque or a school of architecture or ornamental art, since styles of this kind are definable and imitable.'[6]

Yet what seems like praise of style can, of course, cut both ways. What is Napoleon if not a polarizing figure who both created and destroyed? The wilfully 'individual' can tip over into individuality for its own sake; pure style can become purely style. Valéry's views on style harden markedly when he historicizes them, and this is where his ideas of 'style' and 'form' most obviously part ways. In essence, he starts to identify style with rhetoric, of which he is deeply suspicious. The best-known example is his series of polemical statements about Pascal:

The finest *thoughts* of Pascal don't take us very far. Sometimes they are models of style; but they don't increase our knowledge, i.e. our power. He gives us no weapons, more often the opposite. (*Notebooks* II: 283)

Here Valéry seems to be saying that, despite his fine style, Pascal does not ultimately illuminate the reader. Elsewhere he goes further, arguing that it is actually *because* of his style that Pascal does not move him: 'To say: *eternal silence* etc., is to enunciate clearly: *I want to terrify you with my profundity and terrify you with my style*' (*Œuvres* II: 696). The problem, as Valéry sees it, is that Pascal's *Pensées* are too well written to be convincing:[7] their polished surface implies that they have been rewritten after the event, that they are not a true record of spontaneous emotion. Since the impression of metaphysical depth engendered by Pascal's writing paradoxically reposes, for Valéry, on its glittering but ultimately misleading surfaces, 'depth' is not to be trusted. Tellingly, Valéry writes in one notebook entry: 'Profundity is a hundred times easier to obtain from oneself than rigour' (*Œuvres* II: 630). The development of his poetry after the period of silence, the insistence on formal 'rigour' instead of the stylistic binary of surface/depth, attests to this view. Style becomes the seal of insincerity:

Distress that writes well is never so complete that it cannot save from the shipwreck some freedom of spirit, [...] some symbolism that contradicts what it is saying. (*Œuvres* I: 463)

It was statements such as these, and other comparable pronouncements on the insincerity of writers such as Stendhal and Verlaine, that caused the critic Jean Paulhan (to whom we shall return in the following chapter) to term Valéry a *rhétoriqueur*. Paulhan essentially accused him of *mauvaise foi*, drawing out the pattern to Valéry's denunciations, which consisted, so Paulhan averred, in taking the self-professed strength of an author and turning it against him. So Verlaine's claim that his poems are *naïf* is for Valéry necessarily false, since a true poet can by definition not be naïve; so Stendhal's horror of mere rhetoric is itself to be understood as a kind of rhetoric, that of the 'natural' writer trying too hard to be natural.[8] Paulhan's analysis obtains equally for Valéry's views on the writers that underlie modernist style. Of the realists, Valéry writes in 1941 that they seek 'to obtain a *trompe-l'œil* effect through an excess of "style". [...] An extraordinary language is called upon to evoke ordinary objects' (*Œuvres* II: 802). Flaubert's obsession with style would thus become a weakness, not a strength, an attempt to conjure up what Barthes would call *l'effet de réel*, rather than the 'real' itself.[9]

Valéry's description of style as a *trompe-l'œil* is typical of his later views on style, of which he comes to think that there is simply too much in modernist literature. His analysis of decadent style diagnoses a comparable overdetermination:

What characterises a literature of decadence is perfection – or perfections. And it cannot be otherwise. It is [characterized by] increasing skill; and by ever more spirit [*esprit*], more sensuality, more cross-referencing, more dissimulation of tiresome necessities; by more intelligence, more profundity; in short by *more knowledge of mankind,* of the needs and reactions of the reader [*sujet lecteur*], of the resources and effects of language, by more self-mastery – of the author. (*Œuvres* II: 634–5)

Whilst this may seem like praise, when set alongside his other pronouncements about the 'effects' of language, it becomes clear that the compliment is back-handed. 'Perfection is a means of defence,' he writes elsewhere. 'One puts perfection between oneself and the other. Between oneself and oneself' (*Œuvres* II: 485). In an article of 1928 on Veronese, Valéry implies that the 'decadent style' as defined by Bourget – where, through this hypertrophied process of 'perfection', everything decomposes into constituent parts – has extended beyond literature: 'Contemporary artists [...] too often succumb to detail. [...] The part absorbs them; it should be the other way around' (*Œuvres* II: 1294). Indeed, Valéry makes a fundamental distinction between what he calls *le style sec* and *le style gras*, claiming that one can divide all writing into the two camps:

Lean style [*le style sec*] traverses time like an incorruptible mummy, whilst the other styles, swollen with fat and groaning with images, rot under their jewellery. Later on, a handful of diadems and rings are removed from their tombs. (*Œuvres* II: 768)

In short, Valéry views much of modern art as 'swollen', as prostituting truth for the facile pleasures of rhetorical 'style'. 'Haste has entered into the world,' he writes in 1941. 'It has killed posterity, and with it, a certain "style". How many modern works pimp themselves, go kerb-crawling' (*Œuvres* II: 803). Despite the valid reservations of Paulhan, Blanchot and others about his tendency to succumb to rhetorical excess, Valéry astutely notices the dangers of *too much* style, of the risk modernist literature runs in cultivating its surfaces so assiduously.

If Valéry thus loses faith in 'style', equating it with specious rhetoric, then it is the 'form' of his poetry that picks up the slack. Simplifying slightly, one can say that he comes to oppose contingent style to classical form. His attempts to 'govern' style,[10] notes Jean Hytier, develop into a 'praise of constraint'.[11] Both in his poetics and in his poetry, Valéry insists on a formal rigour, claiming that 'freedom' is an illusion that discourages rather than encourages art: 'Amongst the victims of freedom are form, and, in every sense of the term, style' (*Œuvres* II: 965). What Valéry seeks is a classical impersonality; in Hytier's words, Valéry's aim is 'to attain a style where it is less the poet himself speaking than language itself'.[12] The way Valéry obtains this is essentially by sublimating style into form. By making form the determining factor – 'Beautiful works are the daughters of their form, *which is born before them*' (*Œuvres* II: 477) – he makes it seem as though it were indeed language which speaks, rather than the poet.

One can thus distinguish, broadly speaking, between two different kinds of 'style' in Valéry's poetics: one which he associates with rhetoric, and dismisses, and one which he approvingly smuggles back in through its sublimation to form. It is tempting to wonder whether the renewed emphasis on form does not coincide with the ending of the period of silence. Certainly the publication in 1917 of *La Jeune Parque* marked a watershed moment. After 20 years without writing any substantial poetry, it was to the form of strict alexandrines that Valéry looked to give him inspiration: 'anybody who knows how to read me will read my autobiography through form. The content matters little' (*Œuvres* I: 1631–2). By 1922, the time of the publication of *Charms* (which grew out of *La Jeune Parque*), Valéry's subordination of *le fond* to *la forme* had become the driving force behind the complicated metrical structures of his poems. 'That which is "form" for anyone else is "content" for me,' he wrote later in the 1920s (*Œuvres* I: 1456). One might define this aesthetics broadly speaking as Apolline, in Nietzsche's terms, since it favours the clarity of hard-edged form over Dionysian profundity (both in *Charms* and elsewhere, Valéry is constantly returning to the Greeks, for whom 'all things are form' [*Œuvres* I: 112]).

In one of his prefaces for *Charms*, Valéry distinguishes between poetry and prose in terms that bring form very close to style:

> Whilst one can demand pure content of prose, [in poetry] it is pure form that prevails. It is sound, rhythm, the physical relationship of words, their inductive effects, or their mutual influences, that dominate. (*Œuvres* I: 1510)

Valéry's conception of poetry is accordingly one that emphasizes its performative aspects. In essence, one can term this conception 'Orphic'. At the levels of both genetic conception and thematic preoccupations, from its title onwards *Charms* reflects Valéry's view that 'the object [of poetry] seems to me to be to produce *enchantment'* (*Œuvres* I: 1485). The first step in creating this stylistic effect lies in his obsession with rhythm:

Certain poems began with the simple suggestion of a rhythm *which gradually developed its own meaning*. This genesis, which proceeded as it were from the 'form' to the 'content', and finished by stimulating the most conscious work on the basis of an empty structure, is no doubt comparable to the preoccupation which had exercised me over several years, namely the quest for the general conditions of all thought, whatever its content might be. (*Œuvres* I: 1474)

In his recollection of the genesis of the most famous poem of the collection, 'The Graveyard by the Sea', Valéry gave a concrete example of the primacy of rhythm for his work, recalling that the decasyllabic metre which came to him seemed 'poor and monotonous' next to the time-honoured alexandrine (*Œuvres* I: 1503): 'It was born, like most of my poems, out of the unexpected presence in my thoughts of a certain rhythm' (*Œuvres* I: 1687). Born out of rhythm, the poems of *Charms* often seem to *thematize* rhythm as a means of 'enchantment'. Valéry foregrounds 'Voice' (often with a capital 'V') as a way 'to avoid saying I',[13] as in the closing stanza of 'The Pythoness' (itself born of its octosyllabic rhythm [see *Œuvres* I: 1656]):

> Honour of Men, O sacred SPEECH,
> Prophetic, ornate discourse, mesh
> Of lovely fetters in whose reach
> God lost himself and became flesh,
> Illumination and largesse!

> To speak a wisdom here, express
> That august Voice that's understood
> When it resounds to be not voice
> So much of any person's choice
> But voice of waters and of wood![14]

'The Python[ess]', notes Paul Gifford, 'enacts mythically the poet's own interpreted experience of poetic Voice.'[15] Valéry equates Voice with capitalized Speech (*langage*). Its 'lovely fetters' suggest the formal and metrical rigour which he saw as the paradoxical precondition of stylistic freedom; by the closing lines of the poem, the Delphic 'Voice' has become not the voice of any particular person, but rather that of the waves and the woods.

This drive to oracular or Orphic impersonality is Valéry's particular contribution to modernist style. As Gifford remarks, 'Valéry singularly radicalizes and modernizes this nineteenth-century theme.'[16] (Rilke, whose late work, as we shall see, cultivates a comparable Orphism, does not stress the element of impersonality, whilst Eliot's famous doctrine of impersonality is not hieratic in the same way.) It is in passing through the impersonal forms of his poetry that Valéry's notion of Voice becomes style: 'Our style is our voice, altered by our work, completed.'[17] Voice as the vehicle of style depends upon the extreme self-consciousness characteristic of Valéry; as Kirsteen Anderson remarks, 'the more deliberately a poet learns to handle his phonic sensibility, the more possible it becomes to talk of the poetic voice as a consciously exploited imposition of style'.[18] That this is an implicit theme of *Charms* becomes apparent from the first poem onwards, where 'Dawn' seeks to re-establish contact with Being through its oracular music:

> Their spiritual web I breach
> And go through, searching long
> My sensuous forest to reach
> The oracles of my song,
> Being! Universal Hearing!
> The whole soul set to nearing
> Desire's utmost aim ...
> Trembling, herself she hears.
> Sometimes my lip appears
> That thrill of hers to claim.[19]

Charms is thus established from the start as a 'poetry that renders account of itself'.[20] 'Being' is sought through both the quest for, and the enactment of, 'the oracles of my song'. 'The poetic voice works enchantment,' writes Gifford, with reference to Valéry's stated aim; 'it persuades us in the very act of utterance'.[21]

It is instructive at this stage to know that 'Dawn' was originally conceived as one half of a longer poem. The other half became the final poem of the collection, 'Palm', written in the same metrical and stanzaic structure. The palm is a figure of harmonious, serene form, one that mediates between 'shade and sun', the humans and the gods. Its formal structure is its very essence:

> For in as much as it may bend
> To the abundance of its yield,
> Its form will have achieved its end,
> Its bonds by heavy fruit revealed.[22]

This division of a single long poem into the first and last poems of the collection points towards a stylistic idiosyncracy of Valéry's. Deferral of meaning, and the patience it implies, is one of the major themes of the two poems:

> Patience, have patience in this.
> Wait patiently in the blue!
> Every atom of silence is
> Also the chance of ripe fruit, too![23]

Strikingly, this is reflected elsewhere in the collection in what one could call a syntax of deferral (inspired, perhaps, by the same Greek syntax which so inspired Hölderlin, and through him Rilke).[24] 'I'll hold back longer | One word, none fonder,'[25] writes Valéry in 'The Insinuant', and this poetic shapes much of his style, which hesitates between conveying meaning and deferring it – and in doing so becomes the vehicle of this double movement. The sonnet 'The Bee' opens with an evocation of the bee's sting which depends on the extended clauses for its effect: 'Whatever, and how fine, how fell, | Your barb may feel, my blond bee.'[26] 'The Steps' evokes the motion of the eponymous steps through its deferral of the main verb 'tread':

> Your steps, children of my silence,
> Saintly, gently, unrushed
> Towards the vigil of my bed
> They tread, polished and hushed.[27]

The closing sestet of the sonnet 'The Sleeping Woman', meanwhile, provides a virtuoso example of Valéry's style (I cite it here in French in order to retain the stylistic aspects of the original):

Dormeuse, amas doré d'ombres et d'abandons,
Ton repos redoutable est chargé de tels dons,
Ô biche avec langueur longue auprès d'une grappe,

Que malgré l'âme absente, occupée aux enfers,
Ta forme au ventre pur qu'un bras fluide drape,
Veille; ta forme veille, et mes yeux sont ouverts.

(Sleeper, gold mass of shadows, wanton shifts.
Your awesome peace is loaded with such gifts,
Doe in your long languor beside the grapes,

That, though your soul in hells is occupied,
With its clear belly a liquid arm now drapes,
Your form's awake, awake, and my eyes are wide.)[28]

The sonorous play of internal rhymes and assonance centred around the long vowel sounds of 'a' and 'o' evoke the languor of the sleeping woman. The poem turns on the opposition of absence and presence: the 'absent soul' (*l'âme absente*) is watched over by the physical form of the sleeping body. Valéry's poetics of form thus becomes literal: the repetition of the term 'form(e)' and its attendant verb 'veille' ('is awake') gives the poem its evocative power, like a painting of a woman draped decoratively over a chaise longue. Yet it is the deferral of the main verb 'veille' (*Ta forme ... veille*), contrasting with its subsequent repetition without the deferral, which is the stylistic secret of the poem. Form here, both in the generic poetic sense and with immediate physical reference to the sleeping body, depends upon style; it is Valéry's carefully modulated style which mediates between the presence of the body and the absence of the sleeping soul. Style, through its association to form, becomes the vehicle of meaning.

Valéry's most important contribution to modernist style, in both his aesthetic theory and his poetic practice, arguably consists in refining the distinction between poetry and prose. Despite his protestations against style as rhetoric, his cultivation of style as form betrays his roots in the symbolist movement of the 1880s and 1890s. This is most immediately apparent in his view of poetry as necessarily 'musical', and the doctrine of 'poésie pure' to which this led:

> The musical education [...] of a growing number of French writers has contributed more than any other theoretical considerations to orienting poetry towards a purer destiny, and to eliminating from its works anything that can be expressed exactly in prose. (*Œuvres* II: 1273)

In Valéry's own analysis, it was the symbolists – and in particular Mallarmé – who brought European lyric poetry to an unprecedented pitch of stylistic self-consciousness:

> Poetry forced itself [...] to do its best to distinguish in language those formulations in which meaning, rhythm, the sonorities of voice, and movement, correspond and reinforce each other, whilst attempting on the contrary to proscribe formulations in which meaning is independent of musical form, of all auditory value. (*Œuvres* II: 1273)

A *poésie pure*, for Valéry, is thus a poetry of absolute self-sufficiency. Indeed, he suggests that *poésie absolue* would be a more accurate term:

> It would perhaps be better to say *absolute poetry*, by which one would mean the attempt to create effects through the interrelation of words to one another, or rather the interrelation of the resonances of words to one another, which suggests, in short, *an exploration of the whole realm of sensibility governed by language*. (*Œuvres* I: 1458)

This is the definably modernist element of both Valéry's poetry and his poetics: he constructs an opposable style in analogy to his 'opposable soul', turned back on itself in the modernist manner. Valéry's views on style unite the classical and the modern: he defines the classical writer as one 'who bears within him a critic, and who allies him intimately with his work' (*Œuvres* I: 604), and yet in the same essay he makes it clear that he sees this self-reflectivity as distinctively modern, indeed *modernist*, praising Edgar Allan Poe for having understood that

> modern poetry must conform to the tendency of an epoch which has seen modes and spheres of activity separated ever more distinctly, and [thus] it could aspire to develop its own object and to develop, after a fashion, *in a pure state*. (*Œuvres* I: 609)

The italicized final phrase resonates with a weight of modernist associations – the Proustian 'fragment of time in the pure state', the Joycean epiphany – placing

Valéry's understanding of *poésie pure* squarely within its time. Yet whilst he wants to push poetry as far as possible in the direction of 'pure' self-sufficiency, divorcing it from any external content, he bemoans this same tendency in prose, pointing out, as we have seen, the danger that it may become *purely* style. In other words, it seems that for Valéry, poetry and prose are ultimately distinct realms, where different rules apply: where prose – from Pascal to the realists and decadents – should be wary of losing its sincerity in its stylistic surface, poetry must cultivate this stylistic surface as its very essence, enacting its own 'enchantment'. Modernist poetry, to put it polemically, is conceived as the realm of pure style, turned back on itself as both subject and object, both vehicle and locus of meaning. For Valéry, the style of self-consciousness is the self-consciousness of style.

R.M. Rilke and Orphic style

If Valéry's preoccupation with form and 'Voice' flirts with a latter-day Orphism, Rilke's late poetry places Orpheus at the very centre of poetic modernism. After the publication of *Charms* in 1922, the two poets became firm friends. In the winter of 1922–23, Rilke holed up in his tower in Muzot and translated almost the entire collection into German. 'Rilke viewed Valéry literally as a window to a new kind of poetry,' remarks Rilke's biographer Ralph Freedman. '[Valéry's] precision and ideas about space, time, and motion shaped much of Rilke's post-elegiac thought.'[29] Yet in order to reach this 'post-elegiac' stage where he could begin to write poetry in French, rather than just in his native German, Rilke had to complete, finally, his long-awaited *Duino Elegies*. The great breakthrough of February 1922 is one of the major achievements of the modernist era; what does this much-mythologized moment have to teach us about the self-conceptualization of modernist style?

On the morning of 2 February 1922, the opening words of what would become the first of the *Sonnets to Orpheus* came to Rilke: 'Oh Orpheus sings! Oh tall tree in the ear!' Inspired by a French translation of Ovid's *Metamorphoses* and a reproduction of Cima de Conegliano's drawing *Orpheus*, 'the stream of the sonnets gushed over [Rilke] like a deluge'.[30] The composition of the Sonnets and the later Elegies was so closely intertwined that it is important to establish the order of genesis:

2–5 February: Sonnets I, 1–26
7–8 February: 7th Elegy (early part); 8th Elegy
9 February: 9th Elegy (main part); 6th Elegy
11 February: 10th Elegy
14 February: 5th Elegy
15–19 February: Sonnets II (except II, 1)
23 February: Sonnet II, 1
26 February: 7th Elegy (concluded)[31]

The main lesson here is that it was the arrival of the Sonnets that led to Rilke's finally finishing the Elegies, and not the other way around, as is sometimes assumed. The Elegies had been gestating for ten years since their inception at Schloss Duino in 1912; their triumphant completion was thus a significant event, which Rilke quickly announced to his friends and correspondents. This sequence of events raises the question: what is the nature of the relationship between the Sonnets and the Elegies? How did the composition of the former lead to the completion of the latter? And what conception of poetic style as a response to modernity emerges from their juxtaposition?

It is instructive to compare the earlier Elegies, starting with the two composed in 1912, with their later counterparts. Simplifying somewhat, one might speak in very broad terms of a first half of the Elegies (those composed before the First World War) and a second half (those composed after the Sonnets in 1922). The famous rhetorical question of the opening line, whispered to Rilke by the winds on the cliff-tops in Duino, sets the tone of the first half. Yet the Elegies can be said to 'form a response not so much to this question as to the impulse to ask it'.[32] This distinction is already contained within the syntax of the opening stanza:

Who, if I cried out, would hear me among the ranks
of the angels? Even if one of them clasped me
suddenly to his heart, I'd wither in the face
of his more fierce existence. For their beauty
is really nothing but the first stirrings of a terror
we are just able to endure and are astonished
at the way it elects, with such careless disdain,
to let us go on living. Every angel is terrifying.[33]

As a rhetorical question, the first line can expect no answer; its very form implies that the poet is left to himself, turned back on his own self-consciousness. Related to this is Rilke's use of the subjunctive in this opening stanza, a crucial detail which threatens to get lost in the English translation. The correct translation of the opening line 'wer, wenn ich schriee' would be 'who, if I *were* to cry out', suggesting that the 'elegiac' realm that will be developed over the course of the sequence is the hypothetical sphere of the imagination, not the empirical world of the indicative. This series of conditionals then continues in the original German with the verbs *nähme* and *verginge*: 'Even if one of them *were* to clasp [...] me | suddenly to his heart, *I'd* wither.' Rilke thus develops a spiral of imagined situations: if he were to cry out, none of the angels would hear him; but even if one were to, he would wither and perish. A curious kind of performativity is at work here: through framing it in the subjunctive Rilke is effectively negating the ontological status of his opening cry (he is not saying that it is happening, only imagining what might result were it to happen); yet through turning this into the beginning, the *incipit* of the entire sequence (and through subsequently mythologizing the moment of inspiration on the cliff-tops), he gives form to the cry and thus makes it happen after all.

This syntactical detail is worth pausing over, since it suggests that from the very start the realm of the self-consciously elegiac is configured as one of stylistic tension. The switch from the subjunctive to the indicative is instructive: 'beauty | *is* really nothing but the first stirrings of a terror | we are just able to endure'. Coming after the subjunctives, the first indicative of the sequence is given extra force; raised into a programmatic, ontological statement (tellingly, the first indicative is the verb 'to be'), it recalls Nietzsche's declaration in *Human, All Too Human*: 'Grand style originates when the beautiful carries off victory over the monstrous.'[34] Yet if the elegiac is thus associated in the first instance with the Nietzschean grand style, it is a high modernist version, full of the uncertainty about the 'interpreted world' conveyed by the tentative subjunctives, rhetorical questions and elegiac metre. Indeed, this is one way to clarify the distinction between what we have called the two halves of the Elegies: where the second half of the sequence is transfigured by the appearance of the Orphic into an affirmation of immanent beauty, in the first half it is not at all clear that the beautiful *will* carry off victory over the transcendent 'monstrous'. Will grand style prevail?

Whilst this is not the place for a point by point exposition of the whole cycle, the analysis of the preoccupations of the opening Elegies, and the relationship between style and sentiment implicit in them, could certainly be continued. In the first four Elegies, Rilke thematizes a hierarchy of consciousness, from animal to human to angel. His argument, taken in part from Heinrich von Kleist's essay 'On the Marionette Theatre' (1810), is essentially that man is hopelessly caught in the middle: where animals have no self-consciousness, and angels sublime self-consciousness, man has enough to be aware of his own mortality, but not enough to be able to do anything about it. Variations on this theme, and on the mutually assured destruction of *eros* and *thanatos* implicit in it, recur throughout these opening Elegies. Yet there are also moments which seem to anticipate the triumphant reversal of the later Elegies. Strikingly, these moments tend to be conveyed stylistically, rather than thematically, as though the subconscious of style were rebelling against the conscious of subject matter. 'Rilke uses language itself to transgress the boundaries of logic and categorisation that hold human beings captive within self-consciousness,' observes Kathleen Komar. 'In order to do this, he must force language to violate its own categories and allow the reader to catch glimpses of a unified realm that does not draw such distinctions.'[35] It is as though style were timidly holding open the door which the poet cannot yet sketch out thematically, but through which he will triumphantly stride in 1922.

What are these stylistic moments? To the use of rhetorical questions and subjunctives already discussed one could add, amongst others: paradox ('our point of rest is nowhere', Crucefix: 16); temporal conflations ('the after-taste of so strange a future', Crucefix: 39); spatial–temporal conflations ('street of yesterday', Crucefix: 15 [translation modified]); surrealist genitives ('pollen of flowering Godhead', 'knots of light', 'shields of bliss', Crucefix: 23). It is noticeable that these are all, broadly speaking, stylistic idiosyncracies characteristic of modernism: Rilke is groping towards a modernist conception of absolute poetry in the manner of Valéry which, in the pre-war years, he cannot yet grasp openly.

The advent of Orpheus transforms everything. Indeed, 'transformation' (*Verwandlung*) is arguably the key motif of the sequence, and it is certainly the key to unlocking the despairing view of modern life apparent in the earliest Elegies. 'The lesson of transformation gives the critique of modernity in the cycle a positive twist and provides a new foundation for the task and value of poetry,' writes Rilke's latter-day editor Manfred Engel.[36] Despite the Ovidian provenance of the term 'metamorphosis', Rilke's application of this process of Orphic transformation to his view of poetry is as dialectical as it is mythical, inasmuch as the conception of the role of the poet is turned on its head: where previously the poet had performed the traditional elegiac role of lamentation, now he performs one of celebration; where previously he had resisted the world, now he *rejoices* in it. The ecstatic opening of the first sonnet sets the tone: 'Oh Orpheus sings!' What makes this breakthrough possible is the direct thematization of the poetic voice, the Orphic 'song'. In turning away from the modern world with all its confusion and alienation, and back to the process of singing this world into being, Rilke makes the familiar modernist move of constructing a 'narcissistic', intransitive poetics, one that celebrates its own poetic style rather than the world outside it: 'Song, as you teach it, is not desire, not | a wooing of something that's finally attained; | Song is existence. Easy for the god.'[37]

This reconceptualization of poetry as intransitive, as singing for its own sake, resounds in the opening of the 7th Elegy, written immediately after the first group of sonnets: 'No more wooing, enough of this courting, your voice has outgrown it' (Crucefix: 55). Transposed into the metaphysical language of Rilke's late poetry, this equates to a rejection of transcendence in favour of immanence: 'The world is nowhere, my love, if not within. | Our life passes in transformation. The external world | is forever dwindling to nothing' (Crucefix: 57). This is the great lesson of the Sonnets: where the angels of the earlier Elegies distracted the poet into aspiring to a transcendence that humans can never attain, Orpheus, despite his status as a 'god', does not represent 'the supernatural, but rather a particularly heightened form of humanity'.[38] The 9th Elegy makes this more explicit: 'Earth, is it not this you want: to arise | in our *invisible* sphere?' (Crucefix: 73). Rilke comes to realize 'that the idea of transcendence itself is a distracting trap. The poet finally turns back to the world and to the consciousness he sought to escape. By making the two interact, he creates a form more permanent than either, the aesthetic form.'[39]

It is here that the Sonnets, and in particular the form of the sonnet, played such a crucial role. In a manner not unlike Valéry's insistence on formal rigour as the spark that re-ignited his poetic fire, Rilke turns to formal constraints as a response to what he sees as the formlessness of modernity. This does not imply a slavish traditionalism, but rather a modernist self-consciousness about playing with tradition:

> I keep saying sonnets. Even if this entails the freest or, so to speak, most changed-about things that can be conceived of in the name of this usually so calm and stable form. But precisely this, transforming the sonnet, lifting it, in a sense carrying it whilst 'on the run' without breaking it – this was a peculiar task or trial for me.[40]

Through this increased self-consciousness about form, poetic technique becomes both the means and the end of his later work. Poetry becomes the subject of his poetry. In the group of sonnets which effected the breakthrough, and in the Elegies that followed them, this transformation can be traced most succinctly in the transition from 'lamenting' (*klagen*) to 'praising' (*rühmen*). 'Praising, that's it! Praise was his mission' begins Sonnet 7 (Young: 15); 'praising's the only place | [lament] can live' opens Sonnet 8 (Young: 17). Where the earlier Elegies lament the world to the angels, the Elegies written after the Sonnets *praise* it to them. 'Praising' (*preisen*, *rühmen*), 'saying' (*sagen*) and 'speaking' (*sprechen*) accordingly become the key verbs of Rilke's later conception of poetry, as outlined in the 9th Elegy:

Perhaps we are *here* to say: house,
bridge, fountain, gate, jug, fruit tree, window –
at most: column, tower … But to *speak* them,
you understand, oh, you are to say them
with more intensity than things themselves ever
dreamed they would be. […]
Here is the time for what can be *said* – *here* its home.
So speak out and bear witness! […]
Praise this world to the angel, not some
inexpressible other. (Crucefix: 71)

Rilke's italics stress the two main components of his new poetic: the immanence of 'here', and the poet's role in giving voice to it.[41] Once established, these remain the defining imperatives of both the Sonnets and the Elegies, right up until the final stanza of the whole sonnet sequence:

And if the earthly forgets you,
say to the quiet earth: I flow.
Speak to the rushing water – say: I am. (Young: 113)

If the role of lyric poetry is now to celebrate the world through its singing, then the relationship between style and subject matter is predicated on a typically modernist tension. On the one hand, the Sonnets and the later Elegies seem to advocate an ontological humility on the part of the poet: his role is now simply to 'say' the humble objects listed in the 9th Elegy. On the other hand, this role is defined through the complex formal structures of the sonnet and the elegy, structures which become part of the performative enactment of what Rilke is now advocating. Through writing these poems, he 'transforms' the world into song; 'Rilke's language is not only a medium, but a component of his meaning.'[42] In a sense, then, this is the inverse of the modernist crisis of language à la Chandos: where Hofmannsthal loses faith in the relationship between word and world, renouncing what had become purely style, the later Rilke takes a wager on the potency of pure style to give the world meaning. Ulrich Fülleborn has claimed that the defining 'case' for Rilke's late work is the 'evocative', which he locates 'somewhere between the nominative and the vocative':[43] this is a style, in other words, that seeks to give names to things, but also *evokes* them through the very act of saying that it is giving names to things.

Does this equate to a version of grand style? If we understand the 'beautiful' in the terms of the late Rilke as the immanent, and the 'monstrous' as the lure of the transcendent, then the breakthrough of February 1922 can be said, after Nietzsche, to originate when the immanent carries off victory over the transcendent. Orpheus himself is a figure of 'pure tension', since as well as being the archetypical lyric poet, he is also the mediator between the two worlds of the human and the divine, life and death. The final sonnet of the initial, ecstatic sequence interprets the myth of his death as a vision of the triumph of the beautiful over the monstrous – as a triumph, in other words, of grand style:

But you, godlike, beautiful – when the horde
of scorned Maenads attacked, you went on sounding,
right to the end; drowning their cries with order,
up from that mayhem rose your building song.
(Young: 53)

The three major aspects of the Orpheus myth – his role as the representative lyric poet, his role as mediator between life and death, and his violent, yet strangely serene death at the hands of the maenads – come together here to produce an emblematic moment of 'Orphic style'. Through both conception and execution, Orphic style walks a tightrope between 'pure style' and 'purely style', since it is the realm of absolute poetry, but also of death. The death-drive at the heart of decadent style here finds its consummation at the height of poetic modernism: the purest style is the moment of its own destruction. In Roland Barthes' words: 'Literature is like phosphorus: it shines with its maximum brilliance at the moment when it attempts to die.'[44]

In a letter of April 1923, Rilke suggests how this Orphic 'grand style' can be understood as a response to his view of modernity:

Formidableness has shocked and horrified mankind: but where is there anything sweet and marvellous that on occasion does not wear *this* mask, that of the formidable? Life itself [...] is it not formidable? Anyone who has not acknowledged the fearsomeness of life on occasion, even acclaimed it, will never fully take possession of the ineffable authorities of our existence [...]. To demonstrate how formidableness and blessedness are identical [...]: that is the core meaning of my two books [the Elegies and the Sonnets].[45]

Just as Nietzsche defines grand style as the victory of the beautiful over the monstrous, so Rilke defines his poetry of 1922 as the attempt to juxtapose 'blessedness' and 'formidableness'. Behind both of these pairs, of course, is ultimately the relationship of life to death: in a famous letter to his Polish translator Witold Hulewicz, Rilke writes that 'death is the *face of life* that is turned away from us'.[46] Rilke's late poetry uses an Orphic adaptation of grand style to assert not only the beauty of immanent life, but also its necessary relationship to transcendent death: where Nietzsche writes of the 'victory' of the beautiful over the monstrous, Rilke would argue for their necessary 'unity'.[47]

This vision of style as the reconciliation of life and death through the transformative power of poetic language is in many ways typical of its time: 'After World War I, many modernists returned to some sense of order and their view intensified that the ultimate values of art, its intensity, its difference, needed to be vigorously defended against civilisation,' writes Andreas Kramer. 'Mythic modernism imagines a time-space that is both within and outside modernity.'[48] Rilke's seeming defensiveness towards modernity (discernible in those Sonnets which reject modern technology and the criticism of American 'fake things, *substitute lives*' in the letter to Hulewicz) is crucially not mere reactionary conservatism; he does not dismiss modernity altogether, but rather transforms the elegiac lament about modern alienation into affirmative praise for continuing existence. If Rilke is an 'active antagonist of modernity',[49] his status as a leading protagonist of modernism derives from this ability to impose form on a formless world. For although he is open to the charge of retreating to a poetry that is purely style, to the 'typically modernist belief that cultural transformation can be brought about by formal innovations and revolutionary aesthetics alone',[50] it is the paradox of celebrating life through withdrawing into lyricism that makes his breakthrough in 1922 the paradigm of one strand of post-war poetic style. It is to the other strand that we must now turn.

T.S. Eliot and 'the style of direct speech'

If Valéry and Rilke use traditional forms to respond to the perceived formlessness of modernity, the young T.S. Eliot takes the opposite course. Where his continental contemporaries develop stable, coherent styles through appropriating the decasyllable and alexandrine, the elegy and the sonnet, as a means of taming modernity, Eliot prefers to leave modernity in the wild, deliberately incorporating a catholic cacophony of styles within the one poem. From demotic cockney to the Wagnerian sublime, from Shakespeare to the

Bhagavad-Gita: it is hard to imagine a poem displaying greater stylistic range than *The Waste Land*. One of its original titles illustrates clearly its stylistic conception: where Valéry speaks of a coherent single 'Voice', and Rilke of Orphic 'song', Eliot's Dickensian working title 'He do the police in different voices' suggests that the poem was conceived from the start as an act of ventriloquism, as an attempt to conflate a range of very different styles and registers. The abrupt shifts from meditative speculation to narrative description, from dialogue to soliloquy, seemed bewildering to many contemporary critics: 'Here is a poet capable of a style more refined than that of any of his generation, parodying without taste or skill,' wrote one critic in the *Times Literary Supplement*.[51] What sense can we make of Eliot's conception of style in 1922, and how does it relate to this pivotal modernist moment?

The aesthetic sense behind *The Waste Land* can only be understood in the context of Eliot's development in the years immediately after the war. Although Pound claimed that Eliot 'enjoyed good fortune in arriving in London at a particular date with a formed style of his own',[52] Eliot's criticism of this period suggests that he was still busy theorizing this style. The key term, which recurs with particular frequency in the essays published in *The Sacred Wood* (1920), is what he calls 'the pathology of rhetoric'.[53] In a series of 'Reflections on Contemporary Poetry' published in 1917, Eliot outlined what he saw as the defining agenda for the modern lyric:

One of the ways by which contemporary verse has tried to escape the rhetorical, the abstract, the

> moralizing, to recover (for that is its purpose) the accents of direct speech, is to concentrate attention upon the trivial or accidental or commonplace objects.[54]

Eliot's diagnosis of the modernist flight from 'the rhetorical' places him within the main current of the development of poetic style. In an essay on Arthur Symons' translation of *The Flowers of Evil*, Eliot notes that 'the 'nineties are nearer to us than the intervening generation',[55] and the enduring importance of Verlaine and Laforgue – as well as, crucially, their view of Baudelaire – is well established. In his introduction to *The Oxford Book of Modern Verse 1892–1925*, Yeats tells a similar story: modern poets, he writes, were saying to each other ' "we must purify poetry of all that is not poetry," and by poetry they meant poetry as it had been written by Catullus [...] by the Jacobean writers, by Verlaine, by Baudelaire'.[56]

If the overriding concern of the post-war generation was thus to escape what they saw as the meretricious versifying of their predecessors, in Eliot's case it was also bound up with his interest in Elizabethan drama.[57] For the Elizabethans, wrote Eliot, 'rhetoric, a particular form of rhetoric, was endemic, it pervaded the whole organism; the healthy as well as the morbid tissues were built up on it'.[58] The ambivalence of this statement suggests that Eliot's view of rhetoric in these years was more complicated than the standard narrative of its modernist repudiation might imply. Eliot saw clearly the danger of replacing one dogma with another – 'but what is rhetoric?' he asked in the third of his 'Reflections on Contemporary Poetry' (1919);

'there is rhetoric even among the new poets'[59] – and
so determined to move beyond the Manichean view
of rhetoric as axiomatically bad. His most sustained
discussion of the subject is to be found in the essay
'Rhetoric and Poetic Drama' (1919):

> Let us avoid the assumption that rhetoric is a vice
> of manner, and endeavour to find a rhetoric of sub-
> stance also, which is right because it issues from
> what it has to express.
>
> At the present time there is a manifest prefer-
> ence for the 'conversational' in poetry – the style
> of 'direct speech', opposed to the 'oratorical' and
> the rhetorical; but if rhetoric is any convention of
> writing inappropriately applied, this conversational
> style can and does become a rhetoric [...]. Much of
> the second and third rate in American *vers libre* is of
> this sort; and much of the second and third rate in
> English Wordsworthianism.[60]

Eliot brings out clearly the implicit value judgements
in the term 'style' (positive) and 'rhetoric' (negative).
He is lucid not only about the process whereby the
modern, 'conversational' style runs the risk of solid-
ifying into a new rhetoric, but also about the inherent ambivalence of the term 'rhetoric'. By the end
of the essay, he argues that 'we may apply the term
"rhetoric" to the type of dramatic speech which I have
instanced' (which, in this essay, is mainly Shakespeare
and Rostand).[61]

Where Eliot suggests in 1917, then, that the aim of
modern poetry should be to 'recover [...] the accents of
direct speech', in 1919 he wishes to reappropriate the

vilified term 'rhetoric' for 'dramatic speech'. Understood in these terms, the style of *The Waste Land* appears modernist not in its modish rejection of rhetoric, but rather in its reassertion of a different *kind* of rhetoric. There is an important parallel to be drawn with Eliot's famous doctrine of 'impersonality', which was developed around this time in the essays collected in *The Sacred Wood*. 'Eliot's "escape from personality" is an escape from "opinion" and "rhetoric" which he [...] felt had marred the poetry written in the mid-nineteenth century,' notes C.K. Stead.[62] Yet 'Tradition and the Individual Talent', Eliot's best-known essay, argues for greater impersonality not as a suppression of the subjective self, but rather as its *liberation*: 'the poet's escape from "personality" [...] is not an escape from the self, but an escape *further into* the self', writes Stead. 'The concern of the essay is, in fact, that desire [...] to release the poet from his own rational will.'[63] Just as Eliot's interest in Elizabethan drama led him to a point where he did not merely dismiss rhetoric as a stylistic solution, but rather sought a new kind of rhetoric 'which is right because it issues from what it has to express', so his interest in the psychological processes of poetic creation led him to a point where he sought to get beyond his overdeveloped rational personality, in order to reveal the raw emotional power of the irrational personality.

The key influence here is Rémy de Gourmont,[64] whom Eliot praised as 'the critical consciousness of a generation'.[65] Throughout the essays of *The Sacred Wood*, Eliot quotes repeatedly from Gourmont's *Problème du style* (to which we shall return in the following chapter), culminating, in an essay on Philip Massinger, in the following passage:

> In the fine pages which Rémy de Gourmont devotes to Flaubert in his *Problème du Style*, the great critic declares:
>> La vie est un dépouillement. Le but de l'activité propre de l'homme est de nettoyer sa personnalité, de la laver de toutes les souillures qu'y déposa l'éducation, de la dégager de toutes les empreintes qu'y laissèrent nos admirations adolescentes;
> and again:
>> Flaubert incorporait toute sa sensibilité à ses œuvres...Hors de ses livres, où il se transvasait goutte à goutte, jusqu'à la lie, Flaubert est fort peu intéressant...[66]

Where Gourmont speaks of life as a 'dépouillement', and of how one should seek to 'cleanse one's personality', Eliot correspondingly views the 'progress of an artist [as] a continual extinction of personality'.[67] That this is also a stylistic progress is clear from the title of Gourmont's book. But how is it made manifest in *The Waste Land*?

The lesson of the essays written in the years leading up to the poem, as well as of the subsequent essays that reveal latent tendencies in the earlier work, is that Eliot views style as paradoxically conservative, yet liberating. In creating the mongrel style of *The Waste Land*, he destroys any vestigial notion of 'pure' style; yet in conflating so many different styles – in making his poem dependent on their interplay – he also foregrounds the very importance of style. The subtitle to his 1928 collection *For Lancelot Andrewes: Essays on Style and Order* is suggestive: in giving himself over to the external order of the 'tradition', the poet frees himself from his own conscious control, thereby creating the space for the 'dark embryo'[68] of true feeling to emerge. Whilst the younger Eliot was yet to turn towards the specifically Christian tradition, this relationship between conscious constraint and unconscious liberation is paralleled in his view of poetic form. In the years before he wrote *The Waste Land*, Eliot had written a series of rhyming quatrains in the manner of Théophile Gautier. Pound remembers that he and Eliot had 'decided that the dilutation of *vers libre* [...] had gone too far [...]. Remedy prescribed *Emaux et Camées*,' whilst Eliot recalled that 'we studied Gautier's poems and then we thought, "Have I anything to say in which this form will be useful?" And we experimented. The form gave the impetus to the content.'[69] In 1916, Eliot had announced his classical ideal as '*form* and *restraint* in art',[70] whilst in 1917, he wrote in his 'Reflections on *Vers Libre*' that 'the ghost of some simple metre should lurk behind the arras in even the "freest" verse; [...] freedom is only freedom when it appears against the background of an artificial limitation'.[71] Many years later, in 1942, he stated that 'a poem may tend to realize itself first as a particular rhythm before it reaches expression in words, and [...] this rhythm may bring to birth the idea and the image'.[72] If such statements recall Valéry's insistence on the necessary constraint of form, as well as on how the poem is often born of its own rhythm, it is because Valéry and Eliot share a 'classical' temperament. Yet whilst the former aims to cultivate a 'poésie pure', the latter believes 'that this can never be reached, because I think that poetry is only poetry so long as it preserves some "impurity"'.[73] For the later Eliot, 'a complete unconsciousness of anything but style would mean that poetry had vanished'.[74]

Ironically, this holds perhaps less true for the later work[75] than for the Joycean 'impurity' of *The Waste Land*, in which 'all the difficulties with the late-nineteenth-century idea of style seem to be summed up'.[76] We have seen how style, and its related term 'rhetoric', had become a particular problem for Eliot in the years leading up to the composition of the poem; now Eliot attempted, ingeniously, to find a solution. 'Insofar as style had become a problematic literary value', writes Louis Menand, '*The Waste Land* was a poem that succeeded by presenting itself as a symptom.'[77] Yet if the poem is to be understood as the 'explosion of the nineteenth-century metaphysics of style'[78] – which, Menand suggests, 'was perhaps one of the things Eliot learned from Joyce'[79] – it equally depends on having the nineteenth-century metaphysics of style there to explode in the first place. Just as we saw in the previous chapter how Eliot understands *Ulysses* as 'the gigantic culmination of an old [epoch]' inasmuch as it 'puts an end to the [stylistic] tradition of Walter Pater', so *The Waste Land* equally represents the culmination of this tradition *ex negativo*. As with *Ulysses*, the range of styles incorporated into *The Waste Land* can be explained by the decision to renounce any aspiration to a single, coherent 'style'; if the style of *The Waste Land* is impure, it is necessarily so, as a 'symptom' of an impure time. As Eliot wrote in

1921: 'The [modern] poet must become more and more comprehensive, more allusive, more indirect, in order to force, to dislocate, if necessary, language into his meaning.'[80] From section to section, Eliot pursues 'a rhetoric of substance [...], right because it issues from what it has to express'; he does this through the infamous allusions and snatches of stolen dialogue, which 'provide nuggets of the objective world charged with feelings and untarnished by the deadening, conventional rhetoric of Eliot's personal will'.[81]

In practice, the poem moves, as Harriet Davidson has argued, between 'two distinct ways of speaking': the 'lyric voice' (epitomized by the 'repetitive, stylized syntax' of the opening lines meditating around the hypnotic present participles), and the 'babel of many voices speaking in metonymically rendered narrative scenes'.[82] These latter voices – what Eliot called 'the direct accents of speech' – include, amongst others, Marie, the hyacinth girl, Madame Sosostris and the typist. It is noticeable, of course, that most of them are women; where the controlling, 'lyric voice' is recognizably male, the narrative voices tend to be female, echoes of both Eliot's neurotic wife Vivien and of other, more fugitive figures. Eliot's dramatization of the cruelty of 'memory and desire' can be read here into the shifting styles of the poem, from what Davidson calls the 'sterile propriety' of the male voice to the 'fertile impropriety'[83] of its female counterparts (where the opposition of the solitary male voice to the profusive plurality of female voices is itself significant).

If *The Waste Land* can thus be read 'as a poem about the proper and the improper',[84] it is the lack of any reconciliation between these extremes that is its defining characteristic. The central figure of Tiresias in 'The Fire Sermon', whose symbolic position as mediator between the sexes means that he has often been seized upon as the unifying figure of the poem, in fact represents only a 'negative plenitude', as Michael North writes: '*The Waste Land* does not totalize itself in such figures but rather manifests a deep fear of totalization.'[85] A similar argument applies to Eliot's vision of style more broadly: he can conceptualize it only by 'dramatizing its loss'.[86] If Rilke responds to the fragmentation of post-war modernity by reaffirming the Orphic purity of the poetic mission, Eliot takes the *via negativa* of seeking to 'arriv[e] at new forms by accelerating the destruction of present forms'.[87]

It is not surprising, then, that 'readers in the 1920s argued over whether the poem was too radical and meaningless or too conservative and tied to traditional values'.[88] Depending on one's emphasis, one can view the poem either as elegiacally lamenting a lost stylistic tradition, or as 'exploding' it in order to clear the way forward. For Eliot himself was 'caught between two double binds: a yearning for the vitality of common life combined with a revulsion from its vulgarity; and an inclination toward poetry combined with a horror of literature'.[89] The crucial breakthrough behind *The Waste Land* is ultimately not only that Eliot became conscious of his tendency to rhetoric, but that he found a way to make this self-consciousness a constitutive component of his poetry. The knowing quotations and allusions in the poem (as well as the infamous 'notes') paradoxically open up the space for genuine emotional sincerity: their erudition acts as a lightning-rod, drawing the 'rhetorical' fire in order to free the 'dark embryo'. In his effort 'to achieve something more positive than the aesthete's "beauty", and less deceptive than the rhetorician's "Truth"', writes C.K. Stead, Eliot developed 'a critical theory and poetic practice which gives equal weight to a "structure" provided by the positive rational will, and a "texture" which is the gift of the negative imagination'.[90] The young Eliot refused the twin legacy of late Victorian poetry, accepting neither the pure aesthete's nor the rigorous moralist's role. Yet in incorporating this refusal into his work, he made poetry out of negation, in the process offering the modernist lyric a new model of impure style: 'Eliot's conception of style […] transcends aesthetics as a concern with beauty, and "morals" as a set of truths which imply imperatives for right action, fusing the two in a poetics from which neither is detachable.'[91]

In 1922, then, Valéry, Rilke and Eliot all offered differing versions of modernist style. Where Valéry and Rilke developed variations of pure style as a response to modernity, Eliot insisted that a deliberately impure style was the only way to do justice to modernity. What all three have in common, however, is the implication that poetry is the natural genre for conceptions of style; the genre could be affirmed or attacked, but either way its formal self-consciousness and sense of tradition offered the ideal vehicle for developing a modern style. 'Modern poetry', as we saw Barthes state in the Introduction, 'is saturated with style.'[92] In Eliot's case, the verb is to be taken literally: in *The Waste Land*, traditional notions of style reach a saturation point beyond which they can go no further – and this in itself becomes a constitutive factor of the poem.

From the most traditional of forms, we now turn to what is arguably the most modern.

5
The 'Alibi' of Style: Modernist Manifestos

After charting in the previous chapters conceptions of style in modernist prose and poetry, this final chapter proposes to consider style in relation to a characteristically modernist 'genre', namely the manifesto. One could argue that the two terms 'style' and 'manifesto' are related etymologically: where the former refers implicitly to instruments wielded by the hand (a 'writing-implement', but also 'a weapon of offence'),[1] the latter refers explicitly to the hand ('manus') and to offence ('fendere').[2] Moreover, if manifestos are defined not just by what they advocate, but also by what they oppose (a quality Mary Ann Caws terms their 'againstness'),[3] then equally 'most of the famous statements on style [...] are protests', as John Middleton Murry claimed in 1922.[4] As well as tracing conceptions of style through a representative range of modernist manifestos, a particular emphasis will thus be placed in this chapter on the relationship between the manifesto and style, on what one could call the performative aspect of the manifesto:

what is the relationship between the ideas propounded and the way in which they are propounded? How does this correspondence between substance and style feed back into the concept of style put forward by the manifesto? 'At its peak of performance,' writes Caws, 'its form creates its meaning,'[5] and this is what suggests its particularly modernist inflection: 'high on its own presence, the manifesto is Modernist rather than ironically Postmodernist'.[6] If modernism is the great period of '-isms' (Henri Meschonnic counts 51 between 1886 and 1924),[7] then the manifesto is its defining genre. In texts that are by definition 'programmatic', the heightened relationship between the thematic and the stylistic that is characteristic of modernism assumes a particular importance: style is made manifest as *stylization*.

'Style without rhetoric'? From *Le Problème du style* to *The Flowers of Tarbes*

Published 20 years earlier than John Middleton Murry's *The Problem of Style*, Rémy de Gourmont's book of the same name is a clear illustration of the thesis that statements on style tend to be protests. 'This new collection of essays belongs to a completely obsolete literary genre, the Refutation,' begins Gourmont.[8] Yet he does not seek to 'defend' the status quo in the manner of a *défense*;[9] rather, Gourmont goes on the attack, targeting Antoine Albalat's *De la formation du style par l'assimilation des auteurs* (1901), which he sees as falsely attempting to impose a normative sense of 'good' style through specious imitation of the classics. Gourmont rails against Albalat's efforts to outline 'assimilable procedures' (such as 'ampleness and concision', or his models of 'descriptive style' and 'antithetical style'), a technique which he characterizes as follows:

> 'One must always refer back to the great classical models, maintaining a constant interest in their thought, their form, their style…One should ask oneself with Longinus: how would Homer have said that?' But of course not. It is absurd, and Longinus is merely a cheap rhetorician. One should ask one-self rather: how do I feel about something, how do I perceive it?[10]

The key insult here is Gourmont's dismissal of Longinus as 'a cheap rhetorician' (*un bas rhéteur*). We have seen, with Eliot and others, that a suspicion of style as 'mere' rhetoric runs through much modernist thought, reaching the English-speaking world through Symons' book on the symbolist movement; that this suspicion should have originated in French literature, where there is a strong tradition of rhetorical school-ing, is no accident. Gourmont anticipates Valéry's rejection of Pascal's metaphysics as an empty rhetorical gesture when he notes that:

> It is only in the final chapter […] that M. Albalat approaches what ought to be the important part of his book: 'Style without rhetoric'. One should come to that, and show that there is only one style: an involuntary style, whether rich or poor, imaged or naked.[11]

This aversion to rhetoric leads Gourmont to warn against assertions of the intrinsic value of style. After the excesses of symbolism and the decadent fin-de-siècle, he perceives clearly the danger of pure style becoming purely style, insisting that 'style alone is nothing'.[12] 'Solid' thought is to be preferred to empty style: 'a new fact, a new idea is worth more than a beautiful sentence. [...] Nothing dies more quickly than a style that is not supported by the solidity of strong thought. It shrivels up like a slackened hide.'[13] This image of style as 'a slackened hide' (*une peau déten-due*) tempts Gourmont into identifying style with form as a kind of container for meaning – 'form without substance, style without thought – what misery!'[14] – but he also sensibly concedes that all such distinctions are specious: 'It is perhaps a mistake to try to distinguish form from matter. [...] These distinctions are no longer valuable.'[15] The final words of the book accordingly insist on style as the very essence of thought: 'The sign of the man in the intellectual work is the thought. The thought is the man himself. Style is the thought itself.'[16]

This concluding play on Buffon's famous statement points us back to Gourmont's earlier comment that '"Le style, c'est l'homme même" is the statement of a naturalist, who knows that birdsong is determined by the form of the beak.'[17] Style, in other words, is to be understood *pace* Albalat not simply as a product of the authors a given writer has read, but rather as 'a physiological product, and one of the most constant'[18] (this, in his way, was what Eliot was groping towards with Gourmont's help, ironizing his own rhetorical erudition in order to liberate his 'physiological' self). Gourmont's stated goal is thus to 'develop five or six reasons not to believe in the recipes of rhetoric';[19] he wants to insist on the 'problem' of style, rather than on its use as a rhetorical handbook of *L'Art d'écrire* (the title of another of Albalat's books). The problem with Gourmont's rejection of rhetoric remains, nonetheless, that his own argument can itself be characterized as rhetorical, as merely another counter-attack in the epistemological war of words. This is of course a variation of the classic modernist quandary: how to attack language whilst using it? In all documents of *Sprachskepsis* and rejections of rhetoric, language is both target and arrow: (anti-)rhetoric is marshalled against rhetoric, as Gourmont's rather self-conscious evocation of the genre of 'refutation' suggests. In 'refuting' Albalat's rhetorical view of style, Gourmont uses him as a straw man at which to aim his polemical attack: underlying his rejection of Albalat is an implicit rejection of any normative sense of bourgeois 'good' taste, as though that could be handed down through the generations. Clearly, it requires a certain sleight of hand to reject rhetoric whilst in turn making such a rhetorical move.

Looking back from the other end of high modernism, Jean Paulhan diagnosed this self-conscious relationship to rhetoric as one of the key characteristics of the era. Although Paulhan had begun composing it as early as 1925, *The Flowers of Tarbes* did not appear in book form until 1941 (a shorter version appeared in the *Nouvelle Revue Française* in 1936). As this publication history suggests, it is very much a document of its time (indeed, given Paulhan's central position as editor of the *NRF*, it may arguably be seen as one of *the* key documents of its time): the central distinction between Terror and Rhetoric derives from the currency of the former term in literary debates of the 1930s[20] (the subtitle of the book is 'Terror in Literature'). This distinction boils down to the intense self-consciousness of the 'Terrorists' about language:

> A Rhetorician makes his position on language clear once and for all, and is thereafter free to talk about love or fear, slavery or freedom. But a Terrorist cannot help mixing a constant concern about language and expression into his fear, love or freedom.[21]

In classic French fashion, *The Flowers of Tarbes* has a quasi-dialectical structure: three parts with three chapters each, followed by a concluding synthesis of sorts. Paulhan begins by sketching out 'A Portrait of Terror', by which he means the current state of literature in the 1920s and 1930s. The prevailing mood, he summarizes, is that 'one cannot be a decent writer if one is not disgusted by literature' (FT: 3). Stylistic perfection is accordingly perceived as a 'cause for concern', since, as Paulhan states polemically in the opening sentences, 'beauty means little more to us than a reason to feel wary' (FT: 1).

Paulhan thus identifies the suspicion of a literature that has drifted from pure style to purely style as the defining attitude of high modernism.[22] Yet that does not mean that he personally endorses this view:

> I know of no dangers that are more insidious, nor any curse crueller, than those which belong to a time when *mastery* and *perfection* more or less denote artificiality and empty convention, when *beauty*, *virtuosity* and even *literature* signify above all *what one must not do*. (FT: 9)

Paulhan identifies this suspicion of language, the desire 'to put an end forthwith to the reign of words' (FT: 29), with the term Terror. He takes Gourmont (and, strangely given Gourmont's antipathy towards him, Albalat) as initiators of the critical discourse of Terror. Terrorist critics seek to overthrow what they see as the reign of rhetoric. They abhor clichés, 'verbalism [and] the influence of language'; 'skill, knowledge, and technique [...] become suspect, as if they were covering up some lack of conviction' (FT: 24). The Terrorists find their motto in Verlaine: ' "Above all, avoid style". By which we understand an *accomplished* style,' continues Paulhan, 'a style that is just words and phrases' (FT: 21).

Paulhan is at pains to show that such a position – which he takes as representative of avant-garde orthodoxy (he mentions Cubists, futurists, surrealists both by name and by movement) – has been adopted as a way 'to resist literature' (FT: 23). He even goes so far as to coin a new genre:

> To put it simply: we have witnessed the emergence of a new literary genre these days, which has been very successful, and which could be called 'justification' or 'alibi'. Its common theme would more or less be: 'The author establishes that, despite appearances, he is not an author.' (FT: 17)

Paulhan is essentially characterizing here the modernist manifesto. He takes the manifesto – and more broadly the kinds of modernist texts such manifestos are designed to advocate – to be a kind of 'alibi' which exculpates the author from epistemological responsibility. Paulhan initially outlines two kinds of alibi. The first is entitled 'The Author is Different', and breaks down into differences of personality and syntax: the former are exemplified by the dandies and aesthetes of the turn of the century – ' "I don't have a style", both Wilde and Cocteau said. "I *am* a style"' (FT: 12) – whilst the latter move from the 'style that is constantly changing' of the Goncourts, Huysmans and Loti to a style

> which demands of the poet, through some alchemy, *another* syntax, a new grammar, even forbidden words in which a sort of primitive innocence would come back to life, and some long lost adherence of language to the things in the world. This was the ambition, and sometimes the achievement, of Rimbaud, Apollinaire, Joyce. (FT: 13)

The second kind of alibi is entitled 'The Author is Irresponsible': this includes all manner of defensive strategies abrogating responsibility for a given text, ranging from claims to be 'merely reporting', to claims that one has no right to improve the style of the 'confessions of [the] mind' (FT: 15).

What both kinds of alibi amount to is an elaborate strategy of authorial evasiveness. Paulhan implies that this 'Terrorist' technique stretches all the way from early to high modernism: 'Realism and Surrealism are in the same boat here. Both encode a curious system of alibis. Put simply, in the former the writer disappears behind a human text, and in the latter behind a superhuman one' (FT: 14). Paulhan argues that this is a kind of modernist *mauvaise foi*: on the one hand, meaning is increasingly invested in style, syntax and linguistic surface; on the other hand, writers simultaneously try to distance themselves from any notion of responsibility for their style. There is an implicit dialectic here: the more style is invested with meaning, the more suspicious it becomes. The cultivation of pure style tips over, once again, into the suspicion of purely style.

Section Two of *The Flowers of Tarbes*, 'The Myth of the Power of Words', identifies the Terrorist creation of the 'siren or the minotaur, the power-of-words' (FT: 52). Paulhan interprets this veneration of language in post-Nietzschean terms as a kind of surrogate god, yet he links it dialectically to the 'secret desire to humiliate language' (FT: 31). He traces this dialectic historically through the various different styles of modernism, the 'diverse schools which have followed on from Romanticism':

> Whether it is Symbolism or Unanimism, the Paroxysts or the Surrealists, with each and every one of them we cannot fail to be struck these days by their verbal idiosyncracies. Furthermore, every one of them has believed it was based on a rejection of verbalism and literary artifice – and each one of them begins by discovering, with abundant energy, a particular object (the mind, man, society, the unconscious) which, it seems to them, the previous schools took it upon themselves to hide behind words. (FT: 40–1)

The final section of the book, 'Inventing a Rhetoric', seeks to show that both the Terrorist and the

Rhetorician positions are based on illusions. Whilst the various Terrorist movements as Paulhan understands them – broadly speaking, modernism – have brought about a necessary rebellion against the decorum of traditional rhetoric, it is equally evident that 'Terror is verbal, and more preoccupied with language than rhetoric has ever been' (FT: 76). In the concluding section of chapter nine, Paulhan argues in neat dialectical fashion for a 'Rhetoric, or Terror perfected'. Terror has certainly created a self-consciousness, a 'self-reflexive zone' or 'complicity' about language; but this has now become its own kind of rhetoric. What is needed, suggests Paulhan, is 'a shared Rhetoric (to which these pages would be a fairly good introduction) for the dust of the different parties and individual rhetorics that Terror alludes to in its solitude and its anguish' (FT: 82). He condenses this prescription into a maxim: 'Run away from language and it will come after you. Go after language and it will run away from you' (FT: 82).

These last two statements suggest that *The Flowers of Tarbes* can be read as 'a sustained effort on Paulhan's part to articulate something like an ethical imperative of language and literature', in the words of his translator Michael Syrotinski (FT: xix). In essence, Paulhan expounds what we might term an ethics of style: just as Adorno and Horkheimer in their *Dialectic of Enlightenment* want to enlighten the enlighteners, so Paulhan wants to terrorize the Terrorists, advocating a self-conciousness about language that is yet also self-conscious about itself. 'We have pushed Terror as far as it will go', he notes towards the end of his study, 'and have discovered Rhetoric' (FT: 85). In this spirit of turning arguments back against themselves, it is important to understand Paulhan's own text as part of the debates in which it seeks to intervene. Published towards the end of modernism, *The Flowers of Tarbes* seeks to look back dispassionately at the various modernist and avant-garde movements, yet it is also a product of these movements. Its dialectical approach in both structure and argument (as exemplified by the maxim quoted above), and its strangely picaresque tone (there are chapters with titles like 'In Which the Reader Sees the Author the Other Way Round'), suggest that Paulhan's book is itself beholden to a particular style. Syrotinski describes this performative aspect of the text nicely:

> The book is […] a performance of the very radical ambiguity that it talks about, an ambiguity which is not simply an equivocation about *what* the book is saying, but which suspends it between saying and doing, stating and performing, original and commonplace. (FT: xvii)

The Flowers of Tarbes can thus be read as the last in a long line of modernist manifestos characterized by their tendency both to argue a style thematically *and* to enact it stylistically (indeed, this is perhaps implicit in Paulhan's parenthesis about 'a shared Rhetoric [to which these pages would be a fairly good introduction]'). Gourmont's 'refutation' of *Le Problème du style* in 1902 and Paulhan's diagnosis of the 'alibi' of style in 1941 provide the borders between which we can chart the development of the modernist manifesto and its relationship to its own conceptions of style.

Filippo Marinetti, 'The Founding and Manifesto of Futurism' (1909)

'In the aesthetic field the Italian showman Filippo Tommaso Marinetti wins the all-time Oscar for producing and presenting the ur-manifesto, that of futurism in 1909.'[23] Marinetti's manifesto inaugurates what Mary Ann Caws has called 'the Manifesto Moment',[24] a ten-year period stretching from 1909 to 1919. The first and best known of the many futurist manifestos, it set the tone not only for futurism, but for the modernist manifesto more generally: several critics have proclaimed the twentieth century 'a futurist century'.[25] What, then, are its salient characteristics, and how do they relate to modernist conceptions of style?

Marinetti's title 'The Founding and Manifesto of Futurism'[26] points towards what is perhaps the defining aspect of all modernist manifestos, namely their self-reflexive nature. The modernist manifesto is simultaneously both an argument *for* a particular style, and an example *of* it. By setting his manifesto within the story of its founding, Marinetti not only 'builds into [the manifesto's] surroundings its own conditions for reception',[27] he also *enacts* this founding. The title tells us that the manifesto 'founds' the very movement it is seeking to manifest. As the enactment of its own announcement, it is thus the very definition of a performative document.

This performativity resounds through the style of the manifesto. Marinetti's ecstatic rhetoric is clearly meant to convey the sense of excitement and 'speed' he advocates as the essence of the modern. To say that the text is overwritten would be to miss the point: it is deliberately crammed full of otiose adjectives, abrupt transitions and breathless exclamation marks. One way to test the relationship between style and substance in Marinetti's text is to compare the axioms enumerated in the manifesto with the style of the surrounding text recording its 'founding'. Common to both sections is the immediate adoption of the first person plural, a characteristic of almost all modernist manifestos. *Credemus*, they proclaim, not *credo*.[28] Marinetti takes himself to be speaking for a whole movement – although of course it is only in making this statement, in publishing it in *Le Figaro*, that the movement actually comes into being. The two opening paragraphs of the framing text set the scene; read with a retrospective eye, they read not unlike the beat poets of the 1960s, revelling in their multifarious contradictions. Marinetti throws adjectives and images against each other in the hope that they will spark: the repetition in the second paragraph of the phrase 'alone with' (variations of the phrase recur five times in the one paragraph) provides a particularly striking example, since both its repetition and its very paradoxical structure – the notion of being alone, but with someone – suggest that they are hardly 'alone' (indeed, the use of the first person plural militates against this). Already in the opening paragraphs, it is thus obvious that this is an instance of the manifesto as self-stylization, where style is being used to create the context of its own reception.

If these opening lines can be said to correspond in the manifesto to points 3 ('feverish insomnia'), 6 ('the poet must spread himself with ardour, splendour and generosity') and arguably 11 ('great crowds excited by work, by pleasure and by riot'), then the *coup de théâtre* on which the 'founding' turns ('suddenly we jumped') is related to the famous invocation of the 'beauty of speed' in point 4. In both the manifesto and the main text this is linked to the juxtaposition of old and new, classical and modern: the *Victory of Samothrace* and the 'roaring car', 'mythology' and the 'three snorting beasts'. Just as the bullet points of the manifesto are meant to convey the sensation of speed and 'aggressive action', so the snatches of monologue presented in the main text convey a similar sense of urgency. Marinetti achieves this in particular by repeating the refrain 'Let's go!' Accompanied by its attendant exclamation marks, the hortative is perhaps the defining grammatical mood of the manifesto: Marinetti is enjoining his friends, and by extension his readers, to 'shake the gates of life'. The question of tense and mood is particularly important to the manifesto. In the case of Marinetti's text, this becomes especially apparent in the 11 points of the manifesto itself, where the mood hovers somewhere between the performative ('We say'), the optative ('We intend to', 'We want to') and the direct future ('We will'). It is in this careful calibration of tense that the style of the text sublimates the psychological drive of rejuvenation and 'modernization' into the programmatic framework of a manifesto. In the final, longest point, the initial proclamation in the future tense ('We will sing') rapidly disappears into the 'fervour' of nouns and adjectives. The future tense dissolves into a performative present, where the succession of clauses linked by semi-colons 'sings' technological modernity into existence, whilst at the same time stating that this is what it intends to do.

Marinetti's manifesto thus both displays and defers modernity's annunciation, hovering between the present and an imminent future. Its style lends it both 'epiphanic' and 'programmatic' force, in the terms of Roger Griffin; 'the manifesto, at its height, is a poem in heightened prose'.[29] Futurism inaugurates the tendency of the modernist manifesto to what Henri Meschonnic calls 'the principle of generalization' or 'unifying principle',[30] whereby everything is reduced to a single, underlying ideology. 'We already live in the absolute,' intones Marinetti. It also represents the point of entry for Nietzsche, who is arguably the presiding spirit of the modernist manifesto. Marinetti adopts an historiographical position which one could define as 'critical' in the terms Nietzsche develops in his 'On the Use and Abuse of History for Life' (1873): he rejects the monuments and 'museums' of modern Italy, he wishes to free her of 'Professors [and] anti-quarians'. 'No work without an aggressive character can be a masterpiece,' he proclaims. In its definition of beauty as a 'struggle', moreover, in its understanding of art as a kind of *Überwindung* or overcoming, the futurist manifesto displays something of the folly and ambition of 'grand style'. Where Nietzsche proclaims that 'grand style originates when the beautiful carries off victory over the monstrous', Marinetti announces that 'poetry must be conceived as a violent attack on unknown forces, to reduce and prostrate them before man'. Marinetti's is a more explicitly masculine, tech-nocratic, combative version of grand style, determined to see modern man as the Promethean conqueror, as in the closing words of the text: 'Erect on the summit of the world, once again we hurl our defiance at the stars!' The psychology is palpably Freudian as well as Nietzschean: the machismo of style, famously glorifying fascist war as 'the world's only hygiene', encodes futurism as a deeply masculine aesthetics. The erotics of futurism is enacted stylistically in the arguably very male bullet points of the manifesto, as well as in the apostrophes and ejaculations ('Oh! Maternal ditch') of the surrounding text. *Eros*, moreover, clearly also evokes *thanatos*: the 'young lions [running] after Death' desire nothing more than to become martyrs to modernity, dissolved in the supreme *jouissance* of a dawning age. Marinetti is thus the paradigmatic Terrorist, in Paulhan's terms, both in his desire to tear down existing rhetorical structures and in his inevitable replacement of them with a new kind of rhetoric. The 'manifesto' may be destructive; the 'founding' is by definition (re-)constructive. Whilst Marinetti's style is designed to enact his futurist ideology, it also displays the close relationship between anarchy and aesthetics that is at the heart of modernism.

Mina Loy, 'Feminist Manifesto' (1914)

If the futurist, and indeed more broadly the modernist, manifesto is undoubtedly an overwhelmingly male affair, there are notable exceptions that prove the rule. In 1912, Valentine de Saint-Point (the pseudonym of Desglans de Cessiat-Vercell) wrote a 'Manifesto of the Futurist Woman'.[31] Announced in the subtitle explicitly as a 'Response to F.T. Marinetti', it takes as its epigraph point 9 of Marinetti's manifesto – the point glorifying war as 'the world's only hygiene' and proclaiming the futurist 'scorn for woman'. The striking thing about Saint-Point's manifesto is that it rejects Marinetti only in his emphasis on the masculine – it explicitly does not embrace feminism, which is denounced as a 'political' and 'cerebral' error. It thus constitutes a 'response' but not a 'refutation' in Gourmont's terms: 'Futurism, even with all its exaggerations, is right.' Saint-Point enjoins modern women to become *more* virile, not less; she claims to be freeing woman from 'morals and prejudices', returning her to her 'sublime instinct, to violence, to cruelty'. Saint-Point's manifesto is more of a sequel to Marinetti than a riposte, parodoxically importing futurist machismo into a female perspective. Its stylistic interest, such as it is in a text that is extremely derivative of Marinetti, lies principally in this paradox. Initially the style has a certain dialectical equilibrium, since Saint-Point seeks to mediate between what one could call with Jung the *anima* and the *animus* ('Any exclusively virile individual is just a brute animal; any exclusively feminine individual is only a female'); yet by the end, this balance has more or less disappeared, as she exhorts women to become more masculine. A strange mixture of futurism and (a peculiar kind of) feminism, this is the modernist manifesto as epigone.

A more interesting example of a female manifesto is arguably that written by Mina Loy. Loy was originally English, but emigrated to the United States in 1916 (by way of Paris and Florence). Primarily a poet, her work had some influential supporters: Ezra Pound thought her one of the very few poets of interest in America, whilst Ivor Winter compared her to Emily Dickinson. Nonetheless, she also met with much bafflement: modernist critics objected to her artificial diction and often archaic vocabulary. In the words of her latter-day editor Roger L. Conover: 'They did not understand that she was building a Trojan verse – deliberately hijacking Victorian vocabulary and conceptual posturing in order to subvert the values and expose the mechanisms such constructions were meant to euphemize.'[32] She was also repeatedly patronized as a woman, partly for her celebrated beauty and partly for her style: Conrad Aiken 'encouraged readers to "pass lightly over the [...] tentacular quiverings of Mina Loy" in favour of the "manly metre" of Eliot and Stevens'.[33] In 1914, Loy published some 'Aphorisms of Futurism'; clearly indebted to Marinetti, they advocate the standard emphasis on the 'velocity of velocities' and take a similar 'list' form, although in Loy's case the first word of each statement in the list is printed in block letters.

This typographical playfulness was pursued in a later text of the same year, namely her 'Feminist Manifesto'. The manifesto, unpublished in her lifetime, was included in a letter sent to Mabel Dodge Luhan, a Manhattan *grande dame* and artistic impresario. As Conover notes, the manifesto 'was probably written in part in negation to [Marinetti's] "The Founding and Manifesto of Futurism"'.[34] In terms of Marinetti's reception, the move from Saint-Point's ambivalent 'response' to Loy's more explicit 'negation' is worth noting, yet Loy's manifesto, written in Florence towards the end of her futurist phase, is far from an outright condemnation of Marinetti's founding document. Like Saint-Point, she exhorts women to 'be brave' and recognize that woman is not the 'equal of man' (LLB: 153); like Saint-Point, she encourages women to become more like men. 'Loy makes an older model of manhood meaningful for modern womanhood':[35] she advocates the overcoming of 'virtue' and, in particular, the 'destruction of virginity' (LLB: 155) as a means of emancipating the modern woman. In a manner comparable to those of Saint-Point, Loy's views in the manifesto are a somewhat uneasy mixture of feminism and futurism (although, as her title suggests, they are markedly more focused on the 'feminist question').

Yet it is as a rhetorical performance that Loy's manifesto may retain our interest. Christina Walter notes that the 'Feminist Manifesto' is 'shot through with a dilemma: as a feminist and woman writer, Loy wants to claim women's equality within modernism; yet, she also seems to feel that modernist impersonality [...] is a luxury that women writers cannot afford'.[36] This tension can be felt stylistically: Loy adopts what one could call a masculine style, imitating the strident tone, imperatives and modal verbs of the master Marinetti. This is far from the fluid, 'feminine' style one associates with modernist 'women's writing': *pace* Woolf, Loy's style here *is* 'heavy' and 'pompous'.[37] If Loy 'rhetorically violates the body',[38] she does so through her style and typography (key terms are printed for emphasis in large bold font) as much as through her argument. Indeed, her claim in a subsequent letter to Luhan that she feels 'rather hopeless of devotion to the Woman-cause – Slaves will believe that chains are protectors' (LLB: 216) could be turned back against her style: in mimicking the master's voice, she adopts these chains as her own. If Loy articulates 'a set of dialogues and collisions between competing ideologies',[39] it is not clear that she is fully in control of them, and indeed this suspicion is confirmed by comments in both the letter in which she sent the manifesto and subsequent letters to Luhan. In the initial letter, she writes that 'this absolute resubstantiation of the feminist question [is] easily to be proved fallacious – There is no truth – anywhere'; in a second letter a few months later, she dismisses the manifesto as 'a fragment of feminist tirade. [...] I find the destruction of virginity – *so* daring don't you think – had been suggested by some other woman years ago' (LLB: 216). This seems to be a classic case, in other words, of the manifesto as 'alibi': even as she sends it out, Loy disowns her text as arguably 'fallacious'. Where the modernist manifesto is conceived by its own author as a 'tirade', it is clear that the style of its delivery is as important as its argument.

Ezra Pound, 'A Few Don'ts by an Imagiste' (1913)

The celebrated definition of an 'Image' as 'that which presents an intellectual and emotional complex in an instant of time' forms the opening sentence of Ezra Pound's manifesto 'A Few Don'ts by an Imagiste'.[40] With these few words, Pound defined an era, that of the early war years with their combative juxtaposition of hard-headed intellectualism and harder-edged masculinity. The 'image' of the imagists, and the 'vortex' of the associated vorticists, were coined in reaction against the 'symbol' of the symbolists, perceived as vague and dreamily evocative where the 'Men of 1914' (as Wyndham Lewis characterized them) were precise and dynamic. T.E. Hulme was acknowledged as one of the key sources for the concept of the 'image': Hulme had written in 1907 of 'style short, being forced by the coming together of many different thoughts, and generated by their contact'.[41] The imagists advocated in similar terms what Marsden Hartley, writing in 1919, called 'tensity',[42] which one can understand as a kind of syntactical admixture of tension and intensity. At the level of ideas, this tensity is expressed through defining the image as the dialectical juxtaposition of 'two more or less distant realities', as Pierre Reverdy wrote in 1918: 'the more the relations of the two realities brought together are distant and fitting, the stronger the image'.[43] At the level of style, 'tensity' finds its counterpart in the 'mosaic negative' of Pound's manifesto (if indeed one can call it that).

Pound professes that he is building on two main sources: F.S. Flint's 'Imagisme' (1913), and Georges Duhamel's and Charles Vildrac's *Notes sur la technique poétique* (1910). Flint had drawn up the 'three rules' of imagism:

1. Direct treatment of the 'thing', whether subjective or objective.
2. To use absolutely no word that did not contribute to the presentation.
3. As regarding rhythm: to compose in sequence of the musical phrase, not in sequence of a metronome.[44]

Pound presents his manifesto as a reflection on these axioms. However, he presents them in such a way as to undermine their axiomatic force:

> To begin with, consider the three rules recorded by
> Mr. Flint, not as dogma – never consider anything
> as dogma – but as the result of long contemplation,
> which, even if it is someone else's contemplation,
> may be worth consideration. (EP: 357)

One senses the unease in the equivocations of the syntax: the injunctions to 'consider' and to 'contemplate' are both immediately countermanded by negatives and subjunctives. The command 'never consider anything as dogma' is itself dogmatic, and exemplifies Pound's evident unease with the genre of the manifesto: where imperatives and hortatives are *de rigueur*, he subverts them through negation. Indeed, the very form of the negative imperative is a kind of oxymoron: in being told *not* to do something, the reader is being told to do something.

Pound alludes to this paradox, of course, in the title of his manifesto, and he picks up on this in his response to his opening remarks. After establishing his definition of the image, and stressing in particular its 'instantaneous' nature, he begins to equivocate: 'All this, however, some consider open to debate. The immediate necessity is to tabulate A LIST OF DON'T'S for those beginning to write verses. But I can not put all of them into mosaic negative' (EP: 356). Pound is at pains, in other words, to undermine the dogmatic force of his definition of Imagism. In Paulhan's terms, he is a Terrorist with second thoughts: intuiting the tendency of revolution to reify into a new orthodoxy, he fiddles with his own rhetorical bomb, unsure at the last moment whether he really wants it to go off, since that would mean that the rebel had become the ruler.

The relationship between prescription and proscription in Pound's manifesto must be seen in these terms. For every positive imperative, there is a negative. His recommendations for the aspiring poet centre around imagist conceptions of 'language' and 'rhythm and rhyme' – in other words, around style. We do not need to rehearse these recommendations in detail here, but it is perhaps worth saying a word about Pound's presentation of the relationship between poetry and music, since it is typical of the imagists' ambivalent view of the symbolist legacy. On the one hand, they reject the vague notion of a 'musical style' in the manner of, say, Swinburne (Hartley attacks 'Swinburnian encrustations');[45] on the other hand, Pound enjoins the aspiring poet to 'behave as a musician, a good musician' (EP: 358). The parallel between poetry and music is permitted, then, as long as the 'rhythmic structure [does] not destroy the shape of your words, or their natural sound, or their meaning' (EP: 358). Rhythm remains a key element of poetic style for Pound – it is just that it must have a clearly defined relationship to specific aspects of meaning, and not attempt to impose a blanket of euphony arbitrarily.

This emphasis on rhythm derives from Pound's other acknowledged source, Duhamel's and Vildrac's *Notes sur la technique poétique*. One of the key terms on which the two French critics repeatedly insist is 'rhythmical constancy' (*la constante rythmique*).[46] They too reject the symbolist heritage of musical style – 'We do not believe that modern rhythm has been determined by the influence of Wagnerian art, as has often been said'[47] – although they stress in turn the fundamentals of prosody and rhyme, alliteration and assonance.

In essence, they advocate *vers libre*, although, like Pound, they insist on the necessary craftmanship of the poet: 'Any poetics must be founded on metrical and phonetic relationships.'[48] The real force of their pamphlet, however, is to make modern poets fully self-conscious: 'One should not claim that form is as important as content [...]. But all the same, it is amazing how some poets are so little curious about their art.'[49] In this, Pound's manifesto follows them; indeed, the particular force of his text, of its enumeration of negative imperatives, can be located in its attempt to create a kind of anti-manifesto as a model of critical vigilance. 'Poets today, more than ever, should not let their critical sense slumber,' write Duhamel and Vildrac. 'There is no freedom without responsibility, and now, we are responsible.'[50] Pound's manifesto attempts to impose this aesthetic responsibility; yet its final paradox may be that after enumerating all the things a poet should and should not do, as though he could be trained, Pound concludes with Duhamel's and Vildrac's final words: 'Mais il faut d'abord être un poète' (EP: 359). One last time, Pound thus undermines the rhetoric of the manifesto: if one needs to be a poet *a priori*, then what good is a list of prescriptions and proscriptions? In setting the style of his manifesto against its preconditions, Pound creates a document that becomes more than the sum of its parts.

Tristan Tzara, 'Dada Manifesto' (1918)

If Pound coined the idea of the manifesto as 'mosaic negative', it was Dada that perfected it. Born at the Cabaret Voltaire in Zurich in 1916 'of a desire for independence, of a distrust of the community',[51] Dada consciously drew on existing European avant-gardes, but was the first major movement to be conceived in direct response to the war. As such, it was characterized from the start by a spirit of anger and nihilism. Early Dada performances, led by the impresario Hugo Ball, emphasized simultaneous cacophony (as in the famous multilingual performance of 'L'Amiral cherche une maison à louer') and what they called 'pure' sound, bracketing off 'meaning' (and, in particular, any notion of 'redemptive' meaning) as a bourgeois illusion. As Kandinsky wrote in 1911 in his essay *Concerning the Spiritual in Art* (a work which would have a direct influence on Ball), 'pure sound exercises a direct impression on the soul. The soul obtains to an objectless vibration [...]. In this direction lie great possibilities for the literature of the future.'[52]

Yet it was not until 1918 that Dada found its definitive manifesto. This delay enabled its author, the Romanian poet Tristan Tzara, to look back at a movement already well established: the manifesto opens with the disclaimer that 'The magic of a word – DADA – which has set the journalists at the door of an unexpected world, has not the slightest importance for us.'[53] The scene is thus set for a different kind of manifesto: this is not the manifesto as founding document, but rather as 'refutation' in Gourmont's sense – only in this case, it is a refutation of itself. From the opening words, moreover, it is clear that this is a refutation not only of Dada, but of the genre of the manifesto more broadly:

To proclaim a manifesto you have to want: A.B.C., thunder against 1,2,3, lose your patience and sharpen your wings to conquer and spread a's, b's, c's little and big, sign, scream, swear, arrange the prose in a form of absolute and irrefutable evidence [...]. To impose your A.B.C. is a natural thing – therefore regrettable.[54]

Tzara thus immediately refutes the by this stage well-established conventions of the modernist manifesto. In place of the declamatory imperative, he offers the self-aware infinitive, as though to say that he sees through the rhetorical game of the manifesto and refuses to play it. Yet this is of course – how could it be otherwise? – itself a rhetorical gesture; as the Dadaist Georges Ribemont-Dessaignes observed, 'Dada created anti-aesthetic values. So then it created art.'[55] Tzara is clearly aware of this circularity, and so takes his self-conscious reflections a step further:

I am writing a manifesto and I don't want anything, I say however certain things and I am on principle against manifestos, as I am also against principles [...]. I am writing this manifesto to show that you can do contrary actions together, in one single fresh breath; I am against action; for continual contradiction, for affirmation also, I am neither for nor against and I don't explain because I hate common sense.[56]

Tzara here performs the pirouettes as he describes them. He revels in the paradox of writing a manifesto based on 'principles' whilst proclaiming that he is against manifestos and principles; he revels in the contradiction of being both 'for' and 'against'. If he is both, then he is neither, as he concludes; this is the nihilistic aesthetic of negation at the heart of Dada. Yet even this becomes in turn affirmative: by the end of the manifesto, Tzara has moved to the traditional 'I proclaim' of the manifesto writer, albeit in a further form of negation: 'I proclaim the opposition of all cosmic faculties to the gonorrhea of a putrid sun coming out of the factories of philosophic thought, this fierce battle with all the possible means of DADAIST DISGUST.'[57]

It is at this point that we need briefly to inquire into the status of Dada as an 'avant-garde' movement. A distinction perhaps needs to be drawn between modernism and the avant-garde, as Peter Bürger influentially – if controversially – argued in his *Theory of the Avant-Garde* (1974 German, 1984 English). For Bürger, the distinction turns on the essentially aesthetic nature of modernism on the one hand, and the socio-critical nature of the avant-garde on the other. 'Modernism may be understandable as an attack on traditional writing techniques,' summarizes Jochen Schulte-Sasse in his foreword to the English edition of Bürger's study, 'but the avant-garde can only be understood as an attack meant to alter the institutionalized commerce with art.'[58] Bürger argues against Renato Poggioli's understanding of the avant-garde as a version of modernism, perceiving the transition from aestheticism to the avant-garde rather as contingent on 'criticizing the autonomy status of art in developed bourgeois society':[59] only in doing so can it begin to attack the socio-economic assumptions that underlie the role of art in modernity. Against the metaphysics of the modernist belief in the redemptive powers of art, Bürger articulates a materialist vision of the avant-garde as determined by the way it seeks to undermine its own preconditions.

The implications of this for its conception of style are significant. As Schulte-Sasse notes, since 'aestheticist modernism could not address thematically the social status of art in bourgeois society, [it] could only give body to social criticism by the stylistic weapons it tried to use to undermine the homogenous ideology of bourgeois society'.[60] The art of the avant-garde, on the other hand, defined itself by attacking this ideology head-on, by making this attack a constituent part of its identity.[61] Where modernism uses style to critique society, the avant-garde attacks 'style' as part of the bourgeois institution of art. For Bürger, it is 'a distinguishing feature of the historical avant-garde movements that they did not develop a style. There is no such thing as a dadaist or surrealist style.'[62] Peter Sloterdijk takes the argument further, disagreeing with Bürger about the socio-critical ambitions of the avant-garde and interpreting it rather as a broader revolt against the epistemology of 'meaning':

> Dada does *not* revolt against bourgeois 'institution art'. Dada turns against art as a technique of bestowing meaning. Dada is antisemantics. It rejects 'style' as pretense of meaning just as much as the deceitful 'beautifying' of things.[63]

If modernism cultivates style, in other words, as a response to modernity, then avant-garde art renounces it. 'Style becomes arbitrary,' notes Peter Nicholls; 'Dada assumes no coherent world to be mirrored in art [...] and the success of the work itself will be measured by the degree to which [...] it contravenes accepted notions of symmetry and intelligibility.'[64] By these terms, Tzara's anti-manifesto, with all its deliberate contradictions and incoherencies, is a resounding success: the manifesto finishes with the 'shrieking of contracted colours, intertwining of contraries and of all contradictions, grotesqueries, nonsequiturs: LIFE'.[65] Indeed, in Bürger's terms one can conclude that 'it is no accident that the active, even aggressive artistic manifesto [...] became the preferred medium of expression for the avant-garde artist of the twentieth century':[66] this is the manifesto as anti-style.

Kurt Pinthus, 'Foreword' to *Menschheitsdämmerung* (1919)

The war years in which Dada came to prominence can be characterized in broad artistic terms as the expressionist period. The earliest printed occurrence of the term 'expressionist' is generally taken to be the catalogue to the XXII Berliner Sezession, which opened in April 1911.[67] A German term that was orginally applied to French artists, it soon became associated above all with the German-speaking countries, although it remained very much an international movement. Expressionism had been building for some years, with groups of artists such as *Die Brücke* (based in Dresden) and *Blauer Reiter* (based in Munich) developing similar ideas on colour, form and visual abstraction. Kandinsky, who belonged to the latter group, famously defined 'form' as the outward manifestation of 'inner need' (in his *Concerning the Spiritual in Art* [1911]),[68] and the correspondence of visible style to invisible 'essence' (*Wesen*) remained one of the constant concerns of the various groups of expressionist artists.

This correspondence expressed itself not only in the close relationship during this period between poets and painters, but also in their common call for what one might term an ethical aesthetics. The carnage of the First World War created a sense of apocalyptic crisis, to which expressionist artists of all kinds responded with a reborn sense of mission: nothing less than the 'renewal of mankind' (*die Erneuerung des Menschen*, in the playwright Georg Kaiser's Nietzschean phrase) was at stake. Although the movement does not lack for documents and 'manifestos',[69] its characteristic sense of intensity, and the concomitant implications for a concept of style, can perhaps be most succinctly discerned in the foreword to the defining book of expressionist poetry, *Menschheitsdämmerung*.[70] In 1919, the critic Kurt Pinthus put together a representative selection of the leading German-language poets of the preceding decade, including work by Gottfried Benn, Jakob van Hoddis, Georg Heym, August Stramm and Georg Trakl. Subtitled 'A Document of Expressionism', the aims of the anthology were both historical and political; Pinthus' foreword (I am concentrating here on the original 1919 foreword, and not those to subsequent editions) is not strictly speaking a manifesto, yet its declamatory style and representative status give it a programmatic force comparable to that of other modernist manifestos.

Pinthus' textual strategies certainly seem familiar. He begins by stating apodictically that 'the editor of this book is an enemy of anthologies – that is why he is

editing this collection' (MD: 27). Pinthus thus immediately presents his foreword in Paulhan's terms as a
'justification' or 'alibi': where 'the author establishes
that, despite appearances, he is not an author', so the
anthologist establishes that, despite appearances, he is
not an anthologist. The foreword accordingly begins
by telling us what it is *not* going to do: it will not simply collate a range of poets who happen to live at the
same time, nor will it gather poems around a particular
topic. Pinthus' modernist move is not just to present
the book as a kind of anti-anthology (in the manner
of a Dadaist anti-manifesto), but also to turn the focus
back onto the very concept of 'collection' (*Sammlung*)
itself:

> This book does not just call itself a 'collection'. It *is*
> collection!: collection of strong emotions and pas-
> sions, collection of an epoch's longing, happiness,
> and torment – our epoch. It is the collected projec-
> tion of human movement out of time into time. Its
> purpose is not to show skeletons of poets, but rather
> the frothing, chaotic, bursting totality of our times.
> (MD: 27)

'Collection' is thus established as the key motif of the
anthology: by dropping the indefinite article, Pinthus
takes the form of the book and makes it into its defining concept. That this is also a stylistic principle, both
for expressionism broadly and for his foreword specifically, suggests a confluence of aesthetic style and ethical aim: Pinthus understands the expressionist artist
as responding to the catastrophe of the First World
War through a process of centripetal concentration.

Through this aesthetic process, he seeks to obtain an ethical goal, namely 'a new, better humanity' (MD: 28): 'because deliverance cannot come from the outside – from that direction there was a presentiment of war and destruction long before the World War –, but only from the strengths inside the human being, there took place the great turn towards the ethical' (MD: 33). The ethical imperative is thus associated with a concentration on 'the strengths inside', which is then translated into the style of the foreword. Pinthus explains the stylistic principle of expressionism in the following terms:

> Never before were aesthetics and the principle of *l'art pour l'art* as disdained as in this poetry, which is called the 'newest' or 'expressionist' because it is eruption, explosion, intensity – has to be in order to burst that hostile crust. For this reason it eschews the naturalistic depiction of reality as technique, no matter how palpable this degenerate reality was; instead, it creates with enormous and vigorous energy its own means of expression from the motive power of the spirit. (MD: 35)

The explosive language here is literally that of the Terrorist, in Paulhan's terms. Pinthus depicts the expressionist as seeking to blow up vestigial notions of aestheticism; in order to do this, he needs to use the most violent style possible. Style is linked explicitly to 'spirit': the 'means of expression' arise out of its 'motive power'.

This style is itself performed in Pinthus' foreword, which seeks to enact what it describes. Perhaps unusually for the expressionist period, its main objective correlative is not that of visual art, but of music, 'the music of our time [...], the booming unison of hearts and minds' (MD: 28). Time and again in the ten pages of the foreword, Pinthus returns to the image of a symphony, developing at length the comparison between his 'collection' of poets and the various symphonic movements. In its combination of musical imagery and an idiom of 'unity' and 'intensity' (terms such as 'together' and 'at the same time' frequently recur), it is clear that the presiding spirit of the foreword is Nietzsche's Dionysus: Pinthus stresses not Apolline clarity, but chthonic organicity: 'can such a poetry display a pure and clear countenance? Must it not be chaotic like the times out of whose rent and bloody soil it grew?' (MD: 31).

Yet this paradigmatic example of expressionist style must ultimately be understood dialectically, as a kind of ethical correlative. Pinthus insists that his book contains only 'political poetry, for its theme is the condition of contemporary humanity, which it laments, curses, disdains, destroys while at the same time seeking in terrifying outbursts the possibilities of future change' (MD: 34). The more expressionism cultivates an aggressive, intense style, the more it rages and screams, the more it is actually preparing the ground for a future serenity. As the famous ambivalence of the title *Menschheitsdämmerung* (as well as the progression of the four sections of the anthology from 'Crash and Cry' to 'Love to Human Beings') suggests, dusk precedes dawn. Pinthus' foreword manifests a profoundly utopian dialectics: in its closing words, all that remains for the damned is 'hope in the human being and a faith in utopia' (MD: 37). The foreword to *Menschheitsdämmerung* thus represents a microcosm of expressionist style more broadly: it works itself up to a violent crescendo only in order to reach the other side. That this applies specifically to *style* is implicit in the closing paragraph, where Pinthus writes that the whole purpose of expending so much Dionysian energy is to clear the way for an Apolline serenity: 'As surely as the poetry of our age had to travel down this martyr's path, just as surely shall the poetry of the future manifest itself differently: it will have to be simple, pure, and clear. The poetry of our age is at once an end and a beginning' (MD: 37). If the expressionists were 'Terrorists', then this is the manifesto as suicide bomb, sacrificing itself for future salvation.

André Breton, *Surrealist Manifesto* (1924) and Louis Aragon, *Treatise on Style* (1928)

Less than three years later, in 1922, André Breton announced the death of Dada. Breton, Aragon and various other associated writers had become disillusioned with the pure negativity of Dada, particularly since it had become apparent that the anarchic avant-garde was in danger of becoming the new establishment. Tzara's manifesto had opened up many new paths, Breton later recalled, but none of them seemed to lead anywhere.[71] What was now needed was something more constructive. Breton expressed the distinction between the two avant-garde movements in his second *Surrealist Manifesto* (1930):

There really is torpedoing of the idea in the midst of the sentence which is articulating it, even if the sentence were to be free of any charming liberty taken with its meaning. Dadaism had especially wanted to draw attention to this torpedoing. We know that Surrealism, through its appeal to automatism, was involved in sheltering from this torpedoing a building of some sort: something like a Flying Dutchman [*un vaisseau fantôme*].[72]

Breton's image of the torpedo fits squarely into Paulhan's categories: Breton saw Dadaism as pure Terror for its own sake, whereas surrealism was conceived as Terror with a purpose, as a constructive as well as destructive force. The initial *Surrealist Manifesto* of 1924 accordingly assumes a different form to the 'Dada Manifesto' of 1918. It is certainly critical, in particular of what it terms the 'realistic attitude', but rather than merely revelling in its own nihilistic force and offering nothing in return, it attempts to develop its own aesthetic (although the term is problematic). Whilst there may be no such thing as a coherent surrealist style (as Peter Bürger argues), we can nonetheless say with Rémy de Gourmont that it was born as a 'refutation'.

The first two sentences of Breton's manifesto introduce its two opposing concepts: 'real life' and 'man, that inveterate dreamer' (MS: 3). The subsequent introductory passage bemoans the reduction of 'imagination to a state of slavery' (MS: 4): it is clear that these are to be the terms of the debate. Breton opens his argument by attacking 'the realistic attitude, inspired by positivism'. 'I loathe it,' writes Breton, 'for it is made up of mediocrity, hate, and dull conceit' (MS: 6). Breton quotes and attacks a passage from

Dostoevsky's *Crime and Punishment*, whilst a sentence like 'The Marquise went out at five' he takes as representative of 'the purely informative style' (MS: 7), testament to what he sees as the lack of ambition of realist writers. He opposes to this outmoded realism an emphasis on 'the imagination', expressed in particular through the Freudian insistence on dreams: 'The imagination is perhaps on the point of reasserting itself, of reclaiming its rights' (MS: 10). This culminates in the surrealist credo: 'I believe in the future resolution of these two states, dream and reality, which are seemingly so contradictory, into a kind of absolute reality, a *surreality*, if one may so speak' (MS: 14).

It is important to note, then, that surrealism, a term associated in the first instance with the Freudian unconscious and its arbitrary juxtaposition of images, is defined dialectically in relation to the realism of the mid-nineteenth century. The two ends of modernism meet here: one way of understanding surrealism is to view it as realism taken to an absurd extreme, to the point where the realist attention to detail becomes sur-real. Breton underlines this when he notes that it might have been more accurate to use Gérard de Nerval's term 'Supernaturalism'; as it is, he took the term invented by Apollinaire and applied it to 'the new mode of pure expression' (MS: 24). Yet if realism at one end of modernism cultivated a very strong sense of style, as we saw with Flaubert, then how can surrealism at the other end be defined in Bürger's terms as having no sense of style?

Breton's famous 'dictionary' definition (itself an example of the *Surrealist Manifesto* being used to subvert bourgeois institutions, but in a constructive way) may help us:

> SURREALISM, n. Psychic automatism in its pure state, by which one proposes to express – verbally, by means of the written word, or in any other manner – the actual functioning of thought. Dictated by thought, in the absence of any control exercised by reason, exempt from any aesthetic or moral concern. (MS: 26)

The use of the adjective 'pure' picks up one of the key adjectives of modernism – which is constantly striving to push towards stylistic absolutes – and applies it not to an aesthetic process, but to a 'psychic' one. 'Aesthetic' preoccupations are explicitly excluded: style is circumvented in the attempt to obtain direct access to 'the actual functioning of thought'.

Alongside the games based on chance – such as the use of newspaper cuttings to create poems (as demonstrated by Breton in the manifesto) – one of the main ways the surrealists sought to obtain this access was through 'automatic writing'. Breton explains that he tried to apply to himself techniques which he had practised on traumatized soldiers during the war:

> I resolved to obtain from myself what we were trying to obtain from them, namely a monologue spoken as rapidly as possible without any intervention on the part of the critical faculties, a monologue consequently unencumbered by the slightest inhibition and which was, as closely as possible, akin to *spoken thought*. (MS: 22–3)

The problem with this description is that it can be misunderstood as advocating recourse to a kind of interior monologue, as developed in the tradition from Dujardin to Joyce. Since for these latter writers style is all-important, this would seem to suggest that this is also the case for the surrealists. Yet Breton makes clear in a later essay, 'On Surrealism in its Living Works' (1953), that automatic writing and the interior monologue are to be understood as exact opposites:

> Although they are evidence of a common desire to take up arms against the tyranny of a thoroughly debased language, procedures such as the 'automatic writing' that began Surrealism and the 'inner mono-logue' in Joyce's system are radically different at base. (MS: 298)

Breton describes the Joycean model of interior mono-logue as essentially mimetic, despite its radicality, since it ultimately still attempts to impose aesthetic sense on life. Surrealism, on the other hand, does not pretend to any notion of artistic or 'psychic' control – indeed, it actively renounces it. Echoes of Bürger's distinc-tion between modernism and the avant-garde can be heard here: where the interior monologue cultivates aesthetic style as a response to modernity, the avant-garde denounces it. The distinction can be put in terms of surface and depth: if mainstream modernism fore-grounds its stylistic surfaces, cultivating ever greater variations of 'pure style', then surrealism – which emerged, crucially, towards the end of modernism – views these surfaces as having reified into clichés, and so seeks rather to plumb the psychological depths, as Breton's retrospective summary in 1953 suggests: 'What was it all about then? Nothing less than the rediscovery of the secret of a language whose elements would then cease to float like jetsam on the surface of a dead sea' (MS: 297).

Given this rejection of aesthetic surface as a 'dead sea', it is striking that those who started as surrealists, but then moved away from it, often did so in terms that relate to the conscious cultivation of style. Michel Leiris provides one notable example in his essay 'The Autobiographer as *Torero*' ('De la littérature considérée comme une tauromachie'), written as the preface to his autobiography *Manhood* (1939). This preface is itself a kind of manifesto, arguing for the similarities between literature and bull-fighting, not as a mark of virility à la Hemingway, but as a way of giving existential importance to style: 'The matador who transforms danger into an occasion to be more brilliant than ever and reveals the whole quality of his style just when he is most threatened: that is what enthralled me, that is what I wanted to be.'[73] Leiris notes in this same preface that he had 'broken' with surrealism, and his turn towards style can be read as a mark of this.

A further, more obvious example is provided by Louis Aragon's *Treatise on Style* (1928). Aragon's treatise can be read as marking his break with surrealism; certainly its polemical, Nietzschean tone, as well as its call for a return to 'style', suggest a move beyond the surrealist status quo. 'It is time to return to the close reading of texts,' thunders Aragon, 'to the serious and applied analysis of the author's technique, of his style.'[74] Where he speaks of questions of style (despite his title, he wanders over a range of subjects in his haste to settle scores), Aragon strikes a defensive, self-consciously reactionary pose: 'It seems to be generally understood that one should not talk about style,' he ironizes (TS: 58). 'You don't know how to appreciate style and you see that as a good thing!' (TS: 62). Over the course of the whole first half of his book, Aragon mercilessly satirizes contemporaries from Gide to Valéry, from Freud to Einstein; in the final paragraph of this first section, he finally explains what underlies his diagnosis of the modern malaise:

> I see everything that is lacking as related to a coherent conception of style. All the errors, abuses, and idiosyncracies which have been the object of my attention for the last fifty pages can be explained by the current absence of any kind of coherent conception of style. (TS: 159)

In the second half of his treatise, Aragon makes his attack on surrealism and its attempts to invoke arbitrary moments of 'inspiration' explicit. 'Surrealism is [...] not a refuge against style. It is facile to think that the form and the content of surrealism are irrelevant and unrelated to each other. Neither the one nor the other, my friend' (TS: 189–90). Aragon's philippic thus makes clear *ex negativo* the extent to which an implicit rejection of style underlies the surrealist project. In pointed contrast to Breton, Aragon describes his aim in terms that seek to reinvest style with the authority that modernism ascribes to it, but that the avant-garde movements of Dada and surrealism would deny it: 'I am thus giving a very elevated sense to the word style. I am giving it back its beautiful dress; I am giving it back its purity of expression [*son regard très pur*]' (TS: 210). If Breton's *Surrealist Manifesto* suggests that the story of modernism and style ends with its death at the hands of the avant-garde Terrorists, Aragon's *Treatise on Style* attempts its resuscitation.

Conclusion

At the end of this study, it does not seem overstated to claim that the whole project of modernism is bound to the question of style. Style is, of course, intrinsic to all art. Indeed, one could argue that it is in a sense its very definition: either the aesthetics, ethics and politics of a work of art are contained and expressed through its style – or it is not a work of art. Style goes to the very heart of aesthetics, since it 'opens windows on both truth and beauty – a bewildering double vista'.[1] Both Rémy de Gourmont and John Middleton Murry see style in these terms as the very essence of aesthetic endeavour: the former writes in 1902 that 'if art is important, if civilization is important, the problem of style is important',[2] whilst the latter states in 1922 that 'style is not an isolable quality of writing; it is writing itself'.[3] Yet this latter statement also suggests the specifically modernist relationship to style: 'writing itself', rather than what is written about, emerges as a response to the anarchy of modernity. The turn to style can be understood in these terms as an attempt to make the aesthetic centre hold, to impose coherence on a world perceived as incoherent. In contrast to the classical tendency to identify successive period or national *styles*, the linguistic self-consciousness of modernism thematizes *style*. This is not to conclude that a single, monolithic conception of style imposes itself; as Finn Fordham observes, 'being mindful of the range of processes which emerges should qualify unitary conceptions of modernist styles, so that if modernism is going to be understood as unitary in any way, it is unified as a conflict – a conflict over different styles'.[4] Yet the Schopenhauerian insistence on the aesthetic as one of the few remaining spheres which offer the possibility of redemption inevitably foregrounds stylistic surface: modernist art worships the Flaubertian god of style *faute de mieux*.

This book has sought to trace the constitutive relationship of modernism to its own conceptions of style. Concentrating in particular on the genres of prose, poetry and the manifesto, it has attempted to show that from its earliest roots in the philosophy and literature of the 1850s to the last reverberations of late modernism in the 1940s – from *The Flowers of Evil* to *The Flowers of Tarbes*, so to speak – the relationship can be understood as a double movement, oscillating between the drive towards 'pure style' on the one hand and the suspicion of 'purely style', of mere rhetoric, on the other. Modernist style, in other words, is both skin and mask; it can be the vehicle of the greatest sincerity, and of the greatest insincerity. The pivot, the tipping point between these two extremes, is arguably to be found in the fetishization of 'decadent style': where style is reified, it is not far from the ultimate reification of death. 'Modernism comes into being as a cultural phenomenon unique to modernity', writes Roger Griffin, 'at the point at which the contemporary age is both experienced and expressed (constructed) by a critical mass of artists and intellectuals as an epoch not of progress and evolution, but of regression and involution: in a word, of *decadence*.'[5] Crucially, however, Griffin also suggests that 'modernism can be treated as "the revolt against decadence"',[6] rather than simply as its continuation. This implies that decadent style can be understood as the 'germ' of modernist style in both senses of the word, that is, positively (as a seed, as what Griffin would call a 'palinogenetic' beginning) and negatively (as Cioran's 'virus'). To see decadent style as the 'germ' at the heart of modernist style is thus to see modernism both as a development of decadence, and as a reaction against it (in particular, as an increasingly desperate attempt to refute the death-drive implicit in it). If every age produces the aesthetic tendencies it deserves, then modernism does justice to modernity precisely through this ambivalence: by foregrounding the constructive possibilities, but also the self-destructive difficulties, of its own style – and by making this thematization of style a constituent part of its project – it simultaneously embraces and rejects modernity. The 'doubleness' that this book has identified as characteristic of modernist views of style is a consequence not only of its ambivalent relationship to 'modernity', but also of its ambivalent relationship to its own self-conceptualization. Where nineteenth-century realists could be more or less confident in the validity of their attempts to depict industrialized Europe, twentieth-century modernists call into question not just modernity, but the very possibility of responding adequately to it. In cultivating 'modern' ways of expressing modernity, modernism also cultivates ways of fleeing it.

This opens up, of course, the possibility of a 'political' reading of modernism and style. Marxist critics such as Adorno or Bürger would argue that recourse to style is inherently reactionary, since it implies a flight from prevailing socio-economic conditions; pure style, for them, is by definition purely style. According to Adorno, 'it was plausible that socially progressive critics should have accused the program of *l'art pour l'art*, which has often been in league with political reaction, of promoting a fetish with the concept of a pure, exclusively self-sufficient artwork'.[7] The well-documented conservatism of many of the leading European modernists certainly suggests that this reading could be pursued; in the form of Dada and surrealism, meanwhile, the avant-garde edge of modernism reacted against this perceived reification of aesthetic style by attacking it as a self-fulfilling bourgeois construct. By this stage, then, modernism reacts not only against modernity, but against (previous forms of) modernism.

As this study has attempted to show, however, it is important to differentiate between the inherent expectations of the various genres: through their respective preconditions, the forms of poetry, prose and the manifesto impose differing conceptions of style. Through its formal structures, poetry initially suggests a degree of conservatism; the trick of much modernist poetry since Baudelaire is, of course, to subvert these expectations, developing a contemporary, modern style within traditional formal constraints. Whilst modernist poets either push these constraints to their extreme (Valéry's classical metre, Rilke's sonnets) or react against them (Eliotic *vers libre*), one way or another the sphere of the self-consciously 'poetic' implies expectations of 'grand style' with which to work. If prose, meanwhile, offers a more democratic, pluralistic model of writing, a degree of stylistic self-consciousness unites the modernist novel from Flaubert onwards. Style becomes a model, amongst others, for memory (Proust), morality (Mann), history (Joyce) and femininity (Woolf). The hypertrophied linguistic surfaces of late modernist works such as *Finnegans Wake* (1939) and *The Death of Virgil* (1945) – not to mention their very titles – suggest that by the end of the period, a new kind of decadent style emerges as the funeral march of modernism. The 'genre' of the manifesto, finally, tends by definition to impose an aggressive, polemical style. Nietzsche is arguably the patron saint of the modernist manifesto, not only in his attacks on the academic establishment of the day, but also in the relationship between the style and the substance of his arguments. (Indeed, one can pose the same basic question of Nietzsche's philosophical writings as of modernist manifestos: are they works of art?) Yet if the manifesto seeks to tear down existing stylistic dogma, in doing so it imposes a new orthodoxy, in particular through the performative relationship of argument to aesthetic. This grey area of self-reflexivity is itself characteristic of modernism, where it is often not so much what is being written about as the 'writing itself' that matters.

If modernism is defined by its relationship to its own conceptions of style, then this relationship is ultimately a contradictory one. The extreme 'saturation' of style culminates in its extreme renunciation; the extreme renunciation of style is contingent on its extreme saturation. The founding Flaubertian dream of writing about nothing *but* style is also the dream of writing about everything *through* style. The fact that the self-styled avant-garde movements sought to attack style, meanwhile, merely confirms its centrality to the modernist moment. If the problem of style endures, it is as the legacy of a period that sought to respond to the perceived formlessness of modernity with the form of high artistic seriousness; where 'one of the characteristics of modernism [was] a decline in the transfiguring function of art',[8] it compensated for this loss by an increased preoccupation – whether assenting or dissenting – with its own stylistic surfaces. To adapt the words of George Steiner, style is ultimately the 'metaphysics' of modernism.[9]

Notes

Introduction

1. Malcolm Bradbury and James McFarlane (eds), *Modernism: A Guide to European Literature 1890–1930* (London: Penguin, 1976), p. 29.
2. Fredric Jameson, 'Postmodernism and Consumer Society', in *The Anti-Aesthetic: Essays on Postmodern Culture*, ed. Hal Foster (Port Townsend: Bay Press, 1983), p. 114.
3. For an example of this much-used phrase, see David Harvey, *The Condition of Postmodernity: An Enquiry into the Origins of Cultural Change* (Oxford: Blackwell, 1990), which defines modernism as 'a troubled and fluctuating aesthetic response to conditions of modernity produced by a particular process of modernization' (p. 99).
4. See Roger Griffin, *Modernism and Fascism: The Sense of a Beginning under Mussolini and Hitler* (Basingstoke: Palgrave, 2007), esp. 'Introduction'.
5. Immanuel Kant, *The Critique of Judgement*, trans. James Creed Meredith (Oxford: Clarendon Press, 1952), p. 65.
6. Walter Pater, 'On Style', in *Essays on Literature and Art*, ed. Jennifer Uglow (London: Dent, 1973), p. 77.
7. Stéphane Mallarmé, 'Le Tombeau d'Edgar Poe', in *Poésies* (Paris: Flammarion, 1989), p. 99.
8. T.S. Eliot, 'Four Quartets', in *Collected Poems 1909–1962* (London: Faber & Faber, 1963), p. 218.
9. Paul Valéry, 'Poetry and Abstract Thought', in *The Art of Poetry*, trans. Denise Folliot (London: Routledge & Kegan Paul, 1958), pp. 52–81, here p. 81.
10. Robert Musil, *The Confusions of Young Törless*, trans. Shaun Whiteside (London: Penguin, 2001), p. 1.
11. William Carlos Williams, *Autobiography* (New York: New Directions, 1967), p. 380.
12. See, for instance, Bodo Müller, 'Der Verlust der Sprache. Zur linguistischen Krise in der Literatur', *Germanisch-Romanische Monatsschrift* 16 (1966), 225–43.

13. Letter to Louise Colet, 16 January 1852. *The Selected Letters of Gustave Flaubert*, trans. Francis Steegmuller (London: Hamish Hamilton, 1954), p. 131.
14. Theodor W. Adorno, *Aesthetic Theory*, trans. Robert Hullot-Kentor (London: Continuum, 2004), p. 229.
15. Thomas Mann, *Death in Venice*, trans. David Luke (London: Vintage, 1998), p. 207.
16. Angela Leighton, *On Form* (Oxford University Press, 2007), p. 2.
17. Ibid.
18. Susan Sontag, 'On Style', in *A Susan Sontag Reader* (London: Penguin, 1983), pp. 137–55, here p. 141 (originally published in *Against Interpretation*, New York: Farrar, Straus & Giroux, 1966).
19. Ibid., pp. 142–3.
20. Peter Gay, *Style in History* (New York: Basic Books, 1974), p. 3.
21. Sontag, 'On Style', p. 154.
22. Ibid., p. 153.
23. Thomas Mann, *Reflections of a Nonpolitical Man*, trans. Walter D. Morris (New York: Frederick Ungar, 1983), p. 55.
24. Geoffrey Hill, 'Tacit Pledges', in *Collected Critical Writings*, ed. Kenneth Haynes (Oxford University Press, 2008), p. 407.
25. 'Style signifie donc la manière dont quelqu'un s'exprime, *quoi qu'il exprime*.' Paul Valéry, *Vues* (Paris: La Table Ronde, 1948), p. 311.
26. 'Perfomative' is to be understood in J.L. Austin's famous sense: 'to utter the [performative] sentence is not to *describe* my doing of what I should be said in so uttering to be doing or to state that I am doing it: it is to do it'. J.L. Austin, *How to Do Things with Words* (Oxford University Press, 1971), p. 6.
27. Roland Barthes, *Writing Degree Zero*, trans. Annette Lavers and Colin Smith (London: Jonathan Cape, 1967), p. 9.
28. Adorno also identifies 'technique', which he defines – in terms that evoke the Kantian 'purposiveness without purpose' – as 'that whereby artworks are organized as purposeful in a way that is denied to empirical existence' (Adorno, *Aesthetic Theory*, p. 283).
29. Ibid., pp. 184–7.
30. Ibid., p. 187.
31. Ibid., p. 189.
32. Ibid., p. 269.
33. Ibid., p. 270.

34. See, for instance: 'The rank of an artwork is defined essentially by whether it exposes itself to, or withdraws from, the irreconcilable.' Ibid., p. 249.
35. Ibid., p. 270.
36. Ibid., p. 271.
37. Ibid.
38. In a 1973 essay in the *Times Literary Supplement*, George Steiner writes of how Adorno is 'persuasive on the characteristic narcissism in modern art, the reflexive use of the form of the work of art as the theme of the work. Following Benjamin, [Adorno] has sound suggestions regarding the modification of the concept of style through technological modes of reproduction.' See George Steiner, 'Adorno: Love and Cognition', *Times Literary Supplement*, 9 March 1973, pp. 253–5.
39. Adorno, *Aesthetic Theory*, p. 284.
40. Ibid., p. 328.
41. Ibid., p. 196.
42. Jean-Yves Tadié, *La Critique littéraire au XXe siècle* (Paris: Belfond, 1987), p. 10.
43. Ibid., p. 10.
44. Terry Eagleton, *Literary Theory: An Introduction* (Oxford: Blackwell, 1983), p. 3.
45. Tadié, *La Critique littéraire au XXe siècle*, p. 29.
46. Ibid., p. 30.
47. Roman Jakobson, 'Retrospect', in *Selected Writings I* (Berlin/New York/Amsterdam: Mouton, 1962), pp. 631–2, quoted in introduction to *Language in Literature* (Cambridge, MA: Harvard University Press, 1987), pp. 3–4.
48. Jakobson, 'Futurism', in *Language in Literature*, pp. 28–33, here p. 30.
49. Charles Baudelaire, 'The Painter of Modern Life', in *Selected Writings on Art and Artists* (Harmondsworth: Penguin, 1972), p. 403.
50. Rilke described one of his poems, 'The Ball', in these terms. See Elisabeth Schmidt-Pauli, *Rainer Maria Rilke. Ein Gedenkbuch* (Basel: Schwabe, 1940), p. 20.
51. Jakobson, 'Futurism', p. 32.
52. Erich Auerbach's influential study of realist forms of writing, *Mimesis* (1946), gives an historical overview of the development of these differing registers of style: as Jean-Yves Tadié writes, 'the history of European literature is [for Auerbach] none other than that of a metamorphosis:

that of stylistic levels (*niveaux stylistiques*)', Tadié, *La Critique littéraire au XXe siècle*, p. 59. See also Hans-Ulrich Gumbrecht, 'Schwindende Stabilität der Wirklichkeit. Eine Geschichte des Stilbegriffs', in *Stil. Geschichten und Funktionen eines kulturwissenschaftlichen Diskurselements*, ed. Hans Ulrich Gumbrecht and K. Ludwig Pfeiffer (Frankfurt: Suhrkamp, 1986), pp. 726–88, here pp. 774–6.

53. See Gumbrecht, 'Schwindende Stabilität der Wirklichkeit', esp. p. 753.

54. Letter to Louise Colet, 15 July 1853. *Selected Letters*, p. 155.

55. Quoted by Matei Calinescu, *Five Faces of Modernity* (Durham, NC: Duke University Press, 1987), pp. 72–3.

56. T.E. Hulme, 'Notes on Language and Style', in *Selected Writings*, ed. Patrick McGuinness (Manchester: Carcanet, 1998), pp. 39–40.

57. Quoted in the 'Prefatory Note' to William Empson, *Seven Types of Ambiguity* (London: Penguin, 1995), p. xiii.

58. F.R. Leavis, *The Common Pursuit* (London: Chatto & Windus, 1952), p. 31.

59. F.R. Leavis, *New Bearings in English Poetry* (London: Pelican, 1972), p. 48.

60. Ibid., p. 24.

61. Ibid.

62. Ibid., p. 144.

63. Ibid., p. 119.

64. Ibid., p. 120.

65. Ibid., p. 121.

66. Bridges quotes this in his preface to the 1918 edition of Hopkins' poems (see *Poems of Gerard Manley Hopkins* [London: Humphrey Milford, 1918], p. 12). Also quoted by Leavis, *New Bearings in English Poetry*, pp. 120–1.

67. Leavis, *New Bearings in English Poetry*, p. 121.

68. Ibid., p. 122.

69. Ibid., p. 129.

70. Ibid.

71. Stendhal, 'Racine et Shakespeare', quoted in John Middleton Murry, *The Problem of Style* (Oxford University Press, 1922), p. 3.

72. Murry claims that Swinburne, for instance, suffers from the 'hallucination' of hollow style without true feeling. See Murry, *The Problem of Style*, p. 22.

73. Ibid., pp. 10–11.

74. Ibid., p. 17.
75. Ibid., p. 136.
76. Both quoted in Herbert Read, *English Prose Style* (London: Bell, 1963), p. xvi.
77. Both quoted in ibid., p. xvi.
78. See e.g. K. Ludwig Pfeiffer, 'Produktive Labilität. Funktionen des Stilbegriffs', in *Stil. Geschichten und Funktionen eines kulturwissenschaftlichen Diskurselements*, pp. 685–725, esp. p. 709. Pfeiffer notes the obvious parallel with the rise of 'werkimmanente Interpretation' after the Second World War.
79. Alois Riegl, *Problems of Style*, trans. Evelyn Kain (Princeton University Press, 1993).
80. Wilhelm Worringer, *Abstraction and Empathy: A Contribution to the Psychology of Style* (London: Routledge and Kegan Paul, 1963), p. 9.
81. Ibid.
82. Ibid., p. vii.
83. Ibid., p. 34.
84. Heinrich Wölfflin, *Kunstgeschichtliche Grundbegriffe. Das Problem der Stilentwicklung in der neueren Kunst* (1915), translated as *Principles of Art History: The Problem of the Development of Style in Later Art*, trans. M.D. Hottinger (New York: Dover, 1950), p. 14. Wölfflin also refers to 'categories of beholding', p. 227.
85. Ibid., p. 10.
86. René Wellek, 'Stylistics, Poetics and Criticism', in *Literary Style: A Symposium* (Oxford University Press, 1971), pp. 65–76, here p. 70. Gumbrecht echoes this: 'In the 1920s, the humanities – particularly in Germany – were characterized by an almost "imperial" expansion of the paradigm of style.' Gumbrecht, 'Schwindende Stabilität der Wirklichkeit', p. 772.
87. *Die Insel*, vol. I, ed. Otto Julius Bierbaum, Alfred Walter Heymel and Rudolf Alexander Schröder (Berlin: Schuster & Loeffler, 1899), p. 2.
88. Heinrich Vogeler, *Erinnerungen* (Berlin: Rütter and Loening, 1952), p. 74.
89. Jan Andres, 'Gegenbilder. Stefan Georges poetische Kulturkritik in den "Zeitgedichten" des *Siebenten Rings*', *George-Jahrbuch* 6 (2006–7), pp. 31–54, here p. 41.
90. Stefan George, 'Das Wort', in *Werke*, vol. I (Munich: Deutscher Taschenbuch Verlag, 2000), pp. 466–7.

91. For an illuminating account of George's legacy, see Ulrich Raulff, *Kreis ohne Meister. Stefan Georges Nachleben* (Munich: Beck, 2009).

92. Tadié, *La Critique littéraire au XXe siècle*, p. 47.

93. See *Rainer Maria Rilke / Norbert von Hellingrath. Briefe und Dokumente*, ed. Klaus E. Bohnenkamp (Göttingen: Wallstein, 2008).

94. See Theodor W. Adorno, 'Parataxis. Zur späten Lyrik Hölderlins', in *Noten zur Literatur. Gesammelte Schriften II* (Frankfurt: Suhrkamp, 1974), pp. 447–91. Hölderlin had translated Pindar and Sophocles into a new kind of German, one which attempted to retain the movements of the Greek in the syntax of the German.

95. Friedrich Nietzsche, 'On Truth and Lying in a Nonmoral Sense', in *The Birth of Tragedy*, trans. Ronald Speirs (Cambridge University Press, 2009), p. 146.

96. Ibid., p. 148.

97. Hugo von Hofmannsthal, 'Ein Brief', in *Gesammelte Werke in Einzelausgaben. Prosa II*, ed. Herbert Steiner (Frankfurt: Fischer, 1976), pp. 7–20, here p. 8, my translation ('Rhetorik, die gut ist für Frauen oder für das Haus der Gemeinen, deren von unsrer Zeit so überschätzte Machtmittel aber nicht hinreichen, ins Innere der Dinge zu dringen').

98. Virginia Woolf, *The Waves* (London: Penguin, 1992), p. 121.

99. Equally characteristic of modernism, as we shall see in the course of this study, is the fact that Chandos understands this search as a rejection of 'rhetoric'.

100. Woolf, *The Waves*, p. 123.

101. Fritz Mauthner, *Beiträge zu einer Kritik der Sprache* (Leipzig: Felix Meiner, 1923), p. 6.

102. Rémy de Gourmont, *Le Problème du style* (Paris: Mercure de France, 1902), p. 9. Published in English in: Rémy de Gourmont, 'Selections from The Problem of Style', in *Selected Writings*, trans. Glenn S. Burne (Ann Arbor: University of Michigan Press, 1966), pp. 108–29, here p. 109.

103. Arthur Schopenhauer, 'On Style', in *Essays*, trans. T. Bailey Saunders (London: Allen and Unwin, 1951), pp. 13–28, here p. 13.

104. Walter Benjamin, 'The Image of Proust', in *Illuminations* (London: Fontana, 1973), p. 209. This is possibly the source for Susan Sontag's pronouncement in 'On Style': 'Raymond Bayer has written: [...] "Every work of art embodies a principle of proceeding, of stopping, of scanning; an image of energy or

relaxation, the imprint of a caressing or destroying hand which is [the artist's] alone." We can call this the physiognomy of the work, or its rhythm, or, as I would rather do, its style.' Sontag, *Against Interpretation*, pp. 148–9.

105. Benjamin, *Illuminations*, pp. 209–10.
106. Ibid., p. 197.
107. Albert Thibaudet, 'Marcel Proust et la tradition française', *Nouvelle Revue Française*, January 1923, p. 134.
108. Jean Starobinski, 'Préface' to Leo Spitzer, *Etudes de style* (Paris: Gallimard, 1970), p. 19.
109. Hans-Jörg Neuschäfer, 'Über das Konzept des Stils bei Leo Spitzer', in *Stil. Geschichten und Funktionen eines kulturwissenschaftlichen Diskurselements*, pp. 281–8, here pp. 284–5.
110. Ibid., p. 286.
111. Starobinski, *Etudes de style*, p. 23.
112. Ibid., p. 26.
113. Marcel Proust, *By Way of Sainte-Beuve*, trans. Sylvia Townsend Warner (London: Chatto & Windus, 1958), pp. 72–89, here p. 76.
114. Ibid., p. 92.
115. Ibid., p. 93.
116. Ibid., p. 195.
117. Ibid., p. 196.
118. Ibid., pp. 198–9.
119. Valéry, 'Poetry and Abstract Thought', in *The Art of Poetry*, p. 63.
120. Ibid., pp. 73–4.
121. Paul Valéry, 'Problems of Poetry', in *The Art of Poetry*, pp. 82–99, here p. 98.
122. Paul Valéry, 'Remarks on Poetry', in *The Art of Poetry*, pp. 196–215, here p. 211.
123. Paul Valéry, 'The Necessity of Poetry', in *The Art of Poetry*, pp. 216–30, here pp. 219–20.
124. Paul Valéry, *Tel Quel*, in *Œuvres*, ed. Jean Hytier (Paris: Gallimard, 1960), vol. II, p. 635.
125. Jakobson, 'The Dominant', in *Language in Literature*, pp. 41–6, here p. 46.
126. Jakobson, 'On Realism in Art', in *Language in Literature*, pp. 19–27, here p. 20.
127. See Roman Jakobson, 'Two Aspects of Language and Two Types of Aphasic Disturbance', in *Language in Literature*, pp. 95–114.

128. Quoted in Griffin, *Modernism and Fascism*, p. 94.
129. Henri Meschonnic, *Modernité modernité* (Paris: Gallimard Folio, 1993), p. 25.
130. It is worth noting that the year 1857 can only really be said to have this modernist resonance in France. That this is generally taken to be a milestone of European proportions is a mark of the subsequent influence of Flaubert and Baudelaire.
131. Roland Barthes, 'Style and its Image', in *Literary Style: A Symposium* (Oxford University Press, 1971), p. 10.
132. Ibid., p. 9.
133. Barthes, *Writing Degree Zero*, p. 18.
134. Barthes, 'Style and its Image', p. 6.
135. See F.L. Lucas, *Style* (London: Castell, 1955), p. 15.
136. Letter to Louise Colet, 24 April 1852. Gustave Flaubert, *Correspondance* (Paris: Conard, 1926), vol. II, p. 79.
137. Derrida explores this double movement in his speculations on Nietzsche's style as a 'spur'. See Jacques Derrida, *Spurs: Nietzsche's Styles*, trans. Barbara Harlow (University of Chicago Press, 1978), esp. pp. 37–41.
138. Adorno, *Aesthetic Theory*, p. 269.
139. Barthes, 'Style and its Image', p. 4.
140. Ursula Link-Heer, 'Maniera. Überlegungen zur Konkurrenz von Manier und Stil', in *Stil. Geschichten und Funktionen eines kulturwissenschaftlichen Diskurselements*, pp. 93–113, here p. 93.
141. Rémy de Gourmont praises them in these terms as the two representative modern philosophers. See Gourmont, *Le Problème du style*, p. 152 / Gourmont, *Selected Writings*, p. 128.

1 Philosophical Beginnings

1. Nietzsche writes in a *Nachlass* fragment of 1872 that Schopenhauer's rediscovery is to be credited to 'insignificant, indeed dubious literati'; see Friedrich Nietzsche, *Kritische Studienausgabe*, vol. VII (Berlin/New York: de Gruyter, 1980), p. 481. Where these notes have not been translated in the Cambridge *Writings from the Early Notebooks*, the translations (as here) are my own and the page references are given in the main text (listed as KSA).
2. Christopher Janaway, *Schopenhauer* (Oxford University Press, 1994), p. 101.

3. Bryan Magee adds Turgenev, Zola, Maupassant and Conrad. See Bryan Magee, *The Philosophy of Schopenhauer* (Oxford University Press, 1983), pp. 403–14.

4. Ibid., p. 244.

5. Janaway, *Schopenhauer*, pp. 33–4.

6. Arthur Schopenhauer, *The World as Will and Representation*, trans. E.F.J. Payne (New York: Dover, 1969), vol. I, p. 110.

7. Ibid., p. 196.

8. See the enlightening chapter 'Misunderstanding Schopenhauer', in Magee, *The Philosophy of Schopenhauer*, pp. 440–53.

9. Schopenhauer, *The World as Will and Representation*, p. 233.

10. Janaway, *Schopenhauer*, p. 64.

11. Magee, *The Philosophy of Schopenhauer*, p. 445.

12. Ibid., p. 244.

13. Much of the essay is indeed a tirade against the tendency of German syntax to get bogged down in its own clauses and sub-clauses.

14. Schopenhauer, 'On Style', p. 16.

15. Ibid., p. 13.

16. Hegel's triad recalls (although it is certainly not identical to) Goethe's influential essay of 1789, 'Einfache Nachahmung der Natur, Manier, Stil'. See Gumbrecht, 'Schwindende Stabilität der Wirklichkeit', pp. 757–62: with the help of Foucault, Gumbrecht identifies Goethe's and Hegel's concept of style as an 'epistemological threshold', after which the belief in a reliable correlation between object and representation starts to waver (p. 761).

17. G.W.F. Hegel, *Aesthetics: Lectures on Fine Art*, vol. I, trans. T.M. Knox (Oxford University Press, 1988), pp. 293–4.

18. Schopenhauer, 'On Style', p. 24.

19. Ibid., p. 16.

20. Ibid., p. 22.

21. Murry, *The Problem of Style*, p. 35.

22. Schopenhauer, 'On Style', p. 13. Rémy de Gourmont, who repeatedly describes style in terms of 'physiology', praises Schopenhauer, Taine and Nietzsche as philosophers who are also 'écrivains sensoriels'. See Gourmont, *Le Problème du style*, p. 70.

23. Schopenhauer, 'On Style', p. 24.

24. Ibid., p. 25.

25. The other two main reasons Wellbery gives are that Schopenhauer was 'the first philosopher to conceive of being as sheer enigma', and that 'his philosophy stripped mankind of the last remnants of its godlike status'. See *A New History of German Literature*, ed. David. E. Wellbery (London: Harvard University Press, 2004), pp. 594–6.

26. Ibid., p. 596.

27. Ibid., p. 597.

28. Nietzsche, *The Birth of Tragedy*, p. 33.

29. Schopenhauer, *The World as Will and Representation*, p. 240.

30. Ibid., p. 243.

31. Ibid., p. 244.

32. Ibid., p. 275.

33. Ibid., p. 257.

34. Walter Pater, *The Renaissance: Studies in Art and Poetry*, in *Walter Pater: Three Major Texts*, ed. William E. Buckler (New York University Press, 1986), p. 156.

35. Adorno, *Aesthetic Theory*, p. 270.

36. Edouard Dujardin, *The Bays are Sere and Interior Monologue*, trans. Anthony Suter (London: Libris, 1991), p. 133.

37. Ibid., p. 3.

38. Ibid., p. 116.

39. Antoine Baillot, *Influence de la philosophie de Schopenhauer en France (1860–1900)* (Paris: Vrin, 1927), p. 289.

40. Dujardin, *The Bays are Sere and Interior Monologue*, p. 135.

41. Baillot, *Influence de la philosophie de Schopenhauer en France*, pp. 287–8.

42. Schopenhauer, *The World as Will and Representation*, p. 308.

43. Douglas Thomas, *Reading Nietzsche Rhetorically* (New York: Guilford, 1999), p. 126.

44. He himself writes in a *Nachlass* fragment of his 'great uncertainty as to whether philosophy is an art or a science'. Friedrich Nietzsche, *Writings from the Early Notebooks*, trans. Ladislaus Löb (Cambridge University Press, 2009), p. 112.

45. Walter Kaufmann, *Nietzsche: Philosopher, Psychologist, Antichrist* (Princeton University Press, 1974), pp. 91–2. Kaufmann describes the final works from 1888 – *Twilight of the Idols, The Anti-Christ* and *Ecce Homo* – as 'sui generis'.

46. Friedrich Nietzsche, *Untimely Meditations*, trans. R.J. Hollingdale (Cambridge University Press, 1997), p. 49.

47. Kaufmann, *Nietzsche*, pp. 92–3.

48. Nietzsche, *The Birth of Tragedy*, p. 33.

49. See Eric Hobsbawm and Terence Ranger (eds), *The Invention of Tradition* (Cambridge University Press, 1983).
50. Nietzsche, *Untimely Meditations*, p. 234.
51. Ibid., p. 5.
52. Ibid., p. 6.
53. Ibid.
54. Ibid., p. 48.
55. Ibid., p. 80.
56. Barthes, *Writing Degree Zero*, p. 46.
57. Friedrich Nietzsche, *Nietzsche contra Wagner*, in *The Anti-Christ, Ecce Homo, Twilight of the Idols*, trans. Judith Norman (Cambridge University Press, 2005), pp. 263–82, here p. 282.
58. Thomas, *Reading Nietzsche Rhetorically*, p. 9.
59. See Gilles Deleuze, *Nietzsche and Philosophy* (London: Athlone, 1983 [French 1962]).
60. Thomas, *Reading Nietzsche Rhetorically*, p. 173.
61. Friedrich Nietzsche, *On the Genealogy of Morals,* trans. C. Diethe (Cambridge University Press, 2002), p. 78.
62. Thomas, *Reading Nietzsche Rhetorically*, p. 2.
63. Ibid., p. 163.
64. Nietzsche, *Writings from the Early Notebooks*, p. 110.
65. Nietzsche himself noted in 1874 that 'beautiful style is admittedly nothing more than a new cage' (KSA 7, 834).
66. Adorno, *Aesthetic Theory*, p. 135.
67. Nietzsche, 'On Truth and Lying in a Nonmoral Sense', in *The Birth of Tragedy*, p. 146.
68. Nietzsche, *Writings from the Early Notebooks*, p. 110.
69. Friedrich Nietzsche, *Human, All Too Human*, trans. R.J. Hollingdale (Cambridge University Press, 1996), p. 334.
70. Ibid., pp. 332–3.
71. Ibid., p. 342.
72. Ibid., pp. 337–44.
73. Friedrich Nietzsche, *Writings from the Late Notebooks*, trans. Kate Sturge (Cambridge University Press, 2003), p. 226.
74. Friedrich Nietzsche, *The Gay Science*, trans. Josefine Nauckhoff (Cambridge University Press, 2001), pp. 163–4.
75. Hans-Martin Gauger, 'Nietzsches Auffassung vom Stil', in *Stil. Geschichten und Funktionen eines kulturwissenschaftlichen Diskurselements*, pp. 200–15, here p. 203. See this essay for a close reading of the ten points of 'Zur Lehre vom Stil'.
76. Kaufmann, *Nietzsche*, p. 312.

77. Ibid., p. 128.
78. See section 5 of Nietzsche, *The Birth of Tragedy*, p. 30.
79. Ibid., p. 8.
80. Ibid., p. 9.
81. For a concise account of Nietzsche's views on Schopenhauer, see Christopher Janaway, *Self and World in Schopenhauer's Philosophy* (Oxford: Clarendon Press, 1989), pp. 342–56.
82. See ibid., p. 343.
83. See ibid., p. 345.
84. Ibid., p. 355.
85. Nietzsche, *On the Genealogy of Morals*, p. 78.
86. Friedrich Nietzsche, *The Case of Wagner*, in *The Anti-Christ, Ecce Homo, Twilight of the Idols*, pp. 231–62, here p. 233.
87. Ibid.
88. Nietzsche, *The Case of Wagner*, p. 240.
89. Ibid., p. 242.
90. Ibid., p. 245.
91. Paul Bourget, *Essais de psychologie contemporaine* (Paris: Plon, 1883), p. 20.
92. As Karl Heinz Bohrer notes, however, Nietzsche never really took into account the implications of his political comments for contemporary politics. See Karl Heinz Bohrer, *Großer Stil. Form und Formlosigkeit in der Moderne* (Munich: Hanser, 2007), pp. 25 and 28.
93. Nietzsche, *The Case of Wagner*, p. 243.
94. Ibid., p. 244.
95. Ibid., p. 260.
96. Friedrich Nietzsche, *Twilight of the Idols*, in *The Anti-Christ, Ecce Homo, Twilight of the Idols*, pp. 153–229, here pp. 197–8 (translation modified).
97. Peter Nicholls, *Modernisms* (Berkeley: University of California Press, 1995), p. 72.
98. Bohrer, *Großer Stil*, p. 49.
99. Ibid., p. 48.
100. Friedrich Nietzsche, *Ecce Homo*, in *The Anti-Christ, Ecce Homo, Twilight of the Idols*, pp. 69–151, here p. 104.
101. Bohrer, *Großer Stil*, p. 233.
102. Derrida, *Spurs*, p. 39.
103. Bohrer, *Großer Stil*, p. 232.
104. See ibid., p. 234.
105. Ibid.

2 1857: Literary Beginnings

1. Louis Thomas, *Curiosités sur Baudelaire* (Paris, 1912), p. 34, quoted by Walter Benjamin, *The Arcades Project*, trans. Howard Eiland and Kevin McLaughlin (Cambridge, MA: Belknap, 1999), p. 246.
2. Nicholls, *Modernisms*, p. 12.
3. Letter to Ivan Turgenev, 13 November 1872. *The Letters of Gustave Flaubert 1857–1880*, ed. Francis Steegmuller (Cambridge, MA: Belknap, 1982), vol. II, p. 200.
4. Nicholls, *Modernisms*, p. 11.
5. Ibid., p. 19.
6. Proust's first essay on Flaubert, 'Mondanité et mélomanie de Bouvard et Pecuchet', was published as early as 1896.
7. Marcel Proust, 'A propos du style de Flaubert', in *Chroniques* (Paris: Gallimard, 1927), pp. 193–211, here p. 193.
8. Ibid., p. 196.
9. Ibid., p. 202.
10. Ibid., p. 194.
11. Ibid., pp. 198–9.
12. Ibid., p. 199.
13. Ibid., p. 195.
14. This essay, dated to 1910, was only published in the Pléaide edition of *Contre Sainte-Beuve*. See Marcel Proust, 'A ajouter à Flaubert', in *Contre Sainte-Beuve* (Paris: Pléiade, 1971), p. 299.
15. Ezra Pound, 'Hugh Selwyn Mauberley', in *Selected Poems 1908–1969* (London: Faber & Faber, 1975), p. 98.
16. Rainer Maria Rilke, *The Notebooks of Malte Laurids Brigge*, trans. Burton Pike (Champaign and London: Dalkey Archive, 2008), p. 53.
17. Charles Baudelaire, *The Flowers of Evil*, trans. James McGowan (Oxford University Press, 1993), pp. 59–60.
18. Ibid., p. 63.
19. Gottfried Benn, 'Little Aster', in *Primal Vision: Selected Writings*, trans. Babette Deutsch (London: Marion Boyars, 1976), p. 213.
20. Benn, *Double Life*, in *Primal Vision*, p. 180.
21. Gourmont, *Selected Writings*, p. 124.
22. Murry, *The Problem of Style*, p. 89.
23. Letter to Louise Colet, 16 January 1852. Flaubert, *Selected Letters*, p. 131.

24. Letter to Louise Colet, 15 August 1846. Ibid., p. 87.
25. Maurice Bardèche, *L'Œuvre de Flaubert* (Paris: Les Sept Couleurs, 1974), p. 194.
26. Antoine Baillot implies that one can understand Flaubert's doctrine of 'l'art pur' as a reaction to Schopenhauer's philosophy of pessimism, where art becomes the metaphysical consolation outlined by Schopenhauer. See Baillot, *Influence de la philosophie de Schopenhauer en France*, pp. 210–23.
27. Flaubert implies as much in a later letter to the *frères* Goncourt (3 July 1860), writing that 'the standard of the Doctrine [*l'art pour l'art*] will be boldly unfurled this time, you may be sure' (Flaubert, *Selected Letters*, p. 192).
28. Ibid., p. 123.
29. Ibid., p. 17.
30. Quoted by Pierre Bourdieu, *Les Règles de l'art* (Paris: Seuil, 1992), p. 138. Bourdieu speaks of Flaubert's 'formalisme réaliste' (p. 157).
31. Quoted in *Flaubert*, ed. Claude Mouchard and Jacques Neefs (Paris: Balland, 1986), p. 380.
32. Bourget, *Essais de psychologie contemporaine*, p. 164.
33. Arthur Symons, *The Symbolist Movement in Literature* (New York: Haskell, 1971), p. 103.
34. Paul Valéry, 'La Tentation de (Saint) Flaubert' (1944), in *Œuvres I* (Paris: Gallimard, 1957), pp. 613–19, here p. 614.
35. Valéry makes the oscillation between these two extremes the precondition for literature in general: 'Literature moves between realism and nominalism – between belief in exact description, in the creation of objects through words – and the free play of words.' Valéry, *Tel Quel*, in *Œuvres II*, p. 639.
36. Letter to Louise Colet, 20 March 1852. Flaubert, *Selected Letters*, p. 133.
37. Letter to Louise Colet, 6 July 1852. Ibid., p. 140.
38. Vladimir Nabokov, 'Madame Bovary', in *Lectures on Literature* (London: Weidenfeld & Nicolson, 1980), pp. 125–78, here p. 147. Nabokov's notes include an appendix on 'Style', in which he discusses Flaubert's use of what he calls the 'semicolon-and', 'the unfolding method', his 'method of rendering emotions [...] through an exchange of meaningless words', and the imperfect tense (pp. 171–4).
39. Ibid., p. xxiii.
40. Letter to Louise Colet, 24 April 1852. Flaubert, *Selected Letters*, p. 135.

41. Letter to George Sand, 20 December 1875. Ibid., p. 230.
42. Letter to Louise Colet, 15 January 1853. Ibid., p. 146.
43. Letter to Leroyer de Chantepie, 18 March 1857. Ibid., p. 186.
44. Letter to Ivan Turgenev, 14 December 1876. Ibid., p. 234.
45. Letter to Louise Colet, 18 September 1846. Ibid., p. 90.
46. Letter to Louise Colet, 12 January 1852. Ibid., p. 130.
47. Letter to Louis Bouilhet, 10 February 1851. Ibid., p. 120.
48. Letter to Louise Colet, September 1851. Ibid., p. 127.
49. Letter to Louise Colet, 1 February 1852. Ibid., p. 132.
50. Quoted by Bourget, *Essais de psychologie contemporaine*, p. 190.
51. Ibid., p. 170.
52. See ibid., pp. 127–74, esp. pp. 170–1.
53. Letter to Leroyer de Chantepie, 18 March 1857. Flaubert, *Selected Letters*, p. 186.
54. Jonathan Culler, *Flaubert: The Uses of Uncertainty* (New York: Cornell, 1974), p. 13.
55. There are counter-examples: Proust wrote of the 'mediocrity' of the correspondence, maintaining that the critical statements about style in the letters are not borne out by the style of the letters themselves.
56. Letter to Louise Colet, 27 March 1853. Flaubert, *Selected Letters*, p. 148.
57. Bourget, *Essais de psychologie contemporaine*, p. 182.
58. Nabokov, *Lectures on Literature*, p. 125.
59. Culler, *Flaubert*, p. 15.
60. Letter to Louise Colet, 8 August 1846. Flaubert, *Selected Letters*, p. 74.
61. Quoted in *Flaubert*, ed. Mouchard and Neefs, p. 378.
62. Bourget, *Essais de psychologie contemporaine*, p. 171.
63. Ibid., p. 187.
64. Ibid., p. 173.
65. Michael Hamburger, *The Truth of Poetry* (London: Anvil, 1996), p. 4.
66. Baillot, *Influence de la philosophie de Schopenhauer en France*, p. 19.
67. Ibid., pp. 208–9.
68. Letter to Charles Baudelaire, 13 July 1857. Flaubert, *Selected Letters*, p. 187.
69. Arthur Rimbaud, Letter to Paul Demeny, 15 May 1871. Arthur Rimbaud, *Collected Poems* (London: Penguin, 1962), p. 12.
70. Rimbaud, *Collected Poems*, p. 16.

71. Baudelaire, *The Flowers of Evil*, p. 79.
72. Paul Valéry, 'Situation de Baudelaire', *Œuvres I*, pp. 598–613, here p. 604.
73. T.S. Eliot, 'Baudelaire in our Time', in *For Lancelot Andrewes: Essays on Style and Order* (London: Faber & Gwyer, 1928), pp. 86–99, here p. 97.
74. T.S. Eliot, 'Baudelaire' (1930), in *Selected Essays* (London: Faber & Faber, 1999), pp. 419–30, here pp. 423–4.
75. Adorno, *Aesthetic Theory*, p. 309.
76. Jules Levallois, *Milieu de siècle. Mémoires d'un critique* (Paris: Librairie illustrée, 1895), p. 94, quoted in Benjamin, *The Arcades Project*, pp. 240–1.
77. Letter to Charles Baudelaire, 13 July 1857. Flaubert, *Selected Letters*, p. 187.
78. Letter to Clara Westhoff, 23 October 1907. Rainer Maria Rilke, *Letters on Cézanne*, trans. Joel Agee (London: Jonathan Cape, 1988), p. 85 (translation modified).
79. Rilke to Clara Westhoff, 19 October 1907. Ibid., p. 67.
80. Hamburger, *The Truth of Poetry*, p. 7.
81. Charles Baudelaire, 'Madame Bovary', in *Œuvres complètes* (Paris: Pléiade, 1961), pp. 647–57, here pp. 651–2.
82. J.B. Ratermanis, *Etude sur le style de Baudelaire* (Bade: Editions Art et Science Bade, 1949), p. 19. Ratermanis' own study is a Spitzerian analysis of 'all the "expressive" constants' in Baudelaire's poetry (p. 25).
83. Ibid., p. 495.
84. Sartre dedicated the third volume of his study of Flaubert, *L'Idiot de la famille*, to the author's 'névrose objective'.
85. Hermann Bahr, *Zur Überwindung des Naturalismus. Theoretische Schriften 1887–1904*, ed. Gotthart Wunberg (Stuttgart: Kohlhammer, 1968), p. 87.
86. Clive Scott, 'Symbolism, Decadence and Impressionism', in *Modernism*, ed. Bradbury and McFarlane, pp. 206–27, here p. 214.
87. T.S. Eliot, 'The Love Song of J. Alfred Prufrock', in *Collected Poems 1909–1962* (London: Faber & Faber, 1963), p. 17.
88. Eliot, *Collected Poems*, p. 67.
89. Hugo von Hofmannsthal, 'Briefe des Zurückgekehrten', in *Erzählungen* (Stuttgart: Reclam, 2000), p. 192.
90. T.S. Eliot, 'The Perfect Critic', in *The Sacred Wood* (London: Faber & Faber, 1997), p. 4.
91. Symons, *The Symbolist Movement in Literature*, p. 3.

92. Ibid., p. 35.
93. Ibid., p. 115.
94. Scott, 'Symbolism, Decadence and Impressionism', p. 212.
95. Symons, *The Symbolist Movement in Literature*, pp. 5 and 46.
96. Jean Moréas, 'Le Symbolisme', *Le Figaro*, 18 September 1886, Supplément littéraire, pp. 1–2.
97. Edmond Scherer, *Etudes sur la littérature contemporaine*, vol. IV (Paris, 1886), p. 288, quoted by Benjamin, *The Arcades Project*, p. 249.
98. Théophile Gautier, 'Charles Baudelaire', in *The Works of Théophile Gautier*, trans. F.C. de Sumichrast, vol. XXIII ('Art and Criticism') (New York, 1900), pp. 17–126, here p. 122.
99. Ibid., p. 84.
100. Ibid., pp. 39–40.
101. Ibid., p. 40.
102. Baudelaire, *The Flowers of Evil*, p. 119.
103. Ibid., p. 249.
104. Charles Baudelaire, *Artificial Paradise*, trans. Ellen Fox (New York: Herder and Herder, 1971), p. 69. See Ratermanis, *Etude sur le style de Baudelaire*, p. 25: 'Admittedly Baudelaire is describing the sensations of an opium-eater [he means hashish] – yet he himself was one.'
105. For a useful introduction to this influence, see Hamburger, *The Truth of Poetry*; for a classic, if arguably dated, overview, see Hugo Friedrich, *Die Struktur der modernen Lyrik* (Hamburg: Rowohlt, 1956).
106. Symons, *The Symbolist Movement in Literature*, p. 1.
107. Ibid., p. 6.
108. This is the line Helmuth Kiesel takes in his *Geschichte der literarischen Moderne* (Munich: Beck, 2004), esp. pp. 198–222.
109. Symons, *The Symbolist Movement in Literature*, pp. 111–12.
110. Ibid., p. 110.
111. Baudelaire, *The Flowers of Evil*, p. 293.

3 The 'Virus of Prose': Decadent Style and the Modernist Novel

1. Charles Baudelaire, *Paris Spleen*, trans. Martin Sorrell (London: Oneworld, 2010), p. 3.
2. Virginia Woolf, 'Impassioned Prose', in *Selected Essays* (London: Penguin, 2008), pp. 55–62, here p. 57.

3. Virginia Woolf, 'Poetry, Fiction and the Future', in ibid., pp. 74–84, here pp. 80, 83.

4. E.M. Cioran, 'Style as Risk', in *The Temptation to Exist*, trans. Richard Howard (London: Quartet, 1987), pp. 126–35, here p. 130.

5. See Nicholls, *Modernisms*, p. 47.

6. Clive Scott writes that the '"stream of consciousness" technique is as much a result of Impressionism as of advances in psychology'. See Scott, 'Symbolism, Decadence and Impressionism', p. 222.

7. For a more sustained analysis of the style of Dujardin's novel, see Ben Hutchinson, 'Une Ecriture blanche? Style and Symbolism in *Les Lauriers sont coupés*', *Modern Language Review* 106.3 (July 2011), 709–23.

8. See C.D. King, 'Edouard Dujardin, Inner Monologue and the Stream of Consciousness', *French Studies* 6.2 (1953), 116–28, here 126–7.

9. Dujardin, *The Bays are Sere and Interior Monologue*, p. 113.

10. Melvin J. Friedman, 'The Symbolist Novel: From Huysmans to Malraux', in *Modernism*, ed. Bradbury and McFarlane, pp. 453–66, here p. 453.

11. Karl D. Uitti, *The Concept of Self in the Symbolist Novel* (The Hague: Mouton, 1961), p. 45.

12. Dujardin, *The Bays are Sere and Interior Monologue*, p. 32.

13. Friedman concludes that 'The sameness of Prince's thoughts, the recurrence of certain haunting images, the repeated identifications of time and place, all instruments for separating the novel from an externally defined world or a familiar structure of cause and effect, aptly fit Forster's definition in *Aspects of the Novel* of "easy rhythm": "repetition plus variation".' Friedman, 'The Symbolist Novel', p. 455.

14. See Scott, 'Symbolism, Decadence and Impressionism', pp. 212–14. He gives an example from Arthur Symons' verse, but suggests that Symons takes the technique from Laforgue and Verlaine: 'And now the stealthy dancer comes | Undulantly with cat-like steps that cling.'

15. Dujardin, *The Bays are Sere and Interior Monologue*, pp. 30–2.

16. Ibid., p. 47.

17. Amongst the stylistic idiosyncracies which he lists as characteristic of the period (use of specific suffixes ['-ment', '-erie', '-ité', '-ance', '-ure', '-aire', '-al', '-escent', '-eur']; neologisms; inversions; 'échanges de fonctions' [e.g. adjectives or adverbs used

as nouns]; elisions and omissions [particularly through the use of ellipsis]; misuse of prepositions), Gérald Antoine foregrounds in particular the use of the suffix '-ment' to produce a noun (e.g. 'bougement', 'brillement'), claiming that 'if one combines this with the frequency of adverbs ending in *–ment*, equally abundant, it becomes clear that this is a major characteristic, *both lexically and phonetically*, of poetic language after 1880' (his italics). See Gérald Antoine, 'La Langue poétique', in *Histoire de la langue francaise 1880–1914* (Paris: CNRS, 1999), pp. 435–66, here p. 460.

18. Dujardin, *The Bays are Sere and Interior Monologue*, p. 46.
19. Barthes, *Writing Degree Zero*, p. 82.
20. Ibid., p. 83.
21. Rémy de Gourmont, *Esthétique de la langue française* (Paris, 1913), p. 130. (Quoted in Uitti, *The Concept of Self in the Symbolist Novel*, p. 43).
22. Uitti suggests that 'Dujardin's "deformed" syntax is to the prose of the realist novel what *vers libre* is to metrical verse.' Uitti, *The Concept of Self in the Symbolist Novel*, p. 47.
23. Calinescu, *Five Faces of Modernity*, p. 169.
24. Bourget, *Essais de psychologie contemporaine*, p. 20. Barthes himself says something similar: 'modern poetry destroyed relationships in language and reduced discourse to words as static things'. Barthes, *Writing Degree Zero*, p. 55.
25. Emile Verhaeren, *Impressions* (Paris: Mercure de France, 1926), p. 124.
26. Henri Mitterand, 'De l'écriture artiste au style décadent', in *Histoire de la langue francaise 1880–1914* (Paris: CNRS, 1999), pp. 467–77, here p. 473.
27. Gourmont, *Selected Writings*, p. 118.
28. Nicholls, *Modernisms*, p. 57.
29. Ibid., pp. 45–58.
30. Gautier, 'Charles Baudelaire', p. 40.
31. Nicholls, *Modernisms*, p. 46.
32. Ibid., p. 60.
33. Murry, *The Problem of Style*, p. 86.
34. Well before Freud, scientists such as Richard von Krafft-Ebing in his *Psychopathia Sexualis* (1886) had begun to classify the sexual neuroses and perversions of the late nineteenth-century bourgeoisie, whilst Max Nordau's bestseller *Entartung* (1892–93) famously denounced the whole age as decadent.
35. Nicholls, *Modernisms*, p. 60.

36. This relationship between narrative and sexual tension is explored most famously by Roland Barthes in his *Le Plaisir du texte* (1973), where his discussion of 'rhythm' and 'jouissance' is applied to both the body and the text.

37. Dujardin claims that Schnitzler had not read *Les Lauriers sont coupés* before writing *Lieutenant Gustl*, although he also claims that after the publication of Schnitzler's story, the Danish critic Georg Brandès told the Austrian to read Dujardin's novel. See Dujardin, *The Bays are Sere and Interior Monologue*, p. 97.

38. Sigmund Freud, in *Briefe an Arthur Schnitzler*, ed. Heinrich Schnitzler, *Neue Rundschau* 66 (1955), pp. 95–106, here p. 97.

39. For a comparison of the two stories, see Theodor W. Alexander and Beatrice Alexander, 'Schnitzler's *Leutnant Gustl* and Dujardin's *Les lauriers sont coupés*', *Modern Austrian Literature* 2.2 (1969), 7–15.

40. Arthur Schnitzler, 'Leutnant Gustl', in *Der blinde Geronimo und sein Bruder* (Frankfurt: Fischer, 1989), pp. 9–42, here p. 29.

41. For a discussion of the physical manifestations of Mann's 'decadence', see Anna Katharina Schaffner, 'Richard von Krafft-Ebing's *Psychopathia Sexualis* and Thomas Mann's *Buddenbrooks*: Exchanges between Scientific and Imaginary Accounts of Sexual Deviance', *Modern Language Review* 106.2 (April 2011), 477–94.

42. Thomas Mann, *Tonio Kröger*, in *Death in Venice & Other Stories* (London: Vintage, 1998), p. 158.

43. Ibid., p. 158.

44. Ibid., pp. 158–9.

45. Ibid., p. 160.

46. Ibid., p. 157.

47. Ibid., p. 167.

48. Ibid., p. 194.

49. Mann, *Reflections of a Nonpolitical Man*, p. 398.

50. Ibid., p. 401.

51. Ibid., p. 416.

52. Mann, *Death in Venice*, p. 265.

53. Thomas Mann, 'Der Künstler und der Literat', in *Reden und Aufsätze*, vol. I (Frankfurt: Fischer, 1965), pp. 113–21, here p. 118.

54. Ibid., p. 119.

55. Ibid., p. 116.

56. Ibid., p. 117.

57. Ibid., p. 116.
58. Ibid., p. 117.
59. Virginia Woolf, 'Modern Fiction', in *Selected Essays*, pp. 6–12, here p. 9.
60. See Griffin, *Modernism and Fascism*, pp. 61–4.
61. For an introduction to the motif of the 'privileged moment' in modernist literature, see E.F.N. Jephcott, *Proust and Rilke: The Literature of Expanded Consciousness* (London: Chatto & Windus, 1972), ch. 1 (pp. 15–31).
62. Marcel Proust, *Time Regained*, in *Remembrance of Things Past*, vol. III, trans. C.K. Scott Moncrieff, Terence Kilmartin and Andreas Mayor (London: Chatto & Windus, 1981), p. 905.
63. Ibid., p. 916.
64. Ibid., pp. 931–2.
65. Ibid., p. 921.
66. Ibid., pp. 924–5.
67. Proust, 'A propos du style de Flaubert', p. 193.
68. Gérard Genette, 'Proust Palimpsest', in *Figures of Literary Discourse* (Oxford: Blackwell, 1982), pp. 203–28, here p. 204.
69. This recalls, perhaps, Roman Jakobson's famous distinction between realism as tending to metonymy and romanticism as tending to metaphor.
70. Proust, *Within a Budding Grove*, in *Remembrance of Things Past*, vol. I, pp. 666–7.
71. Proust, 'Chardin', in *By Way of Sainte-Beuve*, pp. 249–50, quoted by Genette, 'Proust Palimpsest', p. 207.
72. Genette, 'Proust Palimpsest', pp. 207–8.
73. Proust, *Time Regained*, p. 1102.
74. Genette, 'Proust Palimpsest', p. 218.
75. Ibid., p. 214.
76. Ibid., p. 213.
77. Woolf, 'Modern Fiction', p. 10.
78. Ibid., p. 9.
79. Quoted by Richard Ellmann in the introduction to Stanislaus Joyce, *My Brother's Keeper* (London: Faber & Faber, 1958), p. 23.
80. In his celebrated essay 'The Fox and the Hedgehog', Isaiah Berlin assigns Proust to the hedgehogs and Joyce to the foxes (see Isaiah Berlin, 'The Fox and the Hedgehog', in *Russian Thinkers* [London: Penguin, 1994], pp. 22–81, here pp. 22–3).
81. Letter of 10 December 1921. *James Joyce: Letters*, ed. Stuart Gilbert (London: Faber & Faber, 1957), p. 179.

82. Arthur Power, *Conversations with James Joyce* (London: Millington, 1974), p. 95.
83. Wolfgang Iser, *The Implied Reader* (London: Johns Hopkins University Press, 1974), pp. 191–2.
84. Ibid., p. 185.
85. See Stuart Gilbert, *James Joyce's Ulysses* (London: Faber & Faber, 1930).
86. S.L. Goldberg, *The Classical Temper: A Study of James Joyce's Ulysses* (London: Chatto & Windus, 1961), p. 288.
87. James Joyce, *Ulysses* (London: Penguin, 1992), p. 500.
88. Iser, *The Implied Reader*, p. 186.
89. Ibid., p. 189.
90. Ibid., p. 192.
91. Ibid., p. 202.
92. Virginia Woolf, *The Diary of Virginia Woolf*, vol. II (London: Harcourt Brace Jovanovich, 1978), p. 203 (entry for 26 September 1922).
93. T.S. Eliot, 'Contemporary English Prose', *Vanity Fair* 20 (July 1923), p. 51. First published in French in *Nouvelle Revue Française* 19 (1 December 1922).
94. Ibid.
95. Iser, *The Implied Reader*, p. 191.
96. Jean Moréas, 'Le Symbolisme', *Le Figaro*, 18 September 1886, Supplément littéraire, pp. 1–2.
97. Rémy de Gourmont, *Esthétique de la langue francaise*, p. 130.
98. Murry, *The Problem of Style*, p. 65.
99. Iser, *The Implied Reader*, p. 201.
100. Nicholls, *Modernisms*, p. 274.
101. Benjamin, *The Arcades Project*, p. 460.
102. Samuel Beckett, *Disjecta*, ed. Ruby Cohn (London: John Calder, 2001), p. 172.
103. Iser, *The Implied Reader*, p. 205.
104. Virginia Woolf, 'Women and Fiction', in *Selected Essays*, pp. 132–9.
105. Ibid., p. 135.
106. Ibid., p. 136.
107. Nicholls, *Modernisms*, p. 202. Nicholls takes the phrase 'Men of 1914' from Wyndham Lewis' *Blasting and Bombardiering* (1937).
108. Nicholls, *Modernisms*, pp. 202–4.
109. Woolf, *The Waves*, p. 58.
110. Finn Fordham, *I do I undo I redo: The Textual Genesis of Modernist Selves* (Oxford University Press, 2010), p. 237.

111. Ibid., p. 238.
112. Virginia Woolf, *A Writer's Diary*, ed. Leonard Woolf (London: Hogarth Press, 1975), p. 137.
113. Rémy de Gourmont, *Decadence and Other Essays on the Culture of Ideas* (New York: Harcourt Brace, 1921), p. 124.
114. Nicholls, *Modernisms*, p. 222.
115. Paul Rosenfeld, 'James Joyce's Jabberwocky', *Saturday Review of Literature*, 6 May 1939, pp. 10–11. Quoted in *James Joyce: The Critical Heritage*, ed. Robert H. Deming (London: Routledge, 1970), p. 663.
116. See http://www.guardian.co.uk/books/2002/aug/17/fromthear chives.jamesjoyce
117. Hermann Broch, *Der Tod des Vergil* (Frankfurt: Suhrkamp, 1976), p. 197.
118. Ibid., p. 454.
119. See for instance ibid., p. 198.
120. Valéry, *Tel Quel*, in *Œuvres II*, pp. 634–5.

4 1922: Style and the Modernist Lyric

1. Paul Valéry, *Mauvaises pensées et autres*, in *Œuvres*, ed. Jean Hytier (Paris: Gallimard, 1960), vol. II, p. 864. Hereafter cited in main text as *Œuvres*.
2. As Charles Whiting amongst others points out, this period of 'silence' is strictly speaking a myth: 'Throughout the silence there was a frequent output of unpublished prose and verse and short prose poems. Between 1892 and 1900 Valéry still appeared in print.' Charles G. Whiting, *Paul Valéry* (London: Athlone, 1978), p. 6.
3. *Correspondance André Gide – Paul Valéry*, ed. Robert Mallet (Paris: Gallimard, 1955), p. 493.
4. Jean Hytier, *La Poétique de Valéry* (Paris: Armand Colin, 1953), p. 40.
5. Paul Valéry, *Cahiers/Notebooks*, ed. Brian Stimpson, trans. Norma Rinsler, Brian Stimpson, Rima Joseph and Paul Ryan (Frankfurt: Peter Lang, 2010), vol. IV, p. 62. Hereafter cited in main text as *Notebooks*.
6. Valéry, *Vues*, p. 313.
7. Rémy de Gourmont anticipates this line of criticism, writing of the Port Royal writers in 1902 that 'beauty suggests neither piety nor contrition, and the glory of God

resounds principally in works of a more humble mentality and more mediocre rhetoric'. Gourmont, *Le Problème du style*, p. 48.

8. See Jean Paulhan, *Un Rhétoriqueur à l'état sauvage. Paul Valéry, ou La Littérature considérée comme un faux* (Brussels: Editions Complexe, 1987).

9. Valéry's ambivalence towards the Flaubertian doctrine of style can be sensed in the following statement from 1937: 'Flaubert was convinced that for every idea, there exists only one correct form, that the task is to find it and to construct it, to labour towards this goal. This lovely doctrine is, unfortunately, meaningless. But it is not a bad idea to follow it. Such efforts are never wasted. Sisyphus honed his muscles' (*Œuvres* I: 1476).

10. Hytier, *La Poétique de Valéry*, p. 144.

11. Ibid., p. 161.

12. Ibid., p. 74.

13. Kirsteen Anderson, *Paul Valéry and the Voice of Desire* (Oxford: Legenda, 2000), p. 13.

14. Paul Valéry, *Charms*, trans. Peter Dale (London: Anvil Poetry Press, 2007), p. 97.

15. Paul Gifford, *Valéry, Charmes* (University of Glasgow Press, 1995), p. 25.

16. Ibid., p. 5.

17. 'Notre style, c'est notre voix, altérée par notre travail, complétée.' Quoted by Anderson, *Paul Valéry and the Voice of Desire*, p. 38.

18. Ibid., p. 40.

19. Valéry, *Charms*, p. 33.

20. Gifford, *Valéry, Charmes*, p. 1.

21. Ibid., p. 33.

22. Valéry, *Charms*, p. 149.

23. Ibid., p. 153.

24. Rilke speaks of Valéry's 'profound repose' (*tiefes Ausgeruhtsein*), and sees this stylistic idiosyncracy as a consequence of his years of silence and waiting. As Curdin Ebneter writes, this term suggests that 'Rilke was particularly attracted to Valéry's art of respiratory rhythms and arcs of tension [*Kunst der Diastole nach Spannungsbögen*].' See Curdin Ebneter, 'Die Beziehungen Rilkes zu Catherine Pozzi und Paul Valéry', *Blätter der Rilke-Gesellschaft*, vol. XXX (2010), pp. 74–90, here p. 89.

25. Valéry, *Charms*, p. 101.

26. Ibid., p. 49.

27. Ibid., p. 55 (translation altered).
28. Ibid., pp. 58–9.
29. Ralph Freedman, *Life of a Poet* (Evanston: Northwestern University Press, 1996), p. 504.
30. Ibid., p. 483.
31. Quoted in ibid., p. 610.
32. Kathleen L. Komar, 'The *Duino Elegies*', in *The Cambridge Companion to Rilke*, ed. Karen Leeder and Robert Vilain (Cambridge University Press, 2010), p. 82.
33. Rainer Maria Rilke, *Duino Elegies*, trans. Martyn Crucefix (London: Enitharmon, 2006), p. 15. Cited hereafter as 'Crucefix' in text.
34. Nietzsche, *Human, All Too Human*, p. 334.
35. Komar, 'The *Duino Elegies*', p. 86.
36. Manfred Engel, 'Die *Sonette an Orpheus* als Beginn des spätesten Werkes', in *Nach Duino*, ed. Karen Leeder and Robert Vilain (Göttingen: Wallstein, 2010), p. 16.
37. Rainer Maria Rilke, *Sonnets to Orpheus*, trans. David Young (Middletown, CT: Wesleyan University Press, 1987), p. 7. Cited hereafter as 'Young' in text.
38. Engel, 'Die *Sonette an Orpheus* als Beginn des spätesten Werkes', p. 15.
39. Komar, 'The *Duino Elegies*', p. 92.
40. Letter to Katharina Kippenberg, 23 February 1924. Rainer Maria Rilke, *Briefe in zwei Bänden* (Frankfurt/Leipzig: Insel, 1991), vol. II, p. 225.
41. The similarity to Valéry's emphasis on 'Voice' seems apparent, yet there is an important difference: Rilke's Orphism does not strive towards a formal impersonality, but rather ties both the possibilities and the purpose of poetry to the person of Orpheus, who becomes the incarnation of the 'absolute', pure poet.
42. Paul Bishop, 'Rilke: Thought and Mysticism', in *The Cambridge Companion to Rilke*, p. 170.
43. Ulrich Fülleborn, *Das Strukturproblem der späten Lyrik Rilkes* (Heidelberg: Winter, 1973), p. 172.
44. Barthes, *Writing Degree Zero*, p. 44.
45. Letter to Countess Sizzo, 12 April 1923. *Briefe* II, p. 296.
46. Letter to Witold Hulewicz, 13 November 1925. *Briefe* II, p. 374.
47. See the letter to Hulewicz.
48. Andreas Kramer, 'Rilke and Modernism', in *The Cambridge Companion to Rilke*, p. 125.
49. Ibid., p. 129.

50. Ibid.
51. Edgell Rickwood, 'A Fragmentary Poem', *Times Literary Supplement* 1131 (20 September 1923), reprinted in *T.S. Eliot: The Contemporary Reviews*, ed. Jewel Spears Brooker (Cambridge University Press, 2004), pp. 110–12, here p. 111.
52. Pound made this statement in the *Criterion* in 1932. Quoted from C.K. Stead, *The New Poetic: Yeats to Eliot* (London: Hutchinson, 1964), p. 114.
53. T.S. Eliot, 'A Romantic Aristocrat', in *The Sacred Wood*, p. 25. First printed as 'A Romantic Patrician', in the *Athenaeum*, May 1919.
54. T.S. Eliot, 'Reflections on Contemporary Poetry' I, *Egoist* IV.8 (September 1917), p. 118.
55. T.S. Eliot, 'Baudelaire in our Time', in *For Lancelot Andrewes*, pp. 86–7.
56. W.B. Yeats, *The Oxford Book of Modern Verse 1892–1925* (Oxford University Press, 1936), p. ix.
57. For a detailed discussion of Eliot's view of rhetoric and the Elizabethans, see the chapter entitled 'A Pathology of Rhetoric', in Ronald Bush, *T.S. Eliot: A Study in Character and Style* (Oxford University Press, 1984), pp. 17–31.
58. Eliot, 'A Romantic Aristocrat', p. 25.
59. T.S. Eliot, 'Reflections on Contemporary Poetry' III, *Egoist* IV.10 (November 1917), p. 151.
60. T.S. Eliot, 'Rhetoric and Poetic Drama', in *The Sacred Wood*, pp. 65–71, here p. 66.
61. Ibid., p. 71.
62. Stead, *The New Poetic*, p. 131.
63. Ibid., p. 127.
64. For a discussion of Gourmont's decisive influence on Eliot's doctrine of impersonality, see Bush, *T.S. Eliot*, pp. 44–7.
65. T.S. Eliot, 'Imperfect Critics', in *The Sacred Wood*, p. 37.
66. T.S. Eliot, 'Philip Massinger', in *The Sacred Wood*, pp. 104–21, here p. 118.
67. T.S. Eliot, 'Tradition and the Individual Talent', in *The Sacred Wood*, pp. 39–49, here p. 44.
68. Eliot coined this phrase in his 'critical note' to the *Collected Poems of Harold Monro*. Stead uses it as a chapter heading (see Stead, *The New Poetic*, pp. 125–47, esp. p. 136).
69. Quoted by Bush, *T.S. Eliot*, p. 24.
70. Ronald Schuchard, 'T.S. Eliot as an Extension Lecturer', *Review of English Studies* 25 (1974), 163–73, here p. 165.
71. T.S. Eliot, 'Reflections on Vers Libre', in *To Criticize the Critic* (London: Faber & Faber, 1965), pp. 183–9, here p. 187.

72. T.S. Eliot, 'The Music of Poetry', in *On Poetry and Poets* (London: Faber & Faber, 1957), pp. 26–38, here p. 38.

73. T.S. Eliot, 'From Poe to Valéry', in *To Criticize the Critic*, pp. 27–42, here p. 39.

74. Ibid.

75. Ronald Bush argues that Eliot turns increasingly towards a symbolist aesthetic, where the 'musical' style is all-important; as early as 1933, notes Bush, Eliot refers to the 'musical qualities of verse' (what he also calls the 'auditory imagination') as 'this virtue of poetic style'. See Bush, *T.S. Eliot*, pp. 76–7.

76. Louis Menand, *Discovering Modernism: T.S. Eliot and his Context* (Oxford University Press, 2007 [1987]), p. 89.

77. Ibid., p. 91.

78. Ibid.

79. Ibid.

80. T.S. Eliot, 'The Metaphysical Poets', in *Selected Essays*, pp. 281–91, here p. 289.

81. Bush, *T.S. Eliot*, p. 58.

82. Harriet Davidson, 'Reading *The Waste Land*', in *The Cambridge Companion to T.S. Eliot*, ed. A David Moody (Cambridge University Press, 1994), pp. 121–31, here p. 125.

83. Ibid., p. 126.

84. Ibid., p. 122.

85. Michael North, 'Eliot, Lukacs, and the Politics of Modernism', in *T.S. Eliot: The Modernist in History*, ed. Ronald Bush (Cambridge University Press, 1991), pp. 169–89, here p. 178.

86. Ibid.

87. Ibid., p. 176.

88. Davidson, 'Reading *The Waste Land*', p. 122.

89. Bush, *T.S. Eliot*, p. 61. Bush pursues this into a stylistic reading of 'The Fire Sermon'.

90. Stead, *The New Poetic*, p. 126.

91. Ibid., p. 184.

92. Barthes, *Writing Degree Zero*, p. 18.

5   The 'Alibi' of Style: Modernist Manifestos

1. See Lucas, *Style*, p. 15.

2. See *Manifesto: A Century of Isms*, ed. Mary Ann Caws (London: University of Nebraska Press, 2001), pp. xix and xxix.

3. Ibid., p. xxiii.

4. Murry, *The Problem of Style*, p. 77.

5. *Manifesto*, ed. Caws, p. xx.
6. Ibid., p. xxi.
7. Meschonnic, *Modernité modernité*, pp. 59–60.
8. Gourmont, *Selected Writings*, p. 108.
9. See *Manifesto*, ed. Caws, p. xxi.
10. Gourmont, *Le Problème du style*, p. 31. Where the passage, as here, is not included in the *Selected Writings*, I have translated it myself and given the reference to the original French edition.
11. Gourmont, *Selected Writings*, pp. 125–6.
12. Ibid., p. 129.
13. Ibid., p. 128.
14. Ibid., p. 129.
15. Ibid., p. 128.
16. Ibid., p. 129.
17. Gourmont, *Le Problème du style*, p. 32.
18. Gourmont, *Selected Writings*, p. 112.
19. Gourmont, *Le Problème du style*, p. 9.
20. For a summary of these debates, see Michael Syrotinski, *Defying Gravity: Jean Paulhan's Interventions in Twentieth-Century French Intellectual History* (Albany, NY: State University of New York Press, 1998), p. 79.
21. Jean Paulhan, *The Flowers of Tarbes*, trans. Michael Syrotinski (Urbana and Chicago: University of Illinois Press, 2006), p. 89. Cited hereafter in text as FT.
22. Although his examples are generally taken from French literature, he adds in a footnote that he could easily have extended the analysis to 'Curtius, E.M. Forster, or Cecchi'. See *The Flowers of Tarbes*, p. 17, n. 1.
23. *Manifesto*, ed. Caws, p. xix.
24. Ibid., p. xxii.
25. Giovanni Lista, *Futurisme, Manifestes, Proclamations, Documents* (Lausanne: L'Age d'homme, 1973).
26. *Manifesto*, ed. Caws, pp. 185–9.
27. Ibid., p. xxiii.
28. Meschonnic suggests that it was this adoption of the first person plural, along with the glorification of war and modern technology, that formed part of the appeal of futurism to Mussolini and the fascists. See Meschonnic, *Modernité modernité*, p. 61.
29. *Manifesto*, ed. Caws, p. xxvii.
30. Meschonnic, *Modernité modernité*, p. 57.

31. *Manifesto*, ed. Caws, pp. 213–16.
32. 'Introduction' to *The Lost Lunar Baedeker: Poems of Mina Loy*, ed. Roger L. Conover (New York: Farrar, Straus, Giroux, 1996), p. xv. Much of this introductory paragraph is taken from Conover's introduction.
33. Ibid.
34. *The Lost Lunar Baedeker*, ed. Conover, p. 216. Cited hereafter in text as LLB.
35. Christina Walter, 'Mina Loy', *The Modernism Lab at Yale University*, http://modernism.research.yale.edu/wiki/index.php/mina_loy, accessed 7 October 2010.
36. Ibid.
37. Woolf, 'Women and Fiction', in *Selected Essays*, p. 136. Quoted in Chapter 3, p. 149, of the present study.
38. Walter, 'Mina Loy'.
39. Ibid.
40. Ezra Pound, 'A Few Don'ts by an Imagiste', in *Manifesto*, ed. Caws, pp. 356–9. Cited hereafter in text as EP.
41. T.E. Hulme, 'Notes on Language and Style', in *Selected Writings*, p. 40.
42. Marsden Hartley, 'The Business of Poetry', in *Manifesto*, ed. Caws, pp. 353–6, here p. 353.
43. Pierre Reverdy, 'The Image', in *Manifesto*, ed. Caws, p. 351.
44. F.S. Flint, 'Imagisme', in *Manifesto*, ed. Caws, pp. 352–3, here p. 352.
45. Hartley, 'The Business of Poetry', in *Manifesto*, ed. Caws, p. 353.
46. Georges Duhamel and Charles Vildrac, *Notes sur la technique poétique* (Paris: Chez les libraires et chez les auteurs, 1910), pp. 26–36.
47. Ibid., p. 47.
48. Ibid., p. 25.
49. Ibid., p. 14.
50. Ibid., p. 46.
51. Tristan Tzara, 'Dada Manifesto', in *Manifesto*, ed. Caws, pp. 297–304, here p. 302.
52. Wassily Kandinsky, *Concerning the Spiritual in Art*, trans. M.T.H. Sadler (New York: Dover, 1977), p. 34.
53. Tzara, 'Dada Manifesto', p. 297.
54. Ibid.
55. Georges Ribemont-Dessaignes, *Déjà jadis, ou Du mouvement Dada à l'espace abstrait* (Paris: René Juillard, 1958), p. 154.

56. Tzara, 'Dada Manifesto', pp. 300–1.
57. Ibid., p. 303.
58. Jochen Schulte-Sasse, 'Foreword' to Peter Bürger, *Theory of the Avant-Garde*, trans. Michael Shaw (Manchester University Press, 1984), p. xv.
59. Bürger, *Theory of the Avant-Garde*, p. lii.
60. Schulte-Sasse, 'Foreword', *Theory of the Avant-Garde*, p. xv.
61. Crucially, however, it could only do this after modernism had cleared the way, as Bürger's historicizing argument suggests: 'In bourgeois society, it is only with aestheticism that the full unfolding of the phenomenon of art became a fact, and it is to aestheticism that the historical avant-garde responds' (Bürger, *Theory of the Avant-Garde*, p. 17).
62. Ibid., p. 18.
63. Peter Sloterdijk, *Critique of Cynical Reason*, trans. Michael Eldred (London: Verso, 1998), p. 397. Quoted in Nicholls, *Modernisms*, p. 228.
64. Nicholls, *Modernisms*, p. 228.
65. Tzara, 'Dada Manifesto', p. 304.
66. Jochen Schulte-Sasse, 'Foreword', *Theory of the Avant-Garde*, p. xxxvi.
67. See *Expressionismus. Manifeste und Dokumente zur deutschen Literatur 1910–1920*, ed. Thomas Anz and Michael Stark (Stuttgart: Metzler, 1982), p. 14.
68. The term 'inner need' recurs *passim* in Kandinsky's study; see Kandinsky, *Concerning the Spiritual in Art*, e.g. p. 35.
69. For a comprehensive anthology, see *Expressionismus. Manifeste und Dokumente zur deutschen Literatur 1910–1920*, which includes Cubists, futurists and Dadaists in its broad orbit.
70. Kurt Pinthus, 'Vorwort' zu *Menschheitsdämmerung* (Berlin: Rowohlt, 2001), pp. 22–32. Translated by Joanna M. Ratych, Ralph Ley and Robert C. Conard as *Menschheitsdämmerung* (Rochester, NY: Camden House, 1994). Cited hereafter from the English edition as MD.
71. See André Breton, *Entretiens (1913–52)* (Paris: Gallimard, 1969), p. 52.
72. André Breton, *Manifestos of Surrealism* (Ann Arbor: University of Michigan Press, 1972), p. 159. Cited hereafter in text as MS.
73. Michel Leiris, *Manhood*, trans. Richard Howard (San Francisco: North Point Press, 1984), p. 135.
74. Louis Aragon, *Traité du style* (Paris: Gallimard, 1928), p. 46. Cited hereafter in text as TS.

Conclusion

1. Gay, *Style in History*, p. 6.
2. Gourmont, *Selected Writings*, p. 109.
3. Murry, *The Problem of Style*, p. 77.
4. Fordham, *I do I undo I redo*, pp. 75–6.
5. Griffin, *Modernism and Fascism*, p. 52.
6. Ibid.
7. Adorno, *Aesthetic Theory*, p. 297.
8. Rolf Wiggershaus, *The Frankfurt School*, trans. Michael Robertson (Cambridge, MA: MIT Press, 1994), p. 218.
9. George Steiner, *Avec George Steiner. Les chemins de la culture* (Paris: Albin Michel, 2010), p. 106

Bibliography

Adorno, Theodor W., 'Parataxis. Zur späten Lyrik Hölderlins', in *Noten zur Literatur. Gesammelte Schriften II* (Frankfurt: Suhrkamp, 1974), pp. 447–91

—— *Aesthetic Theory*, trans. Robert Hullot-Kentor (London: Continuum, 2004)

Alexander, Theodor W. and Alexander, Beatrice, 'Schnitzler's *Leutnant Gustl* and Dujardin's *Les lauriers sont coupés*', *Modern Austrian Literature* 2.2 (1969), 7–15

Anderson, Kirsteen, *Paul Valéry and the Voice of Desire* (Oxford: Legenda, 2000)

Andres, Jan, 'Gegenbilder. Stefan Georges poetische Kulturkritik in den "Zeitgedichten" des *Siebenten Rings*', *George-Jahrbuch* 6 (2006–7), pp. 31–54

Antoine, Gérald, 'La Langue poétique', in *Histoire de la langue française 1880–1914* (Paris: CNRS, 1999), pp. 435–66

Anz, Thomas and Stark, Michael (eds), *Expressionismus. Manifeste und Dokumente zur deutschen Literatur 1910–1920* (Stuttgart: Metzler, 1982)

Aragon, Louis, *Traité du style* (Paris: Gallimard, 1928)

Austin, J.L., *How to Do Things with Words* (Oxford University Press, 1971)

Bahr, Hermann, *Zur Überwindung des Naturalismus. Theoretische Schriften 1887–1904*, ed. Gotthart Wunberg (Stuttgart: Kohlhammer, 1968)

Baillot, Antoine, *Influence de la philosophie de Schopenhauer en France (1860–1900)* (Paris: Vrin, 1927)

Bardèche, Maurice, *L'Œuvre de Flaubert* (Paris: Les Sept Couleurs, 1974)

Barthes, Roland, *Writing Degree Zero*, trans. Annette Lavers and Colin Smith (London: Jonathan Cape, 1967)

—— 'Style and its Image', in *Literary Style: A Symposium* (Oxford University Press, 1971)

Baudelaire, Charles, *Œuvres complètes* (Paris: Pléiade, 1961)

—— *Artificial Paradise*, trans. Ellen Fox (New York: Herder and Herder, 1971)

—— *Selected Writings on Art and Artists* (Harmondsworth: Penguin, 1972)

—— *The Flowers of Evil*, trans. James McGowan (Oxford University Press, 1993)

—— *Paris Spleen*, trans. Martin Sorrell (London: Oneworld, 2010)

Beckett, Samuel, *Disjecta*, ed. Ruby Cohn (London: John Calder, 2001)

Benjamin, Walter, *Illuminations*, trans. Harry Zohn (London: Fontana, 1973)

—— *The Arcades Project*, trans. Howard Eiland and Kevin McLaughlin (Cambridge, MA: Belknap, 1999)

Benn, Gottfried, *Primal Vision: Selected Writings*, trans. Babette Deutsch (London: Marion Boyars, 1976)

Berlin, Isaiah, 'The Fox and the Hedgehog', in *Russian Thinkers* (London: Penguin, 1994), pp. 22–81

Bierbaum, Otto Julius, Heymel, Alfred Walter and Schröder, Rudolf Alexander (eds), *Die Insel*, vol. I (Berlin: Schuster & Loeffler, 1899)

Bishop, Paul, 'Rilke: Thought and Mysticism', in *The Cambridge Companion to Rilke*, ed. Karen Leeder and Robert Vilain (Cambridge University Press, 2010), pp. 159–73

Bohnenkamp, Klaus E. (ed.), *Rainer Maria Rilke / Norbert von Hellingrath. Briefe und Dokumente* (Göttingen: Wallstein, 2008)

Bohrer, Karl Heinz, *Großer Stil. Form und Formlosigkeit in der Moderne* (Munich: Hanser, 2007)

Bourdieu, Pierre, *Les Règles de l'art* (Paris: Seuil, 1992)

Bourget, Paul, *Essais de psychologie contemporaine* (Paris: Plon, 1883)

Bradbury, Malcolm and McFarlane, James (eds), *Modernism: A Guide to European Literature 1890–1930* (London: Penguin, 1976)

Breton, André, *Entretiens (1913–52)* (Paris: Gallimard, 1969)

—— *Manifestos of Surrealism* (Ann Arbor: University of Michigan Press, 1972)

Broch, Hermann, *Der Tod des Vergil* (Frankfurt: Suhrkamp, 1976)

Brooker, Jewel Spears (ed.), *T.S. Eliot: The Contemporary Reviews* (Cambridge University Press, 2004)

Bürger, Peter, *Theory of the Avant-Garde*, trans. Michael Shaw (Manchester University Press, 1984)

Bush, Ronald, *T.S. Eliot: A Study in Character and Style* (Oxford University Press, 1984)

Calinescu, Matei, *Five Faces of Modernity* (Durham, NC: Duke University Press, 1987)

Caws, Mary Ann (ed.), *Manifesto: A Century of Isms* (London: University of Nebraska Press, 2001)

Cioran, E.M., *The Temptation to Exist*, trans. Richard Howard (London: Quartet, 1987)

Culler, Jonathan, *Flaubert: The Uses of Uncertainty* (Ithaca, NY: Cornell University Press, 1974)

Davidson, Harriet, 'Reading *The Waste Land*', in *The Cambridge Companion to T.S. Eliot*, ed. A. David Moody (Cambridge University Press, 1994), pp. 121–31

Deleuze, Gilles, *Nietzsche and Philosophy* (London: Athlone, 1983)

Deming, Robert H. (ed.), *James Joyce: The Critical Heritage* (London: Routledge, 1970)

Derrida, Jacques, *Spurs: Nietzsche's Styles*, trans. Barbara Harlow (University of Chicago Press, 1978)

Duhamel, Georges and Vildrac, Charles, *Notes sur la technique poétique* (Paris: Chez les libraires et chez les auteurs, 1910)

Dujardin, Edouard, *The Bays are Sere and Interior Monologue*, trans. Anthony Suter (London: Libris, 1991)

Eagleton, Terry, *Literary Theory: An Introduction* (Oxford: Blackwell, 1983)

Ebneter, Curdin, 'Die Beziehungen Rilkes zu Catherine Pozzi und Paul Valéry', *Blätter der Rilke-Gesellschaft*, vol. XXX (2010), pp. 74–90

Eliot, T.S., 'Reflections on Contemporary Poetry' I, *Egoist* IV.8 (September 1917), p. 118

—— 'Reflections on Contemporary Poetry' III, *Egoist* IV.10 (November 1917), p. 151

—— 'Contemporary English Prose', *Vanity Fair* 20 (July 1923), p. 51

—— *For Lancelot Andrewes: Essays on Style and Order* (London: Faber & Gwyer, 1928)

—— *On Poetry and Poets* (London: Faber & Faber, 1957)

—— *Collected Poems 1909–1962* (London: Faber & Faber, 1963)

—— *To Criticize the Critic* (London: Faber & Faber, 1965)

—— *The Sacred Wood* (London: Faber & Faber, 1997)

—— *Selected Essays* (London: Faber & Faber, 1999)

Empson, William, *Seven Types of Ambiguity* (London: Penguin, 1995)

Engel, Manfred, 'Die *Sonette an Orpheus* als Beginn des spätesten Werkes', in *Nach Duino*, ed. Karen Leeder and Robert Vilain (Göttingen: Wallstein, 2010), pp. 15–27

Flaubert, Gustave, *Correspondance* (Paris: Conard, 1926)

—— *The Selected Letters of Gustave Flaubert*, trans. Francis Steegmuller (London: Hamish Hamilton, 1954)

—— *The Letters of Gustave Flaubert 1857–1880*, ed. Francis Steegmuller (Cambridge, MA: Belknap, 1982)

Fordham, Finn, *I do I undo I redo: The Textual Genesis of Modernist Selves* (Oxford University Press, 2010)

Freedman, Ralph, *Life of a Poet* (Evanston: Northwestern University Press, 1996)

Friedman, Melvin J., 'The Symbolist Novel: From Huysmans to Malraux', in *Modernism: A Guide to European Literature 1890–1930*, ed. Malcolm Bradbury and James McFarlane (London: Penguin, 1976), pp. 453–66

Friedrich, Hugo, *Die Struktur der modernen Lyrik* (Hamburg: Rowohlt, 1956)

Fülleborn, Ulrich, *Das Strukturproblem der späten Lyrik Rilkes* (Heidelberg: Winter, 1973)

Gauger, Hans-Martin, 'Nietzsches Auffassung vom Stil', in *Stil. Geschichten und Funktionen eines kulturwissenschaftlichen Diskurselements*, ed. Hans Ulrich Gumbrecht and K. Ludwig Pfeiffer (Frankfurt: Suhrkamp, 1986), pp. 200–15

Gautier, Théophile, 'Charles Baudelaire', in *The Works of Théophile Gautier*, trans. F.C. de Sumichrast, vol. XXIII ('Art and Criticism') (New York, 1900), pp. 17–126

Gay, Peter, *Style in History* (New York: Basic Books, 1974)

Genette, Gérard, 'Proust Palimpsest', in *Figures of Literary Discourse* (Oxford: Blackwell, 1982), pp. 203–28

George, Stefan, *Werke* vol. I (Munich: Deutscher Taschenbuch Verlag, 2000)

Gifford, Paul, *Valéry, Charmes* (University of Glasgow Press, 1995)

Gilbert, Stuart, *James Joyce's Ulysses* (London: Faber & Faber, 1930)

—— (ed.), *James Joyce: Letters* (London: Faber & Faber, 1957)

Goldberg, S.L., *The Classical Temper: A Study of James Joyce's Ulysses* (London: Chatto & Windus, 1961)

Gourmont, Rémy de, *Esthétique de la langue française* (Paris: Mercure de France, 1899)

—— *Le Problème du style* (Paris: Mercure de France, 1902)

—— *Decadence and Other Essays on the Culture of Ideas* (New York: Harcourt Brace, 1921)

—— 'Selections from *The Problem of Style*', in *Selected Writings*, trans. Glenn S. Burne (Ann Arbor: University of Michigan Press, 1966), pp. 108–29

Griffin, Roger, *Modernism and Fascism: The Sense of a Beginning under Mussolini and Hitler* (Basingstoke: Palgrave, 2007)

Gumbrecht, Hans-Ulrich, 'Schwindende Stabilität der Wirklichkeit. Eine Geschichte des Stilbegriffs', in *Stil. Geschichten und Funktionen eines kulturwissenschaftlichen Diskurselements*, ed. Hans Ulrich Gumbrecht and K. Ludwig Pfeiffer (Frankfurt: Suhrkamp, 1986), pp. 726–88

Hamburger, Michael, *The Truth of Poetry* (London: Anvil, 1996)

Harvey, David, *The Condition of Postmodernity: An Enquiry into the Origins of Cultural Change* (Oxford: Blackwell, 1990)

Hegel, G.W.F., *Aesthetics: Lectures on Fine Art*, vol. I, trans. T.M. Knox (Oxford University Press, 1988)

Hill, Geoffrey, 'Tacit Pledges', in *Collected Critical Writings*, ed. Kenneth Haynes (Oxford University Press, 2008)

Hobsbawm, Eric and Ranger, Terence (eds), *The Invention of Tradition* (Cambridge University Press, 1983)

Hofmannsthal, Hugo von, 'Ein Brief', in *Gesammelte Werke in Einzelausgaben. Prosa II*, ed. Herbert Steiner (Frankfurt: Fischer, 1976), pp. 7–20

—— *Erzählungen* (Stuttgart: Reclam, 2000)

Hulme, T.E., *Selected Writings*, ed. Patrick McGuinness (Manchester: Carcanet, 1998)

Hutchinson, Ben, 'Une écriture blanche? Style and Symbolism in *Les Lauriers sont coupés*', *Modern Language Review* 106.3 (July 2011), 709–23

Hytier, Jean, *La Poétique de Valéry* (Paris: Armand Colin, 1953)

Iser, Wolfgang, *The Implied Reader* (London: Johns Hopkins University Press, 1974)

Jakobson, Roman, *Selected Writings I* (Berlin/New York/Amsterdam: Mouton, 1962)

—— *Language in Literature* (Cambridge, MA: Harvard University Press, 1987)

Jameson, Fredric, 'Postmodernism and Consumer Society', in *The Anti-Aesthetic: Essays on Postmodern Culture*, ed. Hal Foster (Port Townsend: Bay Press, 1983)

Janaway, Christopher, *Schopenhauer* (Oxford University Press, 1994)

Jephcott, E.F.N., *Proust and Rilke: The Literature of Expanded Consciousness* (London: Chatto & Windus, 1972)

Joyce, James, *Ulysses* (London: Penguin, 1992)

Joyce, Stanislaus, *My Brother's Keeper* (London: Faber & Faber, 1958)

Kandinsky, Wassily, *Concerning the Spiritual in Art*, trans. M.T.H. Sadler (New York: Dover, 1977)

Kant, Immanuel, *The Critique of Judgement*, trans. James Creed Meredith (Oxford: Clarendon Press, 1952)

Kaufmann, Walter, *Nietzsche: Philosopher, Psychologist, Antichrist* (Princeton University Press, 1974)

Kiesel, Helmuth, *Geschichte der literarischen Moderne* (Munich: Beck, 2004)

King, C.D., 'Edouard Dujardin, Inner Monologue and the Stream of Consciousness', *French Studies* 6.2 (1953), 116–28

Komar, Kathleen L., 'The *Duino Elegies*', in *The Cambridge Companion to Rilke*, ed. Karen Leeder and Robert Vilain (Cambridge University Press, 2010), pp. 80–94

Kramer, Andreas, 'Rilke and Modernism', in *The Cambridge Companion to Rilke*, ed. Karen Leeder and Robert Vilain (Cambridge University Press, 2010), pp. 113–30

Leavis, F.R., *The Common Pursuit* (London: Chatto & Windus, 1952)

—— *New Bearings in English Poetry* (London: Pelican, 1972)

Leighton, Angela, *On Form* (Oxford University Press, 2007)

Leiris, Michel, *Manhood*, trans. Richard Howard (San Francisco: North Point Press, 1984)

Levallois, Jules, *Milieu de siècle. Mémoires d'un critique* (Paris: Librairie illustrée, 1895)

Link-Heer, Ursula, 'Maniera. Überlegungen zur Konkurrenz von Manier und Stil', in *Stil. Geschichten und Funktionen eines kulturwissenschaftlichen Diskurselements*, ed. Hans Ulrich Gumbrecht and K. Ludwig Pfeiffer (Frankfurt: Suhrkamp, 1986), pp. 93–113

Lista, Giovanni, *Futurisme, Manifestes, Proclamations, Documents* (Lausanne: L'Age d'homme, 1973)

Loy, Mina, *The Lost Lunar Baedeker: Poems of Mina Loy*, ed. Roger L. Conover (New York: Farrar, Straus, Giroux, 1996)

Lucas, F.L., *Style* (London: Castell, 1955)

Magee, Bryan, *The Philosophy of Schopenhauer* (Oxford University Press, 1983)

Mallarmé, Stéphane, *Poésies* (Paris: Flammarion, 1989)

Mallet, Robert (ed.), *Correspondance André Gide – Paul Valéry* (Paris: Gallimard, 1955)

Mann, Thomas, 'Der Künstler und der Literat', in *Reden und Aufsätze*, vol. I (Frankfurt: Fischer, 1965), pp. 113–21

—— *Reflections of a Nonpolitical Man*, trans. Walter D. Morris (New York: Frederick Ungar, 1983)

—— *Death in Venice*, trans. David Luke (London: Vintage, 1998)

Marinetti, Filippo, 'The Founding and Manifesto of Futurism', in *Manifesto: A Century of Isms*, ed. Mary Ann Caws (London: University of Nebraska Press, 2001), pp. 185–9

Mauthner, Fritz, *Beiträge zu einer Kritik der Sprache* (Leipzig: Felix Meiner, 1923)

Menand, Louis, *Discovering Modernism: T.S. Eliot and his Context* (Oxford University Press, 2007 [1987])

Meschonnic, Henri, *Modernité modernité* (Paris: Gallimard Folio, 1993)

Mitterand, Henri, 'De l'écriture artiste au style décadent', in *Histoire de la langue francaise 1880–1914* (Paris: CNRS, 1999), pp. 467–77

Moréas, Jean, 'Le Symbolisme', *Le Figaro*, 18 September 1886, Supplément littéraire, pp. 1–2

Mouchard, Claude and Neefs, Jacques (eds), *Flaubert* (Paris: Balland, 1986)

Müller, Bodo, 'Der Verlust der Sprache. Zur linguistischen Krise in der Literatur', *Germanisch-Romanische Monatsschrift* 16 (1966), 225–43.

Murry, John Middleton, *The Problem of Style* (Oxford University Press, 1922)

Musil, Robert, *The Confusions of Young Törless*, trans. Shaun Whiteside (London: Penguin, 2001)

Nabokov, Vladimir, *Lectures on Literature* (London: Weidenfeld & Nicolson, 1980)

Neuschäfer, Hans-Jörg, 'Über das Konzept des Stils bei Leo Spitzer', in *Stil. Geschichten und Funktionen eines kulturwissenschaftlichen Diskurselements*, ed. Hans Ulrich Gumbrecht and K. Ludwig Pfeiffer (Frankfurt: Suhrkamp, 1986), pp. 281–8

Nicholls, Peter, *Modernisms* (Berkeley: University of California Press, 1995)

Nietzsche, Friedrich, *Kritische Studienausgabe in 15 Bänden*, ed. Giorgio Colli and Mazzino Montinari (Berlin/New York: de Gruyter, 1967ff.)

—— *Human, All Too Human*, trans. R.J. Hollingdale (Cambridge University Press, 1996)

—— *Untimely Meditations*, trans. R.J. Hollingdale (Cambridge University Press, 1997)

—— *The Gay Science*, trans. Josefine Nauckhoff (Cambridge University Press, 2001)

—— *On the Genealogy of Morals,* trans. C. Diethe (Cambridge University Press, 2002)

—— *Writings from the Late Notebooks*, trans. Kate Sturge (Cambridge University Press, 2003)

—— *The Anti-Christ, Ecce Homo, Twilight of the Idols*, trans. Judith Norman (Cambridge University Press, 2005)

—— *The Birth of Tragedy*, trans. Ronald Speirs (Cambridge University Press, 2009)

—— *Writings from the Early Notebooks*, trans. Ladislaus Löb (Cambridge University Press, 2009)

North, Michael, 'Eliot, Lukacs, and the Politics of Modernism', in *T.S. Eliot: The Modernist in History*, ed. Ronald Bush (Cambridge University Press, 1991), pp. 169–89

Pater, Walter, 'On Style', in *Essays on Literature and Art*, ed. Jennifer Uglow (London: Dent, 1973)

—— *The Renaissance: Studies in Art and Poetry*, in *Walter Pater: Three Major Texts*, ed. William E. Buckler (New York University Press, 1986)

Paulhan, Jean, *The Flowers of Tarbes*, trans. Michael Syrotinski (Urbana and Chicago: University of Illinois Press, 2006)

Pfeiffer, K. Ludwig, 'Produktive Labilität. Funktionen des Stilbegriffs', in *Stil. Geschichten und Funktionen eines kulturwissenschaftlichen Diskurselements*, ed. Hans Ulrich Gumbrecht and K. Ludwig Pfeiffer (Frankfurt: Suhrkamp, 1986), pp. 685–725

Pinthus, Kurt (ed.), *Menschheitsdämmerung*, trans. Joanna M. Ratych, Ralph Ley and Robert C. Conard (Rochester, NY: Camden House, 1994)

—— *Menschheitsdämmerung* (Berlin: Rowohlt, 2001)

Pound, Ezra, *Selected Poems 1908–1969* (London: Faber & Faber, 1975)

—— 'A Few Don'ts by an Imagiste', in *Manifesto: A Century of Isms*, ed. Mary Ann Caws (London: University of Nebraska Press, 2001), pp. 356–9

Power, Arthur, *Conversations with James Joyce* (London: Millington, 1974)

Proust, Marcel, 'A propos du style de Flaubert', in *Chroniques* (Paris: Gallimard, 1927), pp. 193–211

—— *By Way of Sainte-Beuve*, trans. Sylvia Townsend Warner (London: Chatto & Windus, 1958)

—— *Contre Sainte-Beuve* (Paris: Pléiade, 1971)

—— *Remembrance of Things Past* (3 vols), trans. C.K. Scott Moncrieff, Terence Kilmartin and Andreas Mayor (London: Chatto & Windus, 1981)

Ratermanis, J.B., *Etude sur le style de Baudelaire* (Bade: Editions Art et Science Bade, 1949)

Raulff, Ulrich, *Kreis ohne Meister. Stefan Georges Nachleben* (Munich: Beck, 2009)

Read, Herbert, *English Prose Style* (London: Bell, 1963)

Ribemont-Dessaignes, Georges, *Déjà jadis, ou Du mouvement Dada à l'espace abstrait* (Paris: René Juillard, 1958)

Riegl, Alois, *Problems of Style*, trans. Evelyn Kain (Princeton University Press, 1993)

Rilke, Rainer Maria, *Sonnets to Orpheus*, trans. David Young (Middletown, CT: Wesleyan University Press, 1987)

—— *Letters on Cézanne*, trans. Joel Agee (London: Jonathan Cape, 1988)

—— *Briefe in zwei Bänden* (Frankfurt/Leipzig: Insel, 1991)

—— *Duino Elegies*, trans. Martyn Crucefix (London: Enitharmon, 2006)

—— *The Notebooks of Malte Laurids Brigge*, trans. Burton Pike (Champaign and London: Dalkey Archive, 2008)

Rimbaud, Arthur, *Collected Poems* (London: Penguin, 1962)

Schaffner, Anna Katharina, 'Richard von Krafft-Ebing's *Psychopathia Sexualis* and Thomas Mann's *Buddenbrooks*: Exchanges between Scientific and Imaginary Accounts of Sexual Deviance', *Modern Language Review* 106.2 (April 2011), 477–94

Scherer, Edmond, *Etudes sur la littérature contemporaine*, vol. IV (Paris, 1886)

Schmidt-Pauli, Elisabeth, *Rainer Maria Rilke. Ein Gedenkbuch* (Basel: Schwabe, 1940)

Schnitzler, Arthur, *Der blinde Geronimo und sein Bruder* (Frankfurt: Fischer, 1989)

Schnitzler, Heinrich (ed.), *Briefe an Arthur Schnitzler, Neue Rundschau* 66 (1955)

Schopenhauer, Arthur, 'On Style', in *Essays*, trans. T. Bailey Saunders (London: Allen and Unwin, 1951), pp. 13–28

—— *The World as Will and Representation*, trans. E.F.J. Payne (New York: Dover, 1969)

Schuchard, Ronald, 'T.S. Eliot as an Extension Lecturer', *Review of English Studies* 25 (1974), 163–73

Scott, Clive, 'Symbolism, Decadence and Impressionism', in *Modernism: A Guide to European Literature 1890–1930*, ed. Malcolm Bradbury and James McFarlane (London: Penguin, 1976), pp. 206–27

Sloterdijk, Peter, *Critique of Cynical Reason*, trans. Michael Eldred (London: Verso, 1998)

Sontag, Susan, *Against Interpretation* (New York: Farrar, Straus & Giroux, 1966)

Spitzer, Leo, *Etudes de style* (Paris: Gallimard, 1970)

Starobinski, Jean, 'Préface' to Leo Spitzer, *Etudes de style* (Paris: Gallimard, 1970)

Stead, C.K., *The New Poetic: Yeats to Eliot* (London: Hutchinson, 1964)

Steiner, George, 'Adorno: Love and Cognition', *Times Literary Supplement*, 9 March 1973, pp. 253–5

—— *Avec George Steiner. Les chemins de la culture* (Paris: Albin Michel, 2010)

Symons, Arthur, *The Symbolist Movement in Literature* (New York: Haskell, 1971)

Syrotinski, Michael, *Defying Gravity: Jean Paulhan's Interventions in Twentieth-Century French Intellectual History* (Albany, NY: State University of New York Press, 1998)

Tadié, Jean-Yves, *La Critique littéraire au XXe siècle* (Paris: Belfond, 1987)

Thibaudet, Albert, 'Marcel Proust et la tradition française', *Nouvelle Revue Française*, January 1923, p. 134

Thomas, Douglas, *Reading Nietzsche Rhetorically* (New York: Guilford, 1999)

Thomas, Louis, *Curiosités sur Baudelaire* (Paris, 1912)

Tzara, Tristan, 'Dada Manifesto', in *Manifesto: A Century of Isms*, ed. Mary Ann Caws (London: University of Nebraska Press, 2001), pp. 297–303

Uitti, Karl D., *The Concept of Self in the Symbolist Novel* (The Hague: Mouton, 1961)

Valéry, Paul, *Vues* (Paris: La Table Ronde, 1948)

—— *Œuvres*, ed. Jean Hytier (Paris: Gallimard, 1957–60)

—— *The Art of Poetry*, trans. Denise Folliot (London: Routledge & Kegan Paul, 1958)

—— *Charms*, trans. Peter Dale (London: Anvil Poetry Press, 2007)

—— *Cahiers/Notebooks*, ed. Brian Stimpson, trans. Norma Rinsler, Brian Stimpson, Rima Joseph and Paul Ryan (Frankfurt: Peter Lang, 2010), vol. IV

Verhaeren, Emile, *Impressions* (Paris: Mercure de France, 1926)

Vogeler, Heinrich, *Erinnerungen* (Berlin: Rütter and Loening, 1952)

Walter, Christina, 'Mina Loy', *The Modernism Lab at Yale University*, http://modernism.research.yale.edu/wiki/index.php/mina_loy

Wellbery, David. E. (ed.), *A New History of German Literature* (London: Harvard University Press, 2004)

Wellek, René, 'Stylistics, Poetics and Criticism', in *Literary Style: A Symposium* (Oxford University Press, 1971), pp. 65–76

Whiting, Charles G., *Paul Valéry* (London: Athlone, 1978)

Wiggershaus, Rolf, *The Frankfurt School*, trans. Michael Robertson (Cambridge, MA: MIT Press, 1994)

Williams, William Carlos, *Autobiography* (New York: New Directions, 1967)

Wölfflin, Heinrich, *Principles of Art History: The Problem of the Development of Style in Later Art*, trans. M.D. Hottinger (New York: Dover, 1950)

Woolf, Virginia, *A Writer's Diary*, ed. Leonard Woolf (London: Hogarth Press, 1975)

—— *The Diary of Virginia Woolf*, vol. II (London: Harcourt Brace Jovanovich, 1978)

—— *The Waves* (London: Penguin, 1992)

—— *Selected Essays* (London: Penguin, 2008)

Worringer, Wilhelm, *Abstraction and Empathy: A Contribution to the Psychology of Style* (London: Routledge and Kegan Paul, 1963)

Yeats, W.B. (ed.), *The Oxford Book of Modern Verse 1892–1925* (Oxford University Press, 1936)

Index

287